PAINTING WAR

PAINTING WAR

GEORGE PLANTE'S COMBAT ART IN WORLD WAR II

Kathleen Broome Williams

Naval Institute Press
Annapolis, Maryland

Naval Institute Press
291 Wood Road
Annapolis, MD 21402

Library of Congress Cataloging-in-Publication Data
Names: Williams, Kathleen Broome, date, author.
Title: Painting war : George Plante's combat art in World War II / Kathleen Broome Williams.
Description: Annapolis : Naval Institute Press, 2019. | Includes bibliographical references and index.
Identifiers: LCCN 2018048527 | ISBN 9781682474266 (hardback)
Subjects: LCSH: Plante, George, 1914–1995—Biography. | War artists—Great Britain—Biography. | Commercial artists—Great Britain—Biography. | World War, 1939–1945—Art and the war. | BISAC: HISTORY / Military / World War II. | BIOGRAPHY & AUTOBIOGRAPHY / Military. | HISTORY / Military / Pictorial.
Classification: LCC ND497.P57 W55 2019 | DDC 709.2 [B] —dc23 LC record available at https://lccn.loc.gov/2018048527

♾ Print editions meet the requirements of ANSI/NISO z39.48-1992 (Permanence of Paper).
Printed in the United States of America.

27 26 25 24 23 22 21 20 19 9 8 7 6 5 4 3 2 1
First printing

To my mother, Jane, and to my siblings,
Derek, Roger, and Susan,
who encouraged me to write this and
who share so many memories.

CONTENTS

FOREWORD

George Plante was a man who led an active life, or should one say "lives"? He went from a Scottish boyhood, through a very active World War II, to a busy postwar career in two countries.

Administrative chaos made it difficult for young George to join his preferred armed service in the war, so Plante was persuaded that he could serve by training as a Radio Officer on merchant ships. The exigencies of wartime service demanded a vast expansion of the field since ships, which had sailed independently with a single officer, now needed around-the-clock coverage and three radio operators on each. This was a fortunate choice for Plante as it enabled facilitation of his great talent, painting.

Serving on merchant ships, even in war, gave George the opportunity to embrace a whole new range of subjects, including all aspects of seagoing life. With his painting materials conveniently at hand, he had time for painting as a radio officer at sea, time he would not have had as an infantryman. After an initial period in coastal shipping, Plante moved to ocean-going service in the oil tanker *Sourabaya*, a former whale factory ship which processed whales and stored their oil. George sailed on several convoys, both across the Atlantic and into the Caribbean and Gulf of Mexico. It was in this period that he was exposed to the United States and its people.

But back at sea, *Sourabaya* was in the thick of the Battle of the Atlantic. On several convoys, Plante saw ships around him being attacked and burned. *Sourabaya*'s turn came on October 27, 1942, when she was sunk by the German submarine U436. Plante, a late leaver from the ship, was lucky to survive.

From this point on, his wartime career took a different turn and he was sent to the Middle East, where he worked for the clandestine Political Warfare Executive (PWE) producing propaganda illustrations aimed at occupied regions, and, as the war went on, recently-liberated ones. An interesting insight in the book is the sheer volume of material disseminated, mostly by air by the millions, and later by the billions during the remainder of the war. This book also offers an excellent description of the labyrinthine bureaucracies involved in propaganda: agencies, armed services, ministries and, above all, inter-allied cooperation and, sometimes, friction.

All this set Plante up well for a postwar career in advertising, both in London and the United States, where he eventually resettled. Despite the calls on his time, he maintained his artistic skills.

Kathleen Williams is an accomplished, meticulous, experienced, and articulate historian who elucidates her subject well and she can be proud of an informative and entertaining account of George Plante's life. Whether you are interested in art, World War II at sea and ashore, or just the story of a fascinating man's life, well researched and told, this book is thoroughly recommended.

W. J. R. "Jock" Gardner
November 2018

ACKNOWLEDGMENTS

This book could not have been written without the help and encouragement of Derek Plante, my stepbrother and George Plante's son. I am profoundly grateful to Derek for sending me his father's letters, for permission to use them in this work, for electronic copies of his father's sketches and paintings from the Imperial War Museum, and for patiently answering my many questions over the several years of this project. I hope he is happy with the result and that he feels it properly honors his father. I also thank Derek—and my brother Roger Broome—for tracking down long-defunct magazines in which some of George's work appeared.

James Bradford has supported this project from the very beginning. He has consistently encouraged me and his enthusiasm has kept me going. His wise and careful comments at various stages have made this a much better work than it would have been without his guidance. I must also thank, as always, Timothy Nenninger of the National Archives. No documents are too obscure or seemingly inconsequential for him to find, including those relating to *Sourabaya* and *Southern Princess* in New York. Alex Douglas has been a font of information and contacts to help me with the Canadian side of things and I also acknowledge help from Jayne Henry at the Directorate of History and Heritage in Ottawa, and Morgiana Halley for more Canadian sources. The archivists at Kew have all been brilliant, as I have come to expect. I want them to know I do not take them for granted. Alexandra Walton at the Imperial War Museum unearthed letters from George to the WAAC and their replies, which particularly helped to clarify the Ian Fleming connection.

I am indebted to Brian Sullivan for his careful reading of the chapters on George's activities with the PWE. Brian's deep knowledge of the history of southern and eastern Europe, and particularly of Italy, has added immeasurably to my understanding of the issues involved in those areas, and saved me from some embarrassing oversimplifications. Among the other friends and colleagues who have read all or part of this book at various stages I must especially thank W. J. R. Gardner, R. L. DiNardo, George Baer, Frank Delano, and Anthony Coombe. They each brought their areas of expertise to bear and made thoughtful suggestions.

Jacqueline Gutwirth went over the manuscript with the finest of toothcombs discovering not only every grammatical awkwardness and inelegancy of phrase, but also weeding out irrelevancies and information I found fascinating which she bluntly labeled "boring." If this book reads well it is largely thanks to her.

Finally, I must acknowledge my dear friends John and Sara Meadows. I have stayed with them in London on my research trips for so many years now that I am amazed at their patience and forbearance. They are the most gracious, generous, and welcoming of hosts.

Many thanks go to Glenn Griffith of the Naval Institute Press for patiently steering the manuscript of this book to acceptance, Aden Nichols for scrupulous editing, and Rachel Crawford, production editor, for seeing this project through to completion.

With so much assistance, I have been saved from numerous errors of omission and commission. Those errors that remain are entirely my own.

ABBREVIATIONS

AFHQ	Allied Force Headquarters
BBC	British Broadcasting Corporation
BIS	British Information Services
BSC	British Security Coordination
DBS	Distressed British Seamen
DSO	Distinguished Service Order
EDES	National Republican Greek League
ELAS	Greek National Popular Liberation Army
GHQ	General Headquarters
KA Press	Kasr El Aini Press, Cairo
MEF	Middle East Force
MI5	Military Intelligence, Section 5
MI6	Secret Intelligence Service (see also SIS)
MOI	Ministry of Information
NID	Naval Intelligence Department
OSS	Office of Strategic Services
OWI	Office of War Information
PID	Political Intelligence Division (Foreign Office)
PWB	Psychological Warfare Branch
PWD	Psychological Warfare Division
PWE	Political Warfare Executive
PWE ME	Political Warfare Executive Middle East
RAF	Royal Air Force
RNVR	Royal Naval Volunteer Reserve

R/O	Radio Officer
SHAEF	Supreme Headquarters Allied Expeditionary Force
SIS	Secret Intelligence Service (MI6)
SOE	Special Operations Executive
USAAF	United States Army Air Forces
WAAC	War Artists Advisory Committee
Y&R	Young & Rubicam (advertising agency)

PROLOGUE

At its heart this is a book about a Scottish artist, George Plante, and how his art served an alliance. The most critical of World War II alliances, the most long-lasting, and in many ways unique, was that of Britain and the United States. Theirs was a bond based on shared democratic principles that was altogether different from the cooperation of necessity with Stalin's Soviet Union. The wartime production of propaganda art provides a little-known example of one way in which the otherwise much-studied Anglo-American relationship was built up and sustained.

George Plante did not enter World War II as an artist; rather, he volunteered as a radio operator in the British Merchant Navy. There he spent more than two years engaged in the long-running and fiercely fought Battle of the Atlantic, plowing his way between Britain and the United States. But while dodging U-boats and battling the elements he never stopped painting. Every time his tanker docked in New York he pursued contacts in the art and advertising worlds, hoping to interest them in his latest work, persistently promoting his talent. Even in the midst of a devastating conflict, he never lost sight of his ambition to carve out a postwar career devoted to his art.

He soon caught the attention of agents of the British Ministry of Information (MOI) and of the War Artists Advisory Committee (WAAC). They recruited him to use his paintings of the war at sea for what was seen as a vital effort to secure American support for Britain. Almost from the moment he became prime minister in the spring of 1940, Winston Churchill made clear that his "foremost political purpose was to drag the United States into the war because only thus could the embattled island hope to accomplish more than its own survival."[1] Plante, following the artists' tradition of reportage, presented his merchant seaman's view of the war, depicting what he saw as truthfully as he could. From the deck of his tanker he gave visual evidence of the dramatic events that threatened Britain and the enormous demands they placed on the country.[2]

Plante's nautical days ended abruptly in March 1943. He was reassigned to work closely with the Americans in Egypt and Italy—this time to use his art as overt propaganda, both to demonize the Nazi and Fascist enemies and to arouse opposition to them among the occupied peoples under their control. Plante's unusual wartime career spanned three continents, moving from the North Atlantic to North Africa and the Mediterranean. Both at sea and on land, Plante's war was far from the policy making, whether at the strategic or operational level. He took no actions nor made any decisions that directly changed the course of the war—the decisions he was called upon to make dealt with color and style and layout. He was just one very talented man with unusual opportunities and a job to do. Yet seeing the war through George Plante's vivid and articulate letters and memoir—and of course through his art—adds a granular, ground-level view that expands and enriches the historical record.

There are notable gaps in Plante's wartime record as well as obvious evasions. His surviving correspondence consists predominantly of the letters he wrote to his wife, and on the brief but important occasions when they were together there were, naturally, no letters. Neither letters nor art survived the sinking of his ship on his last sea voyage. His correspondence throughout the war was subject to censorship, which may account for some gaps in the chronology and certainly affected his choice of topics and the nature of his comments. His memoir, written many years after the war, is surely subject to faded and imperfect memories and is perhaps somewhat colored by knowledge he later acquired of some of the historic events to which he was a party. But for the most part, where his letters and his memoir diverge, it is in small details or in the order in which events occurred, as well as in his later freedom to name some of those who were necessarily nameless at the time.

My approach to this topic is as a historian. I have neither been trained in, nor am I qualified to discuss, the artistic merit of Plante's work. It is clear, though, how his wartime art was shaped by the circumstances in which he found himself. His bold, somber paintings of the naval war show the highly technological conflict in which he was so closely engaged and that he came to know so well. Once installed in Cairo his art changed with the changed assignment. Tasked to work quickly, producing drawings and paintings in the service of explicit propaganda, his art was often cartoonish, consisting mostly of pen and ink sketches on topics selected for him by the clandestine government organization for which he worked.

After the war, when painting for himself, Plante generally repudiated the harsh realism and somber colors of his nautical paintings as well as the political message art of his propaganda days. His later paintings were notably devoid of technology and message, focusing instead on bright colors, scenic views, and a fascination with buildings —from Park Lane in London to old Italian churches to Amsterdam row houses. And yet his career both before the war and for thirty years after was in advertising. It is not difficult to see the direct connection between selling a product for commercial purposes and selling an idea for national purposes. In each case it was the creative challenge to inspire the desired result that fascinated Plante and at which he excelled.

I have lived with George Plante's art for much of my life. My mother married George in London in April 1956 when I was eleven. My American family and I had lived overseas since I was three, but from then on I lived in an Anglo-American family. At that time George worked for Young & Rubicam, an American advertising agency in London. On one of his trips to the head office in New York he met my maternal grandfather who told him he should look up his daughter who was living in London.

I grew up in a household unlike that of any other I knew. At a time when divorce was unacceptably racy my mother was an American divorcée—and no one in Britain had forgotten Mrs. Wallis Simpson. To make matters worse, we called our stepfather by his first name, George—he was my second stepfather and nothing else seemed to fit—and we told all our friends to call him George, too. Equally unnerving, we soon built and lived in a modern American-style split-level house with floor-to-ceiling windows improbably situated in an area of London dominated by large, red brick Edwardian mansions. George almost invariably returned from his many trips to New York with the jazz and blues records he loved so much. Once he brought back two records just released by Tom Lehrer, the Harvard mathematician turned songwriter-satirist. I memorized many of Lehrer's risqué lyrics, which gave me a rather unconventional notion of my own country. But we also listened to the radio program "Letter from America" by Alistair Cooke, the quintessential Anglo-American. Cooke's clear-eyed and amusing take on both his native and his adopted countries very closely reflected George's own views. I was raised sharing those views and George would often say we were truly mid-Atlantic.

Of course, such biculturalism was not always painless. When I was six a British classmate greeted me with the observation: "We could have won the war without you Yanks." Having just moved to England after three years in Italy I wasn't at all sure what he was referring to, but his remark clearly reflected what he heard from the adults around him. Brian Bond, a military historian, notes that in 1945 there was a widespread public "realization that 'We,' the British and Commonwealth peoples (the American role was under-emphasized) had won the war after so many years of hardship and struggle." That edge can still emerge. Occasionally, over the years, I have felt a certain condescension from some Britons when they find out I am American but also from some Americans who, hearing my accent, assume I'm British. I shrug off both. George taught me to acknowledge the oddities and shortcomings of each country while wholeheartedly appreciating their far greater assets. His good-natured criticisms of Britain and America were delivered with the humor that characterized his approach to life. A man by profession used to the economy of words, he gently mocked the American tendency to verbosity, contrasting, for example, "elevator operator," with the British "lift man." Americans, he loved to point out, proudly wear their politics and their religion on their sleeves, while the inhibited British recoil at the thought of revealing such intimate personal information.[3]

As I later learned, it was his experiences in World War II that developed and nurtured the gently sardonic Anglo-Americanism in George that affected the rest of his life. Unlike many other World War II veterans, George bore his war experiences lightly and with humor. I clearly remember his tales of his years in the British Merchant Navy and—more mysteriously—in Cairo. These stories were always delivered with a characteristic grin and were so amiable and so plausibly rendered that we didn't question the fudging of lines between reality and fiction.

George was bald, and his eyes were blue. The baldness, he would tell us, came from having to wash his hair in salt water while at sea. And his eyes changed from brown to blue, he would say, from peering for long hours at the sea and sky. We knew that he had been a Merchant Navy radio operator and also that he was a war artist who had painted many scenes of the Battle of the Atlantic. Most exciting of all, though, were his tales of serving on oil tankers, two of which were torpedoed and sunk by U-boats. (He told us he chose to serve on tankers because he thought he would see some action that way!)

George explained his move from the Merchant Navy to mysterious assignments in Egypt by telling us that he had been personally recruited by Ian Fleming who had sent him off to spy school somewhere deep in the English countryside. And yet his Cairo stories were disappointing, having surprisingly little to do with international espionage. He told us, for example, not to be taken in by the supposed glamor of belly dancers. They didn't bathe very often, he would say, and were unhealthy. And as for the Cairo cockroaches, he claimed they were as big as rats, bold and pervasive. They were so pervasive that at night he and his roommate, without turning on the lights, would make a leap from the doorway to their beds to avoid stepping on them.

And then there were the stories of his assignment to Bari in Italy. The one we heard most often was of the beautiful Yugoslav partisan whose bandoliers of ammunition across her ample chest sent the very strong message that it would be dangerous to try to get too close. Even though he was serving as a civilian in those days, George also told of accompanying flights over enemy-occupied territory to give final briefings to partisan resistance fighters before they parachuted out to their assignments. If they lost their nerve at the last moment he said he had to encourage them on their way, sometimes with a sharp push. If the plane were to crash George might be captured and shot as a spy unless he was in uniform, so he was given the uniform of an army captain to wear on those missions. George said he would often be strolling along preparatory to making a flight and was surprised when he was saluted and was expected to salute back. He had usually forgotten not only that he was in uniform at all, but even which uniform he was wearing.

Finally, George told us that immediately after the war many of his paintings were sent to the Soviet Union as part of a cultural exchange to demonstrate Britain's role in the recent fighting. With the fall of the Iron Curtain the paintings disappeared. Years later George claimed to be grateful for their disappearance since he came to dislike his wartime painting style. Certainly, we never saw any of his war art. While his later paintings hung all over our house none were from the war years, even though—as we found out later—he still had quite a number. Some of the rest were in the Imperial War Museum's collection of war art, some donated by the War Artists Advisory Committee. Nor did George ever mention or show us any of his anti-Nazi propaganda art although he kept many examples of it. We didn't even know that's what he was working on in Cairo and Bari.

Looking back at World War II through the lens of George's life made me recognize how fortunate we were in our leaders then. In spite of other differences, Churchill and Roosevelt shared a common and deeply held belief in democracy and its values. Each was a patriot first, of course, but they also understood the importance of mutual cooperation. While working on this book I was often amused by the unflattering opinions of each other I came across from both Britons and Americans. Now I realize how easily those differences could have been played upon and magnified by leaders less wise. The successful cohesion of the Anglo-American alliance was far from inevitable. Fortunately, there were those at all levels, including George Plante, whose broad, practical, and humane vision kept any divisive, would-be demagogues at bay.

Because I grew up with George's amusing war stories I never thought seriously about what he had actually done, even as I studied to become a naval historian, and even when I began to focus on World War II. His stories were just too much fun and too fantastical. But when I was writing a book about the use of technology in the Battle of the Atlantic I read Martin Middlebrook's excellent study of the great convoy battles of March 1943. Remembering George's stories, I sent him a copy of the book and was surprised when he told me he had been in one of those beleaguered convoys and on the tanker, *Southern Princess*, whose sinking was so graphically described by Middlebrook. Intrigued, I asked George for more information and he wrote a memoir for me that he called "A Very Personal View of World War II." Even in his memoir he put such a humorous face on that deadly conflict that I have had to keep rereading such accounts as Nicholas Monsarrat's *The Cruel Sea* to remind myself of a harsher reality.

When George's son, Derek, sent me his father's Merchant Navy letters after George died some years ago, I was struck by how unconventional a seaman he must have been. His artist's perceptions shaped all his experiences and eventually dominated his life both at sea and ashore. Then Derek sent me letters his father had written from Cairo. The cryptic return address on those letters, "PWE, MEF, Cairo," (Political Warfare Executive, Middle East Force) yielded the first clues about the clandestine propaganda George had been engaged in in Egypt and I finally accepted that his tales had been tailored not just by natural humor nor even by natural reticence, but by the constraints imposed by the secrecy of his work. What, as a naval historian, I had been unforgivably slow to see was that George's adventure stories formed the framework of his very real and very unusual war and that they were critically interwoven with what became known as the "special" Anglo-American relationship, a relationship that was in his bones, as it is in mine.

Once I moved from enjoying George's tales as amusing family lore to embracing them as historically significant I had to sort out, as far as possible, the fact from the fiction. And as I dug deeper into archives and published histories I also saw more and more connections to World War II in what I remembered about George from later years. As with his war stories, so too George used to amuse us with stories of his various postwar advertising campaigns. I remember vividly the time he explained how they made photographs of stew look so appealing. Usually, all the meat and vegetables would sink to the bottom of a pot of stew so to keep them on the surface they propped them up on toothpicks. There was no cheating here, George would say; the stew was real, as were all the ingredients. But there was a visual sleight of hand! Butter was in short supply in those days and expensive, so margarine was heavily advertised as an alternative. To make it more appealing, George told us, the producers added yellow coloring so it wouldn't look white, like lard. More visuals, more salesmanship.

World War II set an indelible stamp on George and the rest of his life was marked by his clear grasp of the importance of image in shaping behavior. The war also made him keen to use his creative talents in joint endeavors with Americans. The 1950s was the era of the Ugly American and when we traveled abroad George—irreverent and irrepressible as ever—loved to point out how much more popular he was with his British passport than we were with our American ones. That is one of the reasons I remember very clearly the 1956 Suez Crisis. George was essentially uninterested in politics, but because of his wartime experiences and his Egyptian friends, he followed the news of Cairo very closely. Quite apart from the political and military situation, though, my mother greatly enjoyed rubbing in that whereas we as Americans could travel to Egypt, George—with his British passport—could not.

For many years after World War II George kept in touch with those he had known in Egypt. His Russian/Egyptian friend, Milo Miloslavsky, was living in Manhattan when I was there, and George asked me to take him a box of chocolates. I don't remember what George told me about Milo except that he was a friend from wartime Cairo. It was a record-breaking bitterly cold January day in 1969 and I bundled my toddler into his snow suit, wrapped him in a blanket in his stroller, and walked south down Broadway for thirty or so blocks to Milo's apartment to deliver the sweets. Milo seemed old and frail to me and we didn't stay long in his rather gloomy home. Now I have so many questions for him. At the time I was studying British history in graduate school but the only war I was concerned about was Vietnam. I never thought someday I would be writing about George's war. Now, I realize how close George and Milo must have been to stay in contact all those years. I wonder what Milo did after the war and what eventually brought him to New York. I know he was in Egypt for some time because George and my mother visited him there once in the late 1950s. There are so many questions that I'll never be able to answer because I didn't think to ask when I could.

In later years, George often said he knew how and what to paint that pleased people and that would sell. By that time, he was living in South Carolina on Hilton Head Island, famous for its iconic lighthouse at the entrance to Harbor Town. George enjoyed painting scenic views, but he mostly resisted the urge to paint Harbor Town. He told me he could easily produce works that would sell like hot cakes in the galleries around the harbor; all he had to do was include that lighthouse. But he was not interested in such clichés. And while he enjoyed collecting beautiful things and living the good life, outside of work he painted only for his own pleasure. Long gone were the days when he painted to help save his country.

This is the story, then, of what lay behind the imaginative tales George Plante wove for us impressionable children and of his real, if unusual, artist's contribution to Anglo-American successes in World War II.

CHAPTER ONE

"I had chosen my own battleground. Well . . . up to a point."

World War I erupted in August 1914, shattering the peace of Europe. Barely six weeks later, on 18 September, George Plante was born on the top floor of an apartment building in Edinburgh. He was his parents' first child. While not a luxurious penthouse, the apartment at 14 Parkside Street in the Newington district looked out on a vast panorama of what was then called King's Park (now Holyrood Park) where—as Plante remembered eighty years later—"the slopes of the Salisbury Crags swept down from the massive red rib-like rocks and stood out against the wild windswept skies with the towering mountainous Arthur's Seat rising up behind."[1]

George was only four when the war ended but he was left with several vivid memories. Until the end of his life he remembered being held in his mother's arms, watching the searchlights stabbing the skies and the star shells exploding over King's Park, hearing the booming of the antiaircraft guns aimed at the German zeppelins flying overhead. He remembered, too, the wounded, gassed, shell-shocked soldiers convalescing in their bright blue flannel uniforms with blood red ties and white shirts. And he remembered the night he awoke to see some policemen in his candlelit sitting room. Apparently, the family's blackout arrangements were showing cracks of light. Most exciting of all was his memory of huge guns and fearsome tanks in the Waverley Market; they were assembled there, he discovered later, for a war bond rally.[2]

George would become an artist: sophisticated, worldly, always sensitive to landscape, color, and design. Yet the immediate foreground of his childhood view—below the majestic peaks—was the unsightly railroad yard that was endlessly fascinating to him. He spent many happy hours with his face pressed to the window, watching the black steam engines "puffing clouds of white smoke, shunting forwards and backwards." What he enjoyed most was when the train trucks careened along the tracks until they arrived at their assigned place with a resounding and most satisfactory crash. He had no need of a train set to play with—he had the real thing.[3]

That was true of most everything that was fun in George's young life. King's Park was his wild and exciting playground with dangerous high rocks to climb, three different lochs to fish in, and the nearby "Medows" (as it is styled in the Scottish vernacular) for football and cricket. He ignored the many scratches he got climbing up the steep face of Arthur's Seat for the reward of finding himself at the top of the world looking out over "Auld Reekie" and seeing the castle rising up out of the blue smoke haze. When it was blustery and raining or sleeting, which it often was, George would wander into the Scottish National Museum with its model ships, ancient steam engines, stuffed animals and birds from all over the world, Egyptian mummies, and ancient artifacts. Many wet Sundays were spent in the National Art Gallery or the Portrait Gallery. It was there that he discovered for himself how to enjoy art. All these treasures were within walking distance and all were free.

George grew up largely unsupervised, without hovering parents and the usual home life. Instead he lived in that top floor flat with a grandmother and grandfather, an uncle (sometimes two), and a young aunt—but no mother or father. His grandfather was a retired surgical instrument maker who sat quietly all day in his wing chair reading the newspapers and listening to the great opera singers of the time including Caruso, Galli-Curci, Scotti, and Homer. Perhaps this interest had been set off by the fact that the great Scottish lyric tenor Joseph Hislop had been born in that flat, in fact in the very same room as young George. The music was played on a wind-up gramophone and emerged from a large horn. Later on, George's uncle Johnny, a bookbinder by trade, brought home some records by Paul Whiteman, Bix Beiderbecke, Joe Venuti, and Red Nichols and his Five Pennies sparking George's lifelong love affair with American jazz.

There was plenty of affection for the "bonny wee bairn," including hugs from his grandmother. He was introduced to Sunday school but admits that "it didn't really take." His responsibilities were few—the main one was to go to the grocery store with a daunting list and the requisite funds. There he was served by men in long white aprons and the money was dispatched to the cashier in a wooden container pulled along overhead wires "with a lot of banging and clanging of bells." Staggering home with his large string bag bulging with heavy potatoes, turnips, flour, and sugar he still had to face the building's stairs; he understood why his grandfather rarely went out. At the bottom of the street were some stables for horses and ponies that pulled the coal carts and the ice cream van. When George was lucky he was allowed to unharness and brush down the pony for a reward of ice cream.

Most days George went home only when darkness fell. Some nights he listened to the radio if he could "get the cat's whisker to scratch the crystal in the right spot." Otherwise he read exciting books about the Boxer Rebellion or terrifying Chinese tortures in books he got from the public library. He also banged away at his grandparents' square rosewood piano, teaching himself to play. Before his grandfather retired he made George a green wood and brass model engine big enough for him to sit on. The whole family did its best to look after George, although it was Aunt Kitty, his mother Madge's young sister, who assumed primary responsibility. She worked in the nearby post office and was engaged to a young man who was about to graduate from university as an engineer.

Where were George's parents? "My mother was away somewhere," Plante explained somewhat enigmatically to his son, eighty years later, "and my father was serving in the famous Black Watch regiment when he was wounded in Palestine." He remembers seeing his father, Harold Plant, only once. "He was in uniform and performed some drill for my amusement. From what I gathered he was a likeable, quite handsome, sandy-haired man of average height. He was a victuals dealer with his own business and enjoyed an occasional drink, which mother disapproved of."[4]

Apparently, the disapproval was deep. In 1913 Madge Smith married Harry Plant, who had moved to Scotland from England. That very same month Harry went bankrupt. The following year, when Harry left to serve in the war, Madge began a romance with George Handwork (originally spelled Handwerck until he Anglicized it), a German immigrant. On Harry's return from the war he and Madge separated and Madge and George Handwork, as attested to in the divorce papers, "lived and cohabited together as husband and wife." In June 1921 Madge gave birth to a daughter, Marjorie, George Plante's half sister. After Madge and Harry's divorce became final in 1923, Harry apparently disappeared. Madge and George Handwork married soon after.[5]

The Handworks divided their time between Edinburgh and Brighton, on the south coast of England, where they had a shop on the seafront selling souvenirs, primarily postcards and novelties. George had come to Britain to help his older brother, Rudolph Handwerck, with his growing postcard business. Unlike his younger brother, Rudolph never Anglicized his name. When World War I broke out Rudolph reluctantly decided to return to Germany with his family leaving his brother, who was a naturalized British subject, in charge of the shop in Brighton.[6]

By then known as the Brighton Picture Post Card Co., the shop prospered under George Handwork. When he and Madge were down south in England they left George in Scotland, although they took their daughter with them. Apparently, Madge "had a great business interest and drive and possibly not much desire to raise a family."

Despite the fact that, as George later noted, "neither Marjorie nor I had what you might call a normal upbringing," he always spoke well of his stepfather and was saddened by his sudden death in 1953 at the age of sixty-nine. Plante never saw, nor tried to find, his father Harry who, his mother told him, had run off to Australia and left them. "I just accepted," Plante told his son, "that I didn't have a father just as if he had never returned from the war." In fact, Harry had settled in Leek, England, not far from London and close to where Plante spent much of the rest of his life. Years later Plante explained his apparent reluctance to learn more about his father by saying that he knew there had been some sort of scandal in the family and some things were best left unknown.[7]

Eventually George was sent to George Heriot's, a well-regarded Scottish public school. From there he went to the Edinburgh College of Art. Of his time in college he wrote: "Now I wish I had been a better student and paid more attention to the unusually talented painters who were on the faculty at that time and less time playing rugby and soccer." Apparently his love of music pulled him away from his studies as well and he earned his keep by playing drums into the small hours of the morning at the Havana, the Ritz, the Cosmos, and similar nightclubs. For the rest of his life he was seldom without a pencil and sketchpad or far from some source of his beloved music.[8]

While at art school Plante met a shy, pretty fellow student, Evelyn Smith, and by the time they were in their last year he was madly in love. In April 1933, with only one more term to go, he saw Evelyn off on the boat to her home in Kirkwall where she was returning to spend the holidays with her family. Kirkwall was the capital of the Orkney Islands that sit off the northern tip of Scotland. Although these were the Depression years and much of Scotland, especially the highlands, was suffering devastating unemployment and neglect, George never alluded to these concerns in his one surviving letter of that spring. Although we know from that letter to Evelyn how much he loved her, we know little else about their courtship except that he told her about the art exhibits he went to while she was gone (one covering the well known 1920s and '30s art deco posters of the London and North Eastern Railway) and shared his thoughts on the latest jazz recordings he had heard (specifically, Louis Armstrong). "You are the sweetest girl in the world," he concluded, "and I'm just crazy about you. Dear, I am already looking forward to your triumphant return."[9]

What we also know is that both George and Evelyn graduated from the Edinburgh College of Art. George had done well enough to be awarded a traveling scholarship to continue his studies abroad. Everyone assumed he would follow the well-worn path and head for Florence or Rome, but he chose Berlin because he saw the exciting things going on in Germany. German scientists, engineers, and doctors were leading the world with their discoveries and inventions. "Even Hollywood," Plante noted, "when casting geniuses always had them speak with German accents," and the Bauhaus movement was shaking up the art world with new theories of the visual and applied arts.[10]

Plante was thrilled to study at the Contempora School of Applied Arts in Berlin, a progressive private college that, like the Bauhaus, strongly emphasized the unity of all applied arts. He was there in the early days when Adolph Hitler and his National Socialists had come to power in Germany and at that time there were rumors that the Contempora would be closed down by the Nazis because they saw the art of the Weimar Republic as degenerate. Yet according to Plante this was still the "gay, mad Berlin of Isherwood," although he claimed he had been too young to really enjoy it.[11]

In his memoir Plante recalled that while he saw that the rich were enjoying their debaucheries on the Kurfürstendamm—one of Berlin's principal avenues—he also saw that the masses, having survived the miseries of hyperinflation, were unemployed, frustrated, vulnerable, and exploitable. He noted that he himself was in the middle of it all and from that vantage point came to understand that while the older generation on the whole were appalled by the Nazis, the younger generation were energized by Hitler's promise of jobs and the revival of national pride. Traveling through Austria by train in 1936, the author Rebecca West found much the same thing. A group of German businessmen and their wives on the train with her expressed their fear of Nazism while acknowledging "all the young people, they are solid for Hitler. For them all is done."[12]

Plante recalled assiduously avoiding attempts to interest him in joining the Hitler Youth (in spite of the fact that he was too old). He did admit, however, to accepting invitations to join Hitler Youth marches in the Black Forest, singing patriotic songs as they tramped along. He also admitted to participating in many "frantically energetic evenings at the gymnasium," adding that these robust activities were often followed by lengthy and heated arguments about who had won World War I. Plante maintained that the Allies had won, but he found the Germans were convinced that they had. Any suggestion to the contrary, no matter the evidence he might invoke, was dismissed as evil Allied propaganda.[13]

Plante had also been invited to attend meetings of the Stahlhelm, an organization of ex-servicemen—officers as he recalled—who were, he thought, trying to organize some sort of resistance to the National Socialist juggernaut. Even then this had looked like a lost cause, and though the organization moved increasingly to the right—and eventually even had members in Hitler's cabinet—it was disbanded in 1935. Plante probably misread the thrust of the organization, which he found quite benign, although it is possible that the members he met had remained true to its original, inclusive purpose. More troubling to Plante was the fact that when visiting private homes, he was often asked to lower his voice in case the conversation should be overheard and reported to the Nazis. While the atmosphere was clearly tense, Plante did not grasp its broader significance nor did he realize at the time how potentially dangerous the situation in Germany would be for the whole world.[14]

On his return to Edinburgh, Plante realized that much as he loved his hometown, if he were to get anywhere he would have to go to "where it all happened": London! He knew, of course, that this was not the ideal time to start a career. At its height the Depression had put more than three million people in England out of work and recovery was slow. There were large numbers of unemployed from all over the country and strikers and hunger marchers demonstrated up and down Westminster. But Plante was optimistic, tenacious, and ready to work hard, so he left for the south. When he arrived at King's Cross Station he headed straight for a room at the YMCA on Tottenham Court Road. Then, with portfolio in hand he attacked the London art world "like Don Quixote attacking the windmills."[15]

He went hungry. He walked miles and miles to save bus fare. Sometimes he climbed into bed, not to sleep but just to keep warm. Eventually he was lucky and met "kind and encouraging people" who gave him work. His first studio "was a little room in Chelsea. It had just one electric outlet and many attachments. With one turn of the switch you could have light, heat, music, or a boiling kettle. If all four came on at the same time, I got a blinding flash and then total darkness." He lived on the absolute minimum, so there was no question of being distracted from his work. He couldn't take any girls out to a meal or a movie. All he could offer was a walk around the pond in Kensington Gardens or, on fine evenings, they could listen to the band playing in the bandstand there. Years later, on reflection, he thought his penury had been a good thing since it made him concentrate on whatever talent it was he had.[16]

The following year, Plante got a job as a graphic artist for Clement Danes Studio in London. By then he was earning enough to bring Evelyn to London and they were married at Turnham Green in Chiswick, London, on 28 August 1937. As their marriage certificate shows, Evelyn was twenty-five and he was twenty-two, but he later admitted lying about his age telling friends that he was twenty-four. He had already added the "e" to his last name and on the certificate he added it to his father's name as well. Sometime later Plante left Clement Danes and moved to Everetts Advertising. As he would often later say, he knew he was not another Picasso and choosing his path with rational foresight he enthusiastically threw himself into the developing field of commercial art and advertising.[17]

Meanwhile, Hitler and his Nazi party continued their campaign of brutal repression at home and aggrandizement abroad and some were prescient enough to see this as a clear threat to the stability of Europe.

But most in Britain and on the continent wished at all costs to avoid another conflagration like the one they had gone through twenty years earlier. Although there were committed anti-appeasers in the country—most prominently Winston Churchill, Anthony Eden, and Harold Macmillan in Parliament—Prime Minister Neville Chamberlain and his Tory government reflected the majority sentiment when they did everything in their power to appease Nazi Germany. This continued even in the face of Hitler's flagrant violations of the Treaty of Versailles. When Chamberlain returned from Munich in 1938 claiming to have pulled Europe back from the brink of war, one anti-appeaser noted: "you might think we had won a major victory instead of betraying a minor country."[18]

In the autumn of what was most likely 1938, Plante made a short trip back to Berlin where he stayed with his uncle Rudolph Handwerck in the Tegel district of Berlin. Though undated, his letters indicate that this time he saw quite clearly what was going on. When he had been booking his ticket Plante heard a man enquiring about the safety of travel in Germany, afraid in case he might get shot over there. Writing to Evelyn and reassuring her that "things aren't as bad as that" he added that the previous day he had "experienced what things are really like." Plante continued,

> Some Nazis on parade marched past singing their song No. 1. Well, when this song is sung everyone must stand with arm outstretched until it is over. However, all this business to me was just darned funny. But—I didn't think it for long. In a few seconds a bunch of Nazis were round me and it was the mere fact that I was a foreigner that saved me from being arrested. In future I will be more careful.[19]

Uncle Rudolf was a keen sportsman and obviously rather well off. Plante wrote of accompanying his uncle and cousin to their yacht club on Lake Tegel near their home on the outskirts of the city where he kept his "beautiful boat." In the summer the members stayed in the club all weekend, but even though "the season is getting late now" everyone still "strips to the waist and paddles around in the boats." They stopped at a lakeside beer garden and drank Berlin Weiss Bier from a "huge thing like a goldfish bowl on a stand" and watched a Nazi propaganda firework display. "It is really embarrassing at times," Plante noted, "because everyone I meet is only too eager to fix up some kind of entertainment for me with the result that I have difficulty in getting my work done."[20]

From his letters it seems as though Plante's main purpose for this visit was to work on posters. Keen to improve his technique in an important advertising medium he tried to ignore the ugly atmosphere in Germany. He was hoping to work with a Professor Bencke, "a real decent sort," but initially the professor was not working on posters so had no use for Plante.[21]

"Honest, Berlin is alright," he reassured his worried wife. "Beautiful cafes, beautiful women, wine in plenty but—no Evelyn. Isn't it really wonderful to have someone who really loves you and encourages you to work hard," he wrote. "Love is the finest thing in the world." Moreover, it was a love based on shared interests. Much of the rest of his letter was in response to Evelyn's comments on the music of Harry Ray and his band that she had been listening to. Her husband agreed that her analysis was quite right adding, "You will hear snatches of Louis Armstrong and Cab Calloway and that the arrangements are also cribbed. Really, I'm very bucked to see that you can enjoy real 'hot' dance music and can also discriminate. Gosh, dear, do we suit each other or do we?"[22]

The previous day Plante noted that he had had a day off from the studio so had worked at home and then gone into the city and done some sketches in Unter-den-Linden. This day he had been at the studio since 7:30 a.m., taking lunch at an open-air café on the Kurfürstendamm. "Wonderful stunt this," he wrote, "you can sit in the sun with a sausage in one hand and a tankard of beer in the other and watch all the society girls parading up and down." As in many of his early letters, Plante made a quick sketch, this time of his cover design for the *Lady* magazine. "I have had great praise for this from Prof.

Bencke when I finally saw him," he noted. Still, in spite of the seeming normality, the atmosphere was tense and he was glad to return to England. His uncle Rudolph, who loathed the Nazis, moved his family back to England not long after and they remained there trying, unsuccessfully, to secure citizenship. During the war Rudolph was interned for four and a half years on the Isle of Man and in 1949, giving up on Britain he moved to Miami, where one of his daughters still lives.[23]

Hitler's increasing aggression and his takeover of Czechoslovakia in March 1939, despite promises not to, led Britain to pledge military support to Poland in the event of a Nazi invasion. Prompted by the obvious failure of the appeasement policy, this diplomatic move had few teeth. Unlike all other European powers, Britain had no peacetime conscription until April 1939—and even then it only applied to men between the ages of twenty and twenty-two.

In August 1939 George and Evelyn went on holiday to La Napoule, near Cannes on the French Riviera. As they crossed the English Channel to the White Cliffs of Dover on the way back, an unidentified plane crashed into the water just ahead of their ferry; it seemed like an omen. Nazi forces had slammed into Poland the day before and everyone's nerves were on edge. At home the next day they woke up to a lazy Sunday morning. It was 3 September 1939 and Plante went out in search of the milkman to let him know that they were back. Instead he heard the deep sonorous chimes of Big Ben booming out the hour of eleven on the radio and then heard Prime Minister Chamberlain solemnly announce that in spite of all the warnings, Hitler had not responded to Britain's ultimatum to get out of Poland and that Britain was therefore at war with Germany.[24]

Since everyone had been warned that should war break out the skies would fill with hordes of Luftwaffe bombers raining bombs, the air raid sirens came as no surprise. But even before Plante could grab his gas mask and crawl under the table the all clear sounded. Everything was strangely quiet again. Later they heard that a German reconnaissance plane had been spotted while another plane had dropped a couple of bombs in Scotland, near the Forth Bridge and the

Rosyth Naval Base, causing the warning sirens but leaving no damage in its wake.[25]

That same day Parliament passed the National Service (Armed Forces) Act extending conscription to all men between eighteen and forty-one. This began a long, drawn-out process of registration by age groups and progress was made, according to one observer, "with the speed of an elephant trying to compete in the Derby." In part the delay was caused by lack of infrastructure to deal with the sudden large influx of draftees. At first there was not even a way to register those liable for the draft, never mind housing, training, and equipping them.[26]

Like many other young men in their twenties, Plante—who was then twenty-five—was caught in limbo. Artists were not in a reserved occupation and were liable for call-up just like everyone else. George was ready to serve, but until called he had no option but to continue his work as a commercial artist. Fortunately for him, he was kept busy doing illustrations for a couple of national newspapers and several other clients, though many advertising and commercial art departments had been forced to lay off large numbers of staff at the beginning of the war. While eager to serve his country in some capacity, Plante was accustomed to making his own decisions and as he recalled in his memoirs, the thought of being ordered to march up and down by someone in a sergeant major's uniform had little appeal. He needed to find another option.[27]

On the outbreak of war, Britain's pitifully small regular army of fewer than two hundred thousand was short of almost all equipment. Its reserve forces, the Territorial Army, were even smaller, underequipped, and poorly trained. Germany, on the other hand, had more than three million men under arms, while in September 1939 France could muster five million men. The Royal Air Force (RAF), while better funded than the army, was also undermanned and underequipped, and aircraft production was well behind that of Germany. Indeed, Britain's tentative rearmament campaign, begun in the mid-1930s, had progressed slowly despite the critical nature of the international situation. Even the economic sector had continued business as usual with little acceleration of armaments production or stockpiling of raw materials and other essential supplies.[28]

Watching the destruction of Warsaw in newsreel footage, Londoners continued to expect German bombers to attack them at any moment. But the bombers didn't come and there followed a surreal six months known to British troops as the "bore war." In America it was called the Phony War, when neither the British Army nor the RAF nor France took action but waited to be attacked. Britain's contribution was to drop not bombs but millions of propaganda leaflets over Germany assuring Germans that it would be impossible for them to continue the war much longer. This inactivity abruptly ended when Winston Churchill became prime minister.

Alone of the British armed forces the Royal Navy, under the guidance of Winston Churchill as First Lord of the Admiralty, had seen real combat in those first months. Churchill immediately put his department on a war footing and instituted convoy tactics employing scarce naval vessels to protect merchant ships from German U-boats and surface raiders as best they could. Nevertheless, the navy was also restricted to largely defensive action, even when U-boats and raiders started taking a toll on British and neutral merchant ships.

By the spring of 1940, when the shooting war finally began in earnest in Western Europe, Plante and many other men his age still had not been called up. He was certainly an unlikely warrior. A quintessential civilian; an artist by temperament, training, and profession; and a jazz musician by avocation, nothing in his background (except perhaps that he was a Scot) suggested martial tendencies. But when Britain finally faced down the Nazi juggernaut, he decided not to wait any longer to be drafted. Knowing he would hate slogging through the mud with the infantry, Plante decided to present himself to the RAF for service. As he recalled years later, he had been "quite elated at the prospect of wearing the pale blue uniform with a pilot's wings sewn to my chest and flying off into the deep blue yonder to help get this nasty little war over." To his chagrin, the RAF told him to go away and wait until he was sent for. In the meantime, they made clear they would do their best to manage without him.[29]

Plante immediately marched into the navy recruiting office but here the story was the same, although the recruiters listened a good deal more sympathetically. They asked Plante if he would be willing to volunteer to be a radio operator in the Merchant Navy since he seemed determined to go to sea. Radio operators were desperately needed, he was told; in wartime all vessels had to carry three of them to keep two four-hour watches each to effect around-the-clock coverage. In peacetime most vessels had only one or two radio officers, so the push was on to quickly train more. The Merchant Navy was a civilian service that had shifted to a war footing. Radio operators could not be secured through the draft, making the shortfall even more dire. Navy recruiters told him that if he joined up, took the training, and passed the course, they were quite sure he would be given a shipboard assignment. Best of all, he could take the radio course in Edinburgh.[30]

While service in the Merchant Navy had never occurred to him, Plante could see that the work would be of critical importance. Everyone knew that as an island nation, Britain relied on imports brought in by sea, largely shipped across the Atlantic from the United States. Although Britain was self-sufficient in coal, when the new war began in 1939 many other materials vital for a modern industrial state still had to come from overseas, as did half its food. Most metal ores, all rubber, and even key manufactured goods were imported, as was all of the oil. As in World War I, when the Germans employed unrestricted submarine warfare against British merchant shipping, the Nazis were again determined to cut Britain off from these essential supplies.[31]

Under the determined leadership of Admiral Karl Dönitz the U-boats struck immediately, sinking the passenger liner *Athenia* less than nine hours after the British declaration of war on 3 September 1939. At sea there was no Phony War. Although quickly on the offensive, at this early stage the U-boats could not mount a coordinated attack, nor even a very efficient one. Even so, in the first year and a half of war the goods reaching Britain were cut almost in half and Britons were forced to endure a meager, nearly meatless diet. "Everyone was in the front line in one way or another," Plante recalled. "Sugar, chocolate, cheese, butter, meat, petrol, clothing, even such essentials as gin and scotch were strictly rationed! Everything was either in short supply or non-existent." If he could not shoot down Nazi Messerschmitts or sink U-boats, Plante concluded he could at least help fend off disaster by bringing in vital cargoes. Censorship of the media largely obscured the heavy toll on cargo ships inflicted by mines, dive-bombers, and surface raiders, in addition to the deadly U-boats. Also hidden was the extent of the loss of life among merchant seamen. Officially, the civilian population knew little of these escalating disasters, but the results were everywhere apparent, and no one was fooled. Plante had a pretty good idea of what he was getting into.[32]

When he had decided on a course of action, Plante quit his commercial artist's job; he and Evelyn stowed all their belongings in a warehouse in London. They loaded the petrol they had been saving into the back of their small Ford convertible with little room for anything else. This was both illegal and dangerous, but it was the only way they could get themselves and the car to Scotland. They drove the four hundred-odd miles very carefully, coasting downhill in neutral to save on fuel, reaching Scotland without mishap. While they lived cheaply with his mother, Plante enrolled in the radio operator's course at Leith Nautical College outside Edinburgh. He took a job as a night watchman to help make ends meet, sleeping up in the rafters of the Royal College of Surgeons. His duties included being ready to deal with any incendiary bombs that might land on the roof. Fortunately, none did.[33]

On 31 December 1940, upon completion of the seven-month course, Plante received a "Special Certificate of Proficiency in Radiotelegraphy." This made him eligible for commission as a radio officer (R/O) in the Merchant Navy, a role by long custom referred to as "Sparks" by the rest of the crew. The certificate stated that Plante was five feet nine inches tall, had brown eyes and a fair complexion. The attached photograph showed that he had a receding hairline. It seems his baldness was not caused by a regimen of salt water as he later claimed; the mystery of his changing eye color remains unresolved. His course successfully completed, Plante embarked on his new life while Evelyn sought the relative safety of her family home at Kirkwall.[34]

At the beginning of World War II, the British merchant shipping fleet had been the largest in the world with almost one third of all existing merchant ships, even though it had been diminished by the years of depression between the wars. Still, the Merchant Navy Plante joined was considerably smaller than the armed services, numbering some 185,000 members, of whom 144,000 or so were at sea on any given day. Prewar officers were traditionally drawn from seafaring families and were well-educated types who served as masters, deck officers, engineers, radio officers, and pursers. The rest of the personnel fell into three basic categories: seamen, engine-room men, and the catering staff of stewards/stewardesses and cooks. By one account, about half of the seamen came from the British Isles, mostly from such ports as London, Liverpool, Cardiff, Glasgow, Hull, and Southampton, while others came from all over the empire as well as some foreign countries. About a third of all seamen on British ships were lascars, Asians—mainly Indian and Chinese—who were traditionally employed under special agreements giving the ship owners more control over them than they had over other ratings. A great many merchant seamen thus served in mixed crews. The ships themselves also included a very broad range of vessels from tankers to passenger liners and from freighters to tramp steamers to coasters. As opposed to warships their purpose was trade, and for the duration of the war they carried people and merchandise under the direction of the Ministry of War Transport.[35]

There were four basic elements engaged in the Battle of the Atlantic: the convoys of merchant ships carrying vital supplies to Britain; the naval escorts that accompanied the convoys for their protection; the aircraft, both land-based and (later) shipborne, that helped protect the convoys; and the German submarines—the deadly U-boats—whose job it was to prevent the passage of the merchant ships by sinking as many as possible. Limited in range by the geography of their North Sea bases, the U-boats mostly operated in the coastal waters off Scotland and Ireland and in the Bay of Biscay attacking targets of opportunity. Such successes as they had were dictated a great deal by luck. In addition to being very short of escorts at this stage, Britain also had few land-based aircraft assigned to help convoys, so the enormous size of the Atlantic was the convoys' best protection. Both sides had yet to develop effective measures of control and coordination of effort.[36]

By the time Plante was at sea in 1941 the Atlantic campaign had changed considerably. The fall of France and the access this gave the Germans to French ports allowed U-boats to thrust much farther out into the ocean. The development of wolf pack tactics enabled them to converge on convoys in groups directed by radio from their headquarters. The German fleet was also assisted by the great increase in the number of U-boats being built, although Britain was also furiously producing more escorts and using various military intelligence methods to avoid U-boat concentrations.

Although he knew little about the war at sea that awaited him, Plante wrote his wife in February that he had "at least managed to exercise some control over my own destiny and I had chosen my own battleground. Well . . . up to a point." Now he waited for news of his ship. Would he be assigned to the frigid and deadly Murmansk convoys, he wondered? Or perhaps the Malta convoys that faced tremendous bombardment? Despite the rough weather, the North Atlantic would be his first choice because New York was at the other end of the journey. It had long been his dream to visit that mecca of nightclubs with their fabulous jazz.[37]

Plante's first assignment was to serve on a coastal trader, just to help him get his sea legs until a real job came along. To his delight they were headed for the Orkneys and he expected to be able to see his wife, if only briefly.[38]

Plante set sail on Saturday 1 March 1941. Britain had been at war for sixteen months by then. "Feeling proud and just a little self-conscious in my brand new black doeskin uniform with its wavy gold band on each sleeve," he remembered in his postwar memoir, "I reported to the SS *Amelia* tied up at Leith docks. The *Amelia*," he continued, "a rugged little coastal steamer plied its trade up and down the east coast of Scotland between Leith and the Orkney Islands. Its cargo . . . sheep, cattle, motor cars, agricultural machinery—whatever was needed—was stowed in the hold or on deck. It was far too small to carry a radio officer. I was only signed on as a supernumerary to get some feel of life at sea while I waited for my posting to something bigger."[39]

Plante wrote, "On a 'dreachy' cold windy afternoon we cast off and rolled and pitched our way down the Firth of Forth, out into the all-embracing greyness of the North Sea." Sailing in a coastal convoy heading north for the Orkneys and watching out for mines and the sounds of approaching enemy dive-bombers, Plante noted the rest of the crew looking askance at his indoor complexion and decided that the best he could do was to keep out of their way. Retreating to the shelter of the galley, close to the warm open coal stove, he watched as crewmembers burst through the door dripping with water to gulp down a mug of strong, hot tea before going out to face the elements again.[40]

As the little ship rolled and slammed into the waves with resounding thuds, it "creaked and groaned as if it was about to be torn apart at the seams. The very discontented cows we carried bellowed and the sheep bleated their unhappiness." But to the amazement of the crew—and to Plante's own surprise—this novice sailor was still sitting upright and clear-eyed. Unaffected by even a hint of nausea, he seemed to have been made for a life at sea. Later, living through some of the wildest storms imaginable on the North Atlantic, he never suffered the miseries of seasickness. Apparently, however, Plante's hardiness was not matched by his usefulness. Away in the galley he had been enjoying being cozily enveloped in the thick steamy fog created by the sausages, eggs, and bacon, and thick slabs of bread frying in deep fat in an enormous black frying pan three or four feet in diameter. When the crew had eaten, he decided to help out by cleaning the pan. He put some soda in it, went on deck and scrubbed it thoroughly clean, proud that he had remembered to go to the leeward rail. Then he gave a mighty heave, throwing the sudsy contents overboard. Alas, the whole pan disappeared into the sea leaving him hanging onto the wooden handle. His confession to the cook was met first with stunned silence and then by such a torrent of abuse regarding his legitimacy and intelligence, that he almost wished he had joined the army after all.[41]

Time is a great healer, and after some sketch portraits that Plante gave his fellow crewmembers they reluctantly agreed that for a landlubber he was not so bad. Later, on the trip south again, he worked hard to redeem himself even further. Writing to his wife he said that "two German planes were spotted and the gunners became all active removing covers etc. and I was able to make myself useful . . . carrying a box of grenades along to the bomb thrower in the stern." Gunfire from nearby patrol ships soon had the German warplanes climbing away leaving vapor trails in the sky "just like one of the advertising signs. I wouldn't have been a bit surprised if it had spelt Persil [a popular laundry detergent]."[42]

After that threat the crew put up their kite to prevent any dive-bombing. "It was good fun getting this up, it is flown from the foremast, up and up it went and it flew beautifully." A short time later Captain Murray complained that although the ship was going at full speed it did not seem to be making much headway. "He was greatly tickled," Plante wrote, "by my suggestion that the kite was probably lifting the ship several feet out of the water and the propeller was merely turning in thin air!" In response to this explanation it was proposed that when the kite was brought in later they would fit a seat to it and "strap me in as an observer for the rest of the trip." They never got to act on this idea because when they tried to bring the kite in the cable snapped and the kite soared away.[43]

In spite of the danger they were in, Plante never ceased to take note of his surroundings with a painter's eye. "The Orkneys looked really grand in the morning sun," he wrote his wife when they had sailed off early, "and everything was much too lovely for war."[44]

Later, while on the bridge, Plante thought he spotted the vague lines of a cruiser. "After a bit of ragging about me mistaking one of the islands for this imaginary cruiser, Captain Murray said 'can ye read her name?' This was his little joke because it was a mere wisp on the horizon, but I went one better spelling out DEUTSCHLAND as I peered through the glasses." By then it was lunchtime, "boiled beef, turnip and potatoes, broth, tea and biscuits," after which Plante made "one or two perilous journeys from the galley with big tins of hot soup for crew members on duty." Later, Plante had a look through the ship's collection of gramophone records. These were, as he put it "just typical, consisting of hillybillys, jigs and reels, so I didn't trouble to play any." As it turned out the ship's wireless was out of order so "for the remainder of the afternoon I messed around with it and to my surprise was able to mend it."[45]

By then they had joined their convoy. "What a grand sight it is to see these ships all ploughing along together," Plante wrote, still new enough to the business to be enthusiastic. During the rest of the trip they steadily crept up through the convoy and by the following day they were first behind the commodore's ship. Apparently "the vice commodore did not like this and nor did the other ships so after much hooting, and hooting back again from us, we were told to go back." But since by then they were already in the Firth of Forth, "Skipper Murray left the convoy and we made off on our own course." At about 2 p.m. they docked at Leith. Plante wrote his wife, "Murray and I had a glass of beer, I wired you and then made for home." After a hot bath Plante unpacked and had some tea. Edinburgh had just had its heaviest snowfall in years.[46]

And so began—once again—the wait for a new ship and a new destination. But to where?

CHAPTER TWO

"My main duty was to be tethered by the ears to the radio."

In April 1941 Plante had been off the *Amelia* for over a month and was still in his mother's home in Edinburgh waiting to be called to a ship. By then the Germans were in Athens and although Edinburgh was virtually untouched and would remain so, Plante could hear the Luftwaffe bombing the nearby Firth of Forth, especially the port of Leith. From the waves of planes passing over "it appeared that Glasgow," less than fifty miles away to the west, "may have been the main objective for the second night in succession." Everyone knew that Glasgow was taking a terrible beating.[1]

The news from London was bad too. A former colleague of Plante's had been on convoy duty in the Channel "and seems to time his leave nights in London with the high spots of the Blitz—and doesn't like it much! The Regal Marble Arch [movie theater], Selfridges, the Marble Arch itself, Curzon Street and the junction of Park Lane and Piccadilly are a few of the places that suffered the other night. Poor old London—I wonder what it will be like when we get back," Plante wrote Evelyn. Indeed, although the RAF had won the Battle of Britain by the fall of 1940, the Luftwaffe continued to pummel British cities and ports mercilessly and on 10 May had made the greatest raid on London of the entire war so far in an attack by 550 bombers. This feat was repeated on 13 May.[2]

The bad war news, including the German invasion of Yugoslavia and Greece that April, made Plante all the more impatient to get into the fight. He registered at his local Merchant Navy Shipping Pool office not knowing what kind of ship he would be assigned or where it would be headed. If he refused three ships offered by the pool he would immediately be drafted. As he wrote Evelyn, "there may be nothing one day and a great rush the next—so I just live from day to day. In any case . . . , I will just go with whichever [shipping company] calls first."[3]

By early May, Plante had exhausted all patience with waiting to be called. To fill his time he followed his lifelong habit of visiting art exhibitions and gallery shows, commenting extensively and often dismissively on what he saw. "God was it awful," he wrote Evelyn of a private viewing at the Royal Scottish Academy. He found "nothing in the whole show outstanding and 80% the usual muck." The only words of approval he had were for one or two sketches by Feliks Topolski. A few weeks later at an exhibition of war paintings at the Academy, he found two paintings by Eric Ravilious and one by John Nash—both commissioned war artists—"charming," while "by far the best things were sketches by Edward Ardizzone."[4]

During this time Plante admitted to fighting off occasional bouts of depression, made worse by seeing old friends in uniform about to ship out. One afternoon he met a friend, Ian Macdonald, and helped him get his equipment packed. Ian had a commission in the Black Watch and was leaving the next day to join his regiment at Perth. "Though I didn't see him in uniform," Plante wrote his wife, "he should look very smart, tartan trews, a hat the same shape as before but in a better material and with a bright red feather. He will also have a kilt."[5]

Another day Plante bumped into a fellow student from college who was wearing the blue wounded soldier suit. At least he had not lost any limbs "and showed no visible signs of damage," but it still seemed like a rebuke to Plante that he should be loafing around. "Funny how I hated red tape etc.," he complained to Evelyn, "yet it's that and nothing else that has left me out of this war until now. No wonder we 'miss the bus' all over the world if everything is handled in the same manner." In a speech to the House of Commons in April 1940, Prime Minister Neville Chamberlain had confidently asserted that "Hitler has missed the bus," and that British victory seemed assured. After May, when the Germans invaded France and the Low Countries, Chamberlain's unfortunate phrase was widely used with heavy sarcasm. "We need trained men desperately." Plante continued, "and here I am ready and willing, but there is all this monkey business. As I remarked before, it appears to be a private war."[6]

Plante did see one good result of his prolonged wait though—"America is now taking part in the Atlantic business and I'm sure that will make a huge difference to my comfort when I do go." Here Plante was referring to the fact that in February President Roosevelt had established the Atlantic Fleet, commanded by Admiral Ernest King, and construction had begun of a U.S. naval base at Argentia, Newfoundland. The Support Force, Atlantic Fleet was organized to escort eastbound convoys as far as Iceland. The Icelandic government had declared neutrality in 1940 but continued to cooperate with the Allies and had given permission for the development of air and sea bases on both Greenland and Iceland. In the event, the convoy escort service that had been due to begin in April 1941 was delayed until that September. Still, U-boats were now sinking British vessels faster than shipbuilders could replace them. As Churchill wrote Harry Hopkins, Roosevelt's close confidant, "The strain at sea on our naval resources is too great for us . . . we simply have not got the escorts to go round and fight at the same time." Although the U.S. Navy was patrolling the western North Atlantic, without more American naval support Britain would be starved into submission.[7]

Surprisingly, even in the midst of this extraordinarily tense time, some civilities from a more benign time were still observed. Writing to Evelyn on Sunday, 11 May, Plante told her that the previous Friday he had received a "charming letter" from the Ministry of Shipping advising him that he was free to sail with any company he wanted and "wishing me the best of luck in the future." Plante thought this "most unusual for a government department," particularly one in crisis mode.

Finally, that same evening the word Plante was waiting for came through. The chief steward and the first radio officer of SS *Sourabaya* arrived at Plante's home at 7 p.m., "pretty tight too, but seemed decent fellows. They seemed keen that I should go with them. When I discovered that their ship was bound for New York I didn't hesitate for a moment." By 9:45 that night Plante joined his new shipmates, already half asleep in the blacked-out carriage at Waverley Station on the train bound for Liverpool. They were all veteran sailors returning from a few days leave, about to battle with the elements and the U-boat attacks yet again. Well-fortified from time spent in the Rob Roy, the Heart of Midlothian, the Abbotsford, and several other establishments down Rose Street—Edinburgh's street of a thousand pubs—a nice, long, uninterrupted train ride was just what they needed.[8]

That, however, was not to be. They journeyed as far as Carlisle where after a short wait they joined another train that was completely packed. They stood all the way to Wigan, a two-plus hour journey away. At Wigan they changed trains again. They finally arrived at Liverpool's Lime Street station at six the next morning. "Here I came right bang into the war," Plante wrote.

> Groups of people wearing black and looking very drawn and pale wandered around with suitcases. Queues of people were waiting amidst ruined buildings for cigarettes at the tobacconists. No trams were running, water was scarce (no pots of tea, only cups in restaurants) gas and electricity was disorganized and workmen were tearing down dangerous buildings. Streets were roped off and long detours had to be made to reach your destination. Meanwhile, the sirens started their dismal wail. In Edinburgh this meant nothing, but here—it has quite a different implication. As one stood amidst the ruins, the inclination is to make straight for a shelter; we didn't though. Very few actually did go, strangely enough; they were more inclined to grin sheepishly at one another, while the more haggard and drawn looked even more so. People with bandaged heads and legs are quite common sights here.[9]

West Coast ports had become increasingly important for supplying Britain since the beginning of the war. The ports on the river Mersey, including Liverpool and Birkenhead, were the most important gateways of all. With the steady increase in the number and size of convoys using the docks there, they became valuable targets. As a result, over the first five months of 1941 Merseyside bore the brunt of Nazi bombing runs. The raids of the first week of May decimated the area as wave after wave of night bombers saturated Merseyside with high explosive and incendiary devices. As one historian recorded, "the city of Liverpool's outline was altered forever."[10]

Noted author Nicholas Monsarrat, who was born in Liverpool, joined the Royal Naval Volunteer Reserve (RNVR) at the beginning of the war and spent the best part of the next six years on convoy duty, ending as a lieutenant commander in charge of a frigate. His famous novel, *The Cruel Sea*, based on his wartime experiences, vividly portrays the reality of Britain's deadly struggle against the U-boats. Monsarrat captured the devastation of Liverpool very well. As his fictional corvette, HMS *Compass Rose*, made its way upstream toward the city, the following scene unfolded:

> Many of the crew clustered on the upper deck, shading their eyes against the strong May sunlight and looking towards the city they had come to know as home . . . there seemed to be a lot of smoke about, and here and there a jagged edge of the skyline which he [Sub-Lieutenant Morell] had never noticed before . . . At his side he suddenly heard Leading-Seaman Phillips exclaim: 'Christ! It's copped a packet!' and then he smelt—they all smelt—the acrid tang of smoke blowing down river, and his eyes, focusing suddenly on a big warehouse just above Gladstone Dock, discovered that it was split from top to bottom, that one half of it was a gigantic heap of rubble, that the rest was blackened and smoldering. His binoculars, traversing steadily across the city and over to the Birkenhead side, showed him many such buildings, and scores of small houses lying ruined in the centre of a great scorched circle: there were fires still burning, there was a heavy pall of smoke lying over the northern part of the city, there were gaps, whole streets missing, rows of houses misshapen and torn. He dropped his glasses, shocked by the scale of the destruction, the naked ruin of a city.[11]

Since public transportation was nonexistent, Plante and his colleagues had to walk. Eventually, after stepping over fire hoses, wading through puddles, and picking their way over rubble they reached *Sourabaya*. The tanker was tied up at the end of a long oil pier in Dingle—moored alongside a nest of oil tanks on the river. The ship was not a pretty sight, according to Plante.

> She was a large and clumsy looking hulk, not at all enhanced by the battleship grey and black wartime livery. It looked a bit like an oil tanker, but there was something different. As with a tanker, the bridge and accommodations were aft. Behind the bridge, two large funnels were arranged side by side. Forward of the bridge, a large uninterrupted expanse of flat deck stretched out like a football field. But strangest of all, there was a huge hole in the stern . . . looking very unsafe and a bit obscene.[12]

In fact, *Sourabaya* was a 10,107-ton whale factory ship. In peacetime, it operated in the Antarctic off South Georgia. Once the fleet of small, fast whale catchers with their harpoon gunners had done their job, giant whale carcasses would be hauled up through the hole in *Sourabaya*'s stern. Dismembered chunks of whale meat were stuffed down the deck hatches into the boilers and the oil was then stored in the ship's tanks. Requisitioned at the beginning of hostilities, *Sourabaya* had been converted to carrying fuel oil for the war instead of whale oil. The ship was owned by Christian Salvesen, a shipping company founded in the nineteenth century by a Norwegian who had moved to Scotland. Evidently, the Norwegian connection remained strong as Plante noted that "half the crew are Norwegian, including the cook," adding that this accounted for the "unusual but pleasant" food.[13]

There was nothing pleasant about the extremely strong, sickening odor that greeted Plante the moment he stepped on board. Eventually, he got used to the dreadful smell of *Sourabaya*'s former trade—the odor of rancid whale blubber now mixing with diesel oil fumes—but he never learned to like it. During the war, Cunard White Star, Ltd., operated the ship under the direction of Britain's Ministry of

War Transport. At its stern flew the "Red Duster," the red ensign with its Union Jack, flown by British Merchant ships—in contrast to the white ensign flown by Royal Navy warships. *Sourabaya* had recently returned from New York loaded with fuel oil, tank parts, lubricating oil and fifty-five airplanes. It also carried thirty passengers of five different nationalities.[14]

Just as Plante was settling into his cabin to write to Evelyn, a huge explosion rocked the ship "as if a bomb had been dropped on our bow." Rushing to the deck he saw a small ship, about *Amelia* size, "the end half blown to hell," lying partly submerged about seventy yards off *Sourabaya*'s bow. It could not sink further as it was resting on the bottom. Apparently, it had struck a mine—one that Plante could see they themselves might well have hit if she had not. In addition to bombs, German warplanes dropped many magnetic mines during the Merseyside bombings. Here was another reminder that this was the real war now.[15]

Undeterred, by his third day on board Plante was certain he would be very happy with his assignment. To this point, he had done no work at all because the wireless cabin was always sealed in port. He had, however, been kept fully occupied—eating. At 7:30 a.m. "the boy" called him for breakfast consisting of Norwegian porridge, coffee or tea, liver and bacon, bread and jam or marmalade. Coffee was served again at 11 and then at noon a lunch of soup, meat and vegetables, a sweet (dessert), and biscuits and cheese. Tea followed at 5 p.m. (a light meal) and then tea or coffee again and sandwiches at 9 p.m. For a landlubber coming from food rationing and endless shortages, all this eating seemed like heaven.[16]

The social aspects of this new life were also appealing. "Stewards and boys are responsible for cleaning cabins and serving at table," Plante wrote. "Officers are certainly officers at sea." Furthermore, his "little extra danger money" would entitle him, after his first voyage, to the luxury of a different badge on his cap—one almost identical to the Royal Navy with the wide laurel wreath. "The chief [radio] officer is almost permanently tight," he continued, "but he seems a decent fellow and so does the second." The chief was a Shetland Islander who loved his Scotch. He was

> a bit frayed at the edges after countless crossings of the Atlantic, so much so that he had to steady his shaking hand when drinking by taking a napkin or towel in one hand, passing it behind his neck, and holding the other end with his glass and pulling on it as a kind of hoist to raise the glass to his lips. He argued that Scotch was a far healthier drink than water. Didn't they preserve human body specimens in alcohol in hospitals? Water only rusted the insides. When I roused him one night to report that there was a U-boat right bang in the middle of the convoy he solemnly advised me not to touch it! I didn't![17]

Sourabaya's captain was a gruff, ruddy-faced Norwegian. These Norwegians had been caught at sea when their country had been invaded with no news of the fates of their families at home and no prospect of seeing them again until the war ended. Plante had great sympathy and respect for them and the quiet way they went about their duties. In fact, all the officers seemed quite a good crowd, although "they all drink pretty hard." While American ships were dry, by longstanding tradition alcohol was available on British ships and the regulation tot of rum, sometimes served up in a mug of hot tea, was a welcome part of life at sea. Plante wrote that he did not think the drinking on board would bother him. He would continue to enjoy his one glass of beer and save his money for New York and for things like American underwear, and stockings for his wife. Then too, he thought he would save some money so he could visit the Museum of Modern Art and some of the cafes in Greenwich Village.[18]

As he was engaged in these happy thoughts sirens began sounding. When they stopped, others took up the call from another part of the river and a ship started hooting short blasts. Through the deep haze hanging over Liverpool, Plante could hear planes droning overhead. He had no idea if they were British or German. In the coming months he would have many opportunities to hone his aircraft recognition skills.

Sourabaya's cargo for this trip consisted of a load of training planes destined for Halifax, carried as deck cargo. Delivering oil and unloading and loading the deck cargoes meant that tankers could not be turned around in a day but had to spend longer in port than other types of vessels. *Sourabaya* would also be embarking about one hundred RAF pilots so Plante foresaw having to share a cabin with the second radio operator.[19]

On 15 May, three days after embarking, the seals were broken on the wireless cabin to install some new equipment. Plante found his first view of the amount of gear "simply staggering—and beautiful equipment it is too. Let's hope I don't wreck it too soon!" He did not wreck anything, and just two weeks later, at the end of the voyage, he wrote to Evelyn in high confidence that he had taken this work in stride without "the slightest difficulty whatsoever. Really it is very, very easy—when you know what you're doing."[20]

"If you don't hear from me for weeks," Plante wrote to Evelyn, "for heaven's sake don't worry dear. Letters that were posted air-mail in New York etc. last trip are just reaching the sailors' homes now. You will know this much," he continued,

> that whether you receive letters or not, I'll certainly be writing them and thinking about the day when you and I will be together to share the happy times we know. . . . Our planes are being shipped aboard as I write this and we will be ready to sail in the morning. Don't be surprised if this should be my last letter, because I may not manage to get ashore again.[21]

On 19 May the *Sourabaya* was "somewhere in the Irish Sea." They had cast off from the jetty at Birkenhead, the vast complex of docks and miles of quays just across the river from Liverpool, where they had moved three days earlier. Tugs steered them down the Mersey through the churning tidal waters that marked the river's entrance and out to sea to join their convoy. Because it could sustain a speed of 12 knots, *Sourabaya* sailed with fast outward-bound north (ON) convoys. These were convoys for all ships that could maintain speeds of no less than 9 knots and no more than 14.8 knots. They were directed to Halifax, Nova Scotia.[22]

As the junior radio officer, Plante had the middle watch, from midnight to 4 a.m., which he kept in the chart room on the bridge instead of in the usual—and more comfortable—radio cabin. One of his memorable sketches is of *Sourabaya*'s radio room. It shows a radio officer (identified by the wavy band on his sleeve) wearing headphones and leaning back comfortably in a chair in front of an array of wireless equipment. A large calendar on the wall sets the date as 29 May 1941. When on watch, everyone was careful to wear rubber-soled shoes so that their pacing of the deck would not disturb the men sleeping below. The previous night, Plante's greatest difficulty was fighting off sleep at 3:30 a.m. When four o'clock finally arrived he dropped onto his bunk and slept until eleven, with just an hour before his next watch from noon to 4 p.m. "The charts lying on the table before me are lovely things," he wrote Evelyn. "Just like those old maps we like. Also I can see from this," he went on, "that each minute I get nearer to you. The Clyde lies away to our right now, but in a day or so, instead of getting nearer to you I'll be going further and further away. This means that the day when I come back to you is getting nearer."[23]

At sea, Plante acquired some habits he continued for the rest of his life whenever he was traveling. He washed his own clothes by hand—not only underwear, but also socks, pants, and shirts. Before leaving Liverpool, he had bought a pair of navy blue trousers from Marks and Spencer for working in, but to his regret he found they were not the bargain he had imagined. The dye quickly rubbed off leaving his legs looking very dirty "though it does make me wash them every night; my legs I mean." He also sustained his passion for music with the gramophone and the ship's collection of outdated but charming records such as Layton & Johnstone singing "That's My Weakness Now." When he discovered that there was a piano in the salon he was even more pleased with his choice of service. He had been told that the piano had been made in Shanghai "and my God," he wrote, "bits of it certainly sound like it."[24]

The following evening, Tuesday 20 May, the crew was advised that an air attack was probable, but nothing materialized. By then they were much farther north, just off Tiree, above the entrance to the Caledonian Canal. Later the next morning they were to pass between the Hebrides and the mainland. At 4 a.m., just as Plante came off watch, the alarm was given to abandon ship. This was intended to be a surprise boat drill but as Plante pointed out to his wife, "like all these things there was very little surprise attached to it. Everyone had been hanging around with their life jackets on for quite five minutes!"[25]

Sourabaya may not have been a glamorous ship, but in wartime it was particularly valuable, so it was assigned a good position, well on the inside of the convoy. Plante paced the bridge, scanned the horizon through heavy binoculars hung around his neck, and watched, as he recalled, "the wonderful skies and changing moods of the seas. For the first few days I had been wrapped up in thick sweaters, a duffel coat and a balaclava helmet to protect me from the elements. In no time at all, I was so toughened up all I needed was a shirt, jacket and a cap." Still, he found it hard to believe that this was not just a little diversion, some kind of a holiday from his work as an artist and that he would soon be returning to his easel and brushes.[26]

Plante found the convoy escort very impressive; it consisted of something like four destroyers and several corvettes. This was a great comfort but, as he noted, even then "the second engineer (Norwegian) refuses to sleep until he can see one of our planes circling above. Then he is alright, but he has been known to go for days without sleep when out of range of land-based air cover." Until very long-range aircraft and small escort carriers were introduced into the Battle of the Atlantic in 1943, a mid-ocean gap in the air defense left convoys without protective cover. Most of the men slept in their day clothes until they were well out of this danger zone, Plante wrote to his wife although—with the bravado of the uninitiated—he insisted that he didn't feel he had rested unless he had worn his pajamas! He did notice, though, that men who had already been torpedoed wore their life jackets all the time and often stayed up on deck when others slept. This was probably very prudent.[27]

"My main duty," Plante recorded, "was to be tethered by the ears to the radio—but I managed to extend the leads so I could occasionally stick my head out of the cabin and fortify myself with deep gulps of that wonderful air." All ships observed radio silence to avoid giving their positions away to the ever-vigilant U-boats. So all Plante had to do was listen to the stream of coded messages relayed from shore stations and decipher any that were directed to his convoy. As time went on, he noted that his "ears became responsive to the applicable call signs and I could instantly detect the ones that I was meant to hear. It became so instinctive, I hardly had to listen at all." Often, he picked up calls for help from other convoys under attack or from individual ships that had been damaged or had lost contact, but there was nothing he could do about it.[28]

All the orders for *Sourabaya* and the other ships in the convoy came from the commodore's ship. The commodore, often a retired naval officer, was in command of all the merchant vessels in the convoy though the captain of the senior escort vessel, whose rank was usually far below that of the commodore, was always in overall command. While Plante had to listen all the time for messages from shore or from the commodore, he had little to occupy his hands or his brain. Indeed, one historian of the Battle of the Atlantic has called the radio officer's job "the most boring job at sea." Helping to relieve the tedium, Plante also had to direct signals by flag and blinker light to other ships in the convoy; during action his job sending messages from the bridge to the radio room kept him very busy.[29]

By their third day out, excitement picked up considerably. During the previous night's watch a depth charge was released close by giving *Sourabaya* quite a shake. At eight o'clock the next morning Plante was awakened by the alarm bell. After donning his life jacket he ran to his action station on the bridge, greeted by a dark sky and rough seas. Evidently, their destroyer escorts had opened fire on an enemy plane.

"We are certainly in the danger zone now," Plante wrote his wife from the radio cabin a little later. "The chief who I have just relieved picked up submarine radio signals."[30]

Just as he was writing that last sentence, the alarm sounded once more and machine guns rattled. When he raced back to his action station on the bridge, Plante was told that a submarine or submarines were lying aft and that the aircraft warning was also on. They did not have long to wait. "Out of the haze," Plante later reported to Evelyn, "a two-engine plane, probably a Heinkel 111 swooped low and raked us with machine guns. My position on the bridge is well protected by concrete slabs against this kind of thing," he reassured his wife.[31] "We opened fire," Plante continued, "but though the gunner on the port side reckons he hit her, we're quite sure any damage would be negligible. This I rather think is a spotter for the submarines so we can expect something to happen, perhaps this evening or tomorrow. The 'old man,'" he went on, referring to the captain, "has just been in checking our position on the charts and seems to have great faith in the radio picking up the plane's signals to the subs. I certainly hope we do!" In fact, they were able to successfully evade both the enemy planes and the U-boats.[32]

Although that night (21 May) went off without incident, just before Plante's middle watch, his ship passed an upturned lifeboat. By now Plante admitted that even *he* slept in his clothes and they all carried around their life jackets "like mascots." "Things can happen very quickly at times and this is certainly the hot spot. Will be until Sunday [25 May] I reckon. The destroyers have their submarine chasing flags up and keep darting around looking very impressive and efficient, [like] highland sheepdogs, coaxing and shepherding the stragglers." Evidently, someone had a sense of humor as one destroyer signaled the steamer *Mary McGuire* to "come a little closer Mary."[33]

Station keeping in a convoy of thirty-plus ships organized in a huge grid was a challenge. The commodore assigned each ship a position in a column, with his own ship leading from the middle of the front row. He kept in constant touch with his naval escorts by radiotelephone and with his charges in the same way or, whenever possible, by semaphore signal flags by day and lamps by night. Sometimes one of the ships in convoy would get up too much of a head of steam, or miscalculate, and get a little too close to another ship. "It was alarming," Plante recalled, "to look out and suddenly see a big ship bearing down on you, especially if it was loaded with benzene."[34]

By Friday, 23 May, Plante estimated (optimistically, as it turned out) that *Sourabaya* was about half way to its first landfall at Halifax, Nova Scotia. This was the farthest north Plante had ever been—and ever wanted to be. When he went on watch at midnight it was still broad daylight, although it did get quite dark later. The weather had been pretty rough, he noted, and "everything is grey outside, the sea, the sky and the ships." That morning there had been a submarine warning, "but I was so tired I just turned over and went back to sleep." At 11:45 each night, the chief called him and he usually made a cup of chocolate in the galley before going to the radio cabin. "Here, of course, I just sit and listen, and listen and listen. Rather awful to think of all the good programmes I could get with that wonderful equipment but instead I just have to sit and wait for messages!"[35]

On Saturday, 24 May, Plante wrote, "our escorts left us and I thought the convoy was about to break up, but since then we have been joined by two new destroyers. . . . On the last watch a coast guard cutter from the U.S. had been requesting information from ships to assist in the search for survivors from a convoy. We should be in the area tomorrow or the day after—so we may be lucky enough to pick up some of them. It is pretty far west so it would appear the damage has been done by a raider and not submarines but—that is mere conjecture."[36]

Continuing an explanation of his routine, Plante described how, after waking the second radio officer at about 3:45 a.m., he usually headed straight for his bunk. "We still sleep in our clothes but I'm getting a bit tired of this. From 4 a.m. I sleep until about 10:30 a.m., missing breakfast. Then, by the time I have washed, shaved etc. it is lunchtime, 11:30, after which I am on watch again at mid-day."

Coming off watch at 4 p.m. he had free time until tea at 5 p.m. He usually spent the evening chatting and doing odd jobs until he felt tired enough to rest before going on again at midnight.[37]

Often, Plante chatted with the passengers and on this trip one in particular proved to be very interesting. He was from the Ministry of Information (MOI), a professorial type who, as it turned out, really was a professor. Plante found him "rather a nice old gentleman." But "when we were in the thick of the excitement . . . he wanted to know if he could be allowed into the wireless cabin to listen to the news bulletin. We were much too busy right here to trouble with the news from anywhere else." The radio in the wireless cabin was the only one on board as only one radio was allowed on each ship because it was feared that "re-radiation" from many radios might enable U-boats to take bearings on a convoy's location.[38]

Sometimes, those listening in to all the radio chatter learned of important events beyond the narrow focus of the convoy. "My theory that the convoy I spoke of yesterday was shattered by a surface raider has been quite right," Plante wrote Evelyn on Sunday, 25 May. "The fate of the *Hood* yesterday has proved that. . . . We are dodging about the North Atlantic now, zigzagging. There is no doubt in my mind that the raider—according to the BBC [British Broadcasting Corporation] the *Bismarck* and according to Germany the *Gneisenau*—has slipped our forces." The British battlecruiser HMS *Hood* sank in three or four minutes on the morning of Saturday, 24 May, in an engagement with the German battleship *Bismarck*. All but 3 of the crew of 1,418 officers and men were lost. The significance of the possible close proximity of a German warship was not lost on anyone on board. Plante wrote:

> Today, when everyone was waiting for news of this raider, the news from Rugby Radio [a large radio transmission facility in England] had the damned impertinence to send out a yarn about one Hurricane [British aircraft] fighting three ME110s [German Messerschmitts] over Calais. Then, after all this there came a long explanation of how difficult it was to keep in contact with

> a ship at sea due to bad visibility, local storms, etc. etc. So from this I gather we are being prepared for the announcement that the raider has made its escape. Bad news indeed for us, and our ship has an air of expectation about it.[39]

By this time the sea was very rough with a strong wind whipping the spray off the tops of the waves. Plante was glad *Sourabaya* rode the sea well and he was relieved not to be on board one of the other ships in the convoy which he could see pitching and tossing with their decks awash. He watched, fascinated, as the destroyers and other escort vessels, designed for speed and maneuverability, "twisted and turned and burst through the huge waves only to be tossed on the top of another wave like a feather in the breeze." Even on *Sourabaya*, his arm and leg muscles ached from hanging on and trying to stay reasonably upright. They expected the next couple of days could be very eventful and everyone was alert and keeping a sharp lookout. That night they would have to return to their watches on the bridge instead of in the radio cabin which was not good, but it appeared that another day or two would see them out of the submarine area.[40]

The following day the convoy was still ploughing along. "This convoy has certainly dodged about the Atlantic these last few days," Plante wrote. "No doubt when we get through the commodore will get a DSO [Distinguished Service Order] etc. He certainly has been using all his wits and at times we wondered if it would be Glasgow and not Halifax that would be our destination."[41]

And yet, amidst all this excitement, Plante never lost sight of the fact that this was, for him, merely a break from his real life. "Last night I was thinking about New York," he wrote of the evening after the disastrous sinking of HMS *Hood*. He mused about the possibility, while in New York, of getting a temporary job in an advertising agency. Of course he could not be paid but thought the experience would be "invaluable." Failing that, he thought he would like to attend some classes, maybe on illustration. "There is no doubt," he concluded, "that illustration is the way to make a name, and money. So from now on," he resolved, "I'm going to keep drawing and drawing with that object in view. I know I can do it, so even a fortnight or so experience in America will be valuable."[42]

On Tuesday, 27 May, *Sourabaya* received a signal that *Bismarck* had been sunk. Even before confirmation from the BBC or Rugby Radio this was the occasion for huge relief on board and a celebration involving the consumption of large amounts of liquor. The celebration was even more warranted than they may have suspected as the sinking of *Bismarck* marked the end of commerce raiding by German warships, except for a few attacks on convoys to Russia. In the first quarter of 1941 alone, commerce raiders had sunk thirty-seven valuable merchant ships, inflicting enormous damage and disrupting British convoy cycles. Later that night, when Plante went on watch, the convoy split, the vessels each going off in different directions to their various destinations. The seas were calm under an overcast sky and *Sourabaya*, now apparently alone in the Atlantic, was making good speed. The captain estimated that they would reach Halifax in six days.[43]

With the return of some calm, Plante could reflect on his time at sea. He was somewhat unnerved to find that there seemed to be some sort of "invisible barrier" between himself and the rest of the crew, especially the Scots. Though he had "taken great care," he wrote his wife, "not to talk about art or appear arty," and everyone was quite friendly, he realized that temperamentally he had little in common with the others. Their conversation seemed to consist of only two topics: women and drink. "Since joining the ship," he concluded, "apart from chats with the passengers I haven't heard five minutes of intelligent conversation. There is no comradeship such as one experienced in the studio."

"They may think that by swearing they are tough," he continued the next day, "but in reality they have as many petty differences about entirely unimportant things, as little girls in school." In a letter some time later, he described many of the crew as "in reality . . . just men with undeveloped minds."[44]

Plante found the passengers "entirely different" though, and he enjoyed some very interesting conversations—especially with Flying

Officer Seymour and with the Ministry of Information professor. Also, the chief radio officer with whom Plante worked all the time, "though living only for women and liquor is apart from this very decent to work with and not at all boorish like the rest of the men." Plante was sure, too, that he would have found the same thing, maybe worse, in the army or the RAF. He wasn't unhappy, he hastened to reassure his wife. "On the contrary, I'm as happy as I could be during a war, and the anticipation of seeing New York is grand." Moreover, during his night watches he could sketch undisturbed. He was also studying the theory of music and dreamed of owning a baby grand piano someday.[45]

"Last night," (now on page 25 of his letter) "practically everyone on the ship was gathered in the vicinity of the wireless cabin to hear Roosevelt's speech." In a radio address delivered from the White House, FDR, angered by the foray of *Bismarck* into the Atlantic, announced a state of unlimited national emergency, repeating his famous remark that "the only thing we have to fear is fear itself." He also described how German U-boats were attacking British shipping in the Atlantic and threatened American shipping, warning Germany that the United States was ready to go to war if attacked. Plante found the president a "wonderful speaker" who "certainly said some things that sounded good to us. America is certainly well in now—and a damned good job too. One great fear I have, though, is that America may be so much in the war when we arrive that New York will be blacked out and *that* would be a blow!" He need not have feared. Even when America officially entered the war that December it still took several months before coastal cities were persuaded to impose blackout. Floridians, in particular, resisted this move as damaging to their tourist trade.[46]

Close on the heels of Roosevelt's speech American warships "looked us over," Plante recorded with interest. "For a while we wondered who they could be but as they came closer our fears were soon put to rest." He wrote with mounting excitement, "American radio stations are now interfering with our radio—so as you see, the Promised Land is getting nearer."

The next day, Friday 30 May, there was a real storm. Plante noted that he was only on the open deck for about two minutes and had to hang on very tightly indeed. "Rather like a comic picture," he wrote, "gripping a door handle, with my legs lifted in the air in an almost horizontal position. It was only when I saw the great dips the bows took, and the huge waves breaking over, I realized how rough it really was. This is a magnificent sea ship," he concluded, "and in addition I must really have my sea legs now." Although *Sourabaya*'s crew might be uncongenial, in Plante's view, the ocean clearly was not.[47]

"You have no idea how thrilling it was to see little birds hopping around. They were just like sparrows, but were broken up with various colors," Plante noted on 1 June. His keen eye for detail, his interests, and his temperament set him apart, quite markedly, from many of the crew. "This is the first sign of land for a fortnight," he continued, "and it was quite exciting. Of course, I have seen various sea birds but these two little ones were most attractive." The previous night they had played the gramophone with all the good old tunes. Later, Plante sat "chatting and drinking in Squadron Leader Dutten's cabin with Flight Officer Seymour, another fellow, Stewart—an American test pilot—and Mr. Groves of the American Diplomatic Service. Very good company indeed, and as you can imagine the conversation was very interesting. Quite unlike the mess room!"[48]

Sourabaya was expected to reach Halifax the next evening and in the event that he could not get ashore, he had Flight Officer Seymour's promise that he would post Plante's epic letter. "Heaven knows when you will get it though. From Halifax it is only two days sailing to New York, oh boy oh boy!"

On Monday, 2 June, at 7 p.m. *Sourabaya* docked in Halifax after what Plante described as "on the whole quite an uneventful trip, when one considers just how eventful it could have been." The night before, in anticipation of the successful conclusion to the trip there was a bit of a party on board with drinking, singing, and music from the gramophone and the radio going both at once. Later, the foghorn blast at

3 a.m. dispelled any residual drowsiness for Plante on his watch. "We emerged out of the fog to be able to just discern the lights of Halifax flickering in the rain. Even after three weeks at sea it didn't look inviting." The chief constable came on board with the customs officers, likely, it seemed to Plante, for the customary liberal dispensation of duty free Scotch. One of the first things he had learned about life at sea was that it was a good thing to be kind to customs officers. In return, he found, "they might be good to you . . . and they usually were."[49]

"There is still no regret about my choice of service," he finished his letter before going ashore, "and my proverbial luck has held out. This ship is big, clean, and the food good. Then to have three weeks in New York—well if that isn't good fortune!"[50]

But first there was Halifax. It was 10 p.m. before the formalities were completed when Plante got ashore and he found the sights that greeted him amazing. Although "Halifax is reckoned to be a bit of a dump," he found plenty of shops, all lit up, that looked pretty good to him. Every other store was a "drug store," selling everything but drugs—especially fruit and candies, magazines, and soft drinks.

By this time, Plante had met up with some of the other fellows from the ship and those who had been to Halifax before led them in search of drinks. Although Halifax was officially dry, "the reality was quite the opposite. Private civilian clubs serving alcohol to members continued to operate," so first they found their way to the Elks Lodge. By then it was 11:30 p.m. and they were told it was too late to become Elks. There was nothing else for it at that point but to go to the Green Lantern restaurant, "an exceedingly fine place like the atmosphere of the Majestic, but larger and newer." After supper they made their way back to the ship at around 1 a.m. where the drinking continued, mostly of rum. The following day Plante ventured into Halifax again, this time with the American diplomat, Mr. Groves. Because Groves had to carry a huge leather bag with official documents they went everywhere by taxi.[51]

Since the exchange rate was slightly better in Canada than in the United States, Plante bought himself two shirts, "a good Arrow one and a cheaper one, which still looks better than British shirts." After observing that the girls "even in a place like this look very smart indeed, wearing hats similar to your pale blue large brim one or little French berets straight on the top of their heads," he concluded that "Canada appears an attractive place if this is considered one of the poorest spots." The contrast with war-torn Britain was very marked, even here.[52]

The following day, and under way again, Plante wrote his wife that his watch that afternoon "has been just lovely."

> While listening for signals on one set there has been a programme of lovely light music from Boston on the other receiver. In addition, the boy has just brought me my afternoon cakes and tea. In five minutes I go off watch and have a lovely hot bath and then it is time for 5 O'clock dinner. Last night it was cold meat and salad—today we had fruit with lunch. This is all a result of being in port yesterday. Heavens, if only I could enable you to share these things that are so rare at home now—and yet were once so plentiful. If only some reason could prevail in the world.[53]

Just one day out of New York the weather quickly changed and it began pouring with rain. The bad visibility meant extra work for the radio operators who had to take radio bearings to check their position. When he was not on duty Plante mused about what to buy when they arrived in New York. "I'll get you some lipsticks while I'm over here. If only I had a million dollars. I don't think I've ever felt the lack of money as much as I do now. There are so many things I'd like to bring everyone home." Regarding stockings, he could not decide whether to go for quantity or quality. "The nylon ones are expensive, from $1.35, but no doubt they last longer. I feel inclined to buy one or two pairs of ordinary silk at about our normal 3/11d quality—or maybe a pair of each?"[54]

By early Friday afternoon, 6 June, *Sourabaya* had threaded the narrows between Brooklyn and Staten Island and was lying in the East River just off New York City, before going into dry dock the next morning. The Statue of Liberty and the Manhattan skyline were just visible through the summer haze. It had been a hectic day for the ship's officers who had to deal with all the routine paperwork for the crew for the medical authorities as well as for those from immigration. Busy though he was, Plante still took note of how clean everything looked. "Speed launches are painted in pastel colours and even the tug that brought the immigration people on board was shining and polished. The colours were very attractive too. Salmon pink funnel, with all upper decks white and lower part of hull black. Even the mast flag was a primrose yellow."[55]

"The colours of this river are really grand," Plante continued, regretting that he had only watercolors on board with him. "Tomorrow I'll buy some gouache colours. Really, I must make some colour notes of this. It surprises me to see the Statue of Liberty standing out a vivid green—it is really very brilliant. Then all the ferry boats that speed up and down are attractive too. The skyscrapers quite come up to my expectations," he enthused. "I think they make a tremendously impressive pile." He could not wait to see them close up the next day. Not quite able to ignore the war he had so recently left, he shuddered at the thought of what a bomb in the middle of all the skyscrapers would do. Still, he reassured himself, they needn't worry about that yet awhile.[56]

For a long time that afternoon Plante just sat and gazed at the scene in the bright sunshine. He noted the "beautiful modern lines" of several liners that passed down the river. They were "beautifully painted white, with green funnels. What a change from all the drab grey and brown of the British ships' wartime dressing." A gleaming airship passed overhead and everything seemed "so clean and active and all the officials we've had on board were very bright and cheerful. Yes, I'm going to like this." And so began a lifelong love affair with America.

To Plante's intense disappointment, he had to spend practically all the next day on board ship. *Sourabaya* went into dock in the Brooklyn Navy Yard early that morning and soon it was high and dry as workmen immediately began to scrape barnacles off its hull. Until the captain returned with some money there was little point in going ashore so Plante consoled himself by gazing at his surroundings and the superb color and composition of huge ships raised up in dry dock. It was so hot that it was difficult to avoid perspiring and smudging the letter he wrote to his wife. Finally, around 7 p.m., they were issued some money and were off, released into the wilds of New York. Because of threats of sabotage they had to get a pass each time they entered or left the yard.[57]

CHAPTER THREE

"New York . . . is simply magnificent."

As he preferred, Plante set off alone that evening, Saturday, 7 June, aiming for Manhattan. His first challenge was to find the subway station. He had great difficulty just finding someone who could speak enough English to give him directions, as "the language of the country was apparently Italian." Then he made the mistake of asking about the time for the last train back to Brooklyn. Unceremoniously told that any idiot knew the trains ran all night he wondered to himself, "How could they have known that it wasn't at all like that in London?" After some confusion with sorting out the unfamiliar bills and coins he bought a newspaper and decided that Madison Square Garden, with Benny Goodman's band and two other orchestras, would let him see and hear the most for his money.[1]

Taking the subway into Manhattan, Plante got off at Times Square ("deposited among the skyscrapers, and a magnificent spectacle they are") and began walking along Broadway, which he found "absolutely amazing," with "beautiful women and fine semi-open-air cafes like the smartest in Paris. There was that familiar richness of tobacco smoke, mostly cigars. Every woman looks smartly dressed and the men very colourful indeed, a great many with those straw Panama hats with painted bands." The shops were beautiful too, and he missed Evelyn. "It just isn't right that I should see all this without you."[2]

Strolling around with his "eyes absolutely popping out," he came "bang right up against" what he called, with amusement, "American salesmanship." "A man asked me where I was from and what my name was as a girl pinned a banner on my lapel, all inscribed, and charged me ten cents all in a flash. From then on I was on my guard." He needed to be, as he was next confronted by a "most insistent girl who tried to sell me a flower for my buttonhole in aid of the British Relief. I pointed out to her that it was a bit hard to be chased across the Atlantic by a submarine and then asked to buy a flower for my own relief."[3]

Inside, Madison Square Garden was packed and Benny Goodman's band was cheered and cheered. Everyone was jitterbugging madly and once again Plante appreciated all the beautiful girls. "They certainly aren't afraid to use colour or bizarre fashions, with some of the biggest hats I've ever seen and some of the cutest." He watched spellbound until he realized with a shock that it was 2:30 a.m. When he got out to the street it was crowded with people, shops were all lit up and many of them open, as were all the bars—a total contrast to conditions of blackout at home. When he bought a Sunday paper he thought the man had handed him the whole bundle instead of just one. It was so large it was "hardly credible."[4]

The next day, when he took up his pen again, Plante's excitement was still palpable. "Any words I can put together can never express my feelings about New York," he wrote Evelyn. "It is simply magnificent. London, Paris, Berlin—everything they have is thrown together and then some more added. As I sit on deck the sun shines brilliantly, as usual, the sky is clear blue and all the colourful ships and skyscrapers make a grand picture." He did a bit of sketching and then set off for Coney Island.[5]

"Coney Island has to be seen to be believed. Not the kind of place you or I would choose for a holiday, but well worth seeing." After gawking at the miles of soda fountains, hamburger and frankfurter stands, the rides and amusements and the "Girlie Shows," Plante looked for the beach, which he found was of fine, clean sand but rather difficult to see for the crowds of "Jews, Italians and Coloured People." Plante continued walking around the fairgrounds some more, observing every detail, ever sensitive to the aesthetics of the scenes and the people around him. Later he wrote his wife that he "never ceased to be amazed at the colours and the smartness of the girls' clothes."[6]

While enjoying an ice-cold beer some people started chatting to him and it turned out they had English antecedents. One of them had been born and bred in England and his friends later told Plante that he had been very wealthy until the stock market crash. These people insisted on buying him drinks and later, they invited him to supper. Their "wooden bungalow" was just a minute away. "You've seen the type of place in the films," he told his wife. "It only had two rooms plus kitchen and bathroom but was very well fitted with the inevitable huge refrigerator, shower etc." He found himself "very amused" that every so often he was addressed as "Butch." "This seems to have been the equivalent of 'George' or 'Chum' in England." After supper he and his newfound friends talked awhile and they insisted that he stay the night. He was quite tired by then and was happy to do so.[7]

In the morning, Plante's new friends went uptown with him on their way to work and he continued on to Times Square. Next he explored Grand Central Station, which he pronounced "very fine. It certainly is an example of how smart and attractive a railway station can be—it is, of course, immense. I shudder to think what an American must think arriving at any railway station in England," he noted. Before returning to the ship at lunchtime he bought some poster paints and card. He was also weighed down by the souvenirs pressed on him by the Coney Island people, but he was sure his wife would be glad to know that he had managed to keep clear of gangsters. And although no one had taken a shot at him yet, he *had* been trapped by chewing gum sticking to his shoes. Still, his chief difficulty had been with the language; for example, "things aren't what they're called here—camels are cigarettes and suspenders are braces." Back on board, no one on *Sourabaya* could believe he had had such an innocent night ashore.[8]

It was so hot in New York during the day that Plante preferred to leave his visits to town to the late afternoon and evening so he devoted much of the rest of the next day to painting and was very pleased with the progress he was making. When darkness fell that night he remained on board, finding the Navy Yard even more colorful than during the daytime. "Work never ceases in the yards and the coloured lights, the arc lamps, the riveters and welders at work make a grand spectacle with the Statue of Liberty floodlit and the lights of New York in the background." From what he heard the men saying, American workmen were very efficient, getting things done in half the time an English yard would take and working very conscientiously. *Sourabaya's* third radio officer ended his marathon eight-day letter—a paean of praise to America—with a supreme compliment to his wife. "Won't it be grand darling just to see each other again. That will be even more wonderful than seeing New York!"[9]

In addition to the dry dock work on *Sourabaya's* hull, work was begun to convert some of the quarters on board for the use of Distressed British Seamen (DBS), survivors stranded by the loss of their ships, waiting to be transported home. *Sourabaya* was also to undergo degaussing, a process to reduce the ship's magnetic signature in an effort to counter the threat from German magnetic mines. To Plante's delight, all these projects prolonged the ship's stay in New York.[10]

After spending most of Wednesday 11 June on board, Plante still had a good bit of work to do on the painting he was busy with but he already had his next subject in mind. It was easy to be inspired because the place was "packed with interest and colour." He told Evelyn that he would have included a sketch of his effort so far "but no doubt the censor would think I was trying to convey some mysterious information." He thought it would be wonderful if he could sell his painting to *Fortune* magazine for a cover and wrote optimistically that "it suits perfectly and I intend to have a try!"[11]

When Plante went ashore that evening he headed for the Roseland Ballroom where he found the two orchestras quite grand. To his surprise they were broadcasting while he was there, "but nearly everywhere one goes in the entertainment world they seem to be broadcasting. It was strange to see and hear the band and then to stroll over to the bar and hear it through the radio." Of course, Plante had a special interest in radio, but he could not help observing how, in many ways, the States was so much more technologically advanced than Britain. By the time he left Roseland it was two in the morning and though there were plenty of people around and taxis rushed about showing no sign of the lateness of the hour, Plante reluctantly—"because it always seems a great pity in New York"—made his way back to the ship. When he reached the dockyard, work was going full blast and the noise of drills and riveters made sleep difficult. "I'm sure many people are going to suffer badly" from the constant noise and stress, Plante confided.[12]

Early one morning the following week, Plante was awakened by the screaming of police car sirens. Apparently the radio officer on the ship lying alongside *Sourabaya* had shot himself. "This war does get on one's nerves a bit but personally," Plante wrote, "I would have waited until my stay in New York was ended." More seriously he noted, "In all this atmosphere which is free from all war dangers one is rather more inclined to feel nervous about re-entering the danger zone, whereas when you are living in it at home you become kind of accustomed to it." Two days later he wrote, "You know, I had no idea my nerves were so affected by war conditions at home. . . . I was quite unaware it had made any impression on me but time and time again I keep getting little starts, for example when a light is turned on and there is no blackout, or when sirens or hooters go off, or any bang or thud."[13]

Meanwhile, Plante's impressions of New York continued to evolve. "This country is full of people who are devout Catholics," he wrote Evelyn, "and although I don't see eye to eye with them they are certainly most sincere." On the advice of colleagues he had gone to check out the English Club and he stayed so late that when he was ready to go, the room where his coat and cap were held was locked. He had to leave without them. When he got out of the subway near the docks he thought he'd have a drink at a bar his shipmates had told him about. He asked the first person he met how to get there. The man said he'd take Plante there but he didn't think he ought to go there as it was a bit of a dump. His new friend was Irish and in conversation later Plante discovered that he had thought Plante was drunk and had lost his cap and would have been taken for a sucker at the rough bar he asked about. Instead, the man—named Bert—took Plante to a nearby place and ordered steak and chips for two. Several other very friendly Irishmen joined them. One gave Plante a patron saint of travel medal and said it had been blessed. There was almost a fight over who would run Plante back to his ship. They all had cars. "The number of people who asked me what cigarettes I smoked and wanted to adopt me, well, it is quite embarrassing. . . . It is very interesting to hear their views and opinions. The general feeling as I can see it is that America will be in this very soon—and a good job too!"[14]

When Plante got back to the docks he discovered that his pass had been in his coat pocket. When he was finally allowed onto his ship he discovered his cabin key had also been in his coat pocket. As everyone else was in bed he had no choice but to squeeze into his cabin through the porthole. When he emerged the same way in the morning "there was quite a lot of excitement." On top of his lame story about his overnight in Coney Island a few days earlier, he was beginning to get an interesting reputation with his crewmates.[15]

On Sunday 15 June, Plante went to a friend's flat for lunch. "The flat was like all American homes, very well appointed in excellent taste and most comfortable. I can't help thinking how much we could enjoy living there. It all looked like an advert from the *Saturday Evening Post*." Plante's friend gave him a lift back to the ship in his car—"35 horse power which as he mentioned is quite a modest size over here. It was good to hear a radio in a car again. You remember how exhilarating that is." The latest craze, he noted, was for everything South American. "All cabaret and shows feature people like Carmen Miranda and the great dance is La Conga—one, two, three, kick!" When he returned to the ship that evening Plante stayed on board *Sourabaya* and listened to the radio. "I understand Quentin Reynolds of *Collier's* gave a grand talk on the radio addressed to Dr. Goebbels. Did you hear him? I wish I had, it was a magnificent piece of sarcasm from what I hear."[16]

On Tuesday night Plante and "the chief" (R/O) planned to go to Radio City Music Hall, "the greatest show place in New York," at the invitation of the British Club. His daily letter to Evelyn described the evening out. "Jokes say the Americans do everything bigger and better than anyone else but—it is perfectly true." The theater was "huge and very beautiful. The lounge, and the toilet rooms are the most magnificent I've ever seen, everything down to drinking fountains and electric drying machines being beautifully designed. It is the detail that is so fine, even in such a huge place. In the lounge there were grand prints on the wall. Can you imagine similar taste being shown anywhere at home?" He was particularly fascinated by the forty or so "Glee" singers who sang Negro spirituals. The backdrop was a projection "that kept changing with every song. Very ingenious work with what I presume was a film projector." He was also very impressed by the sixty Rockettes. "I understand now how they are so famous."[17]

After lunch the next day, Plante took one of his paintings to the offices of the *New Yorker* magazine. He always had a clear-eyed grasp of the level of his abilities and he also had the self-confidence to actively promote his own work. He enjoyed the hustle and bustle of the artistic marketplace and the war, for all its dangers, served him both as an inspiration and an opportunity. He described to Evelyn how his painting had evolved from an original idea for *Fortune* magazine to one for the *New Yorker* instead:

> It started as a purely decorative painting of work in progress on a big ship which was painted a delicate pink colour. Then, as I put in the little figures all over and climbing up the gangway, it struck me as amusing to put a little ice cream cart on the quayside and one tiny figure throwing an ice cream up to another workman leaning over the rails. To my mind it makes a good cover—decorative, whimsical and with all the shipbuilding in the news, very topical—but I had to leave it for their art conference and telephone tomorrow afternoon so—will see.[18]

The next day Plante saw the *New Yorker* people again but—no luck. "Old story," he explained to his artist wife who would understand, "very charming but not quite suitable. I don't mind it being turned down. I'm certain I can sell it at home—it has a particular interest value." If he was disappointed by his outing that day, the feeling quickly dissipated when he got back to the ship and found his first letter from Evelyn. It had taken nearly a month to reach him. Evelyn had included in her letter the address of a friend in New York, but Plante did not think he would call on her. "Perhaps if I had been lonely I'd have been grateful indeed for this address but the fact is there is so much for me to do and see here that I can't cope with all the hospitality I'm offered."[19]

While Plante admired much of what he saw in the States, he was by no means an uncritical observer. He was bewildered by the great number of pregnant women he saw—until it was explained that these were "draft" babies. If a man were married and supporting a wife, he would not be drafted. If, in addition, he already had children, he *definitely* would not be drafted—unless the country was actually at war. Plante thought these efforts to dodge the draft petty, since the service obligation was only one year's service. "All the problems people have over here seem of no importance at all. . . . Compared with our worries and problems at home, sometimes I want to scream at the kind of things they get worried about over here."[20]

On the other hand, having talked to a good many Americans since arriving in New York, Plante thought some 80 percent of them were solidly behind Britain. He felt they were as good as in the war already, though reluctant to actually send men to fight. The younger people, though, seemed to think, "What the hell, let's get on with it." The universal attitude to "we fellows is one of admiration and they can't do enough for us."[21]

George and Evelyn Plante had several friends and distant relatives in the States, and he spent many pleasant times with some of them in New York. But there was one family in Ohio who persistently urged him to visit and, as he admitted to his wife, only a shortage of money held him back. In his Edinburgh College of Art days Plante had stayed in the home of Evelyn and Yvonne McNish, daughters of a British employee of the American Hoover Company. The two girls were now the guests of Mrs. D. P. Hoover in Canton, and they all invited him to join them. He had reluctantly decided he would have to decline when to his surprise and pleasure, Mrs. Hoover sent him a warm personal invitation and a train ticket. He leapt at the chance to see more of the country. "Travel in an American train is not the same ordeal on a long journey as it is at home. You've seen the trains in films. The coloured porter does everything for you, even to polishing your shoes in the morning. There are such pleasant washrooms etc. that you arrive at the end of the journey completely refreshed and no feeling of having taken a long trip."[22]

Reporting from Ohio, Plante could not restrain his superlatives. His friends, Evelyn and Yvonne McNish, accompanied by Mrs. Hoover's son, met him at the Canton station in a "magnificent Lincoln Zephyr." The Hoover's house was the "most beautiful" he had ever seen and more beautifully furnished than the famous sixteenth-century Lauriston Castle in Edinburgh, though not as large. Mrs. Hoover herself, a widow in her forties, was the "most charming and attractive woman in the world, after my wife." After lunch "served at a table just like the loveliest illustration you've seen in the *Saturday Evening Post*," they enjoyed an afternoon in the garden around the swimming pool.[23]

These were, of course, the Hoovers of the Hoover vacuum cleaner company. The following day Herbert Hoover, together with Mrs. Hoover's father, showed the young Scotsman around the Hoover factory. Plante was suitably impressed. After church on Sunday, with no hint of "that dreadful starchy atmosphere that frightens me away from a church at home," he met "several English kiddies," other children of Hoover company employees who had been evacuated from Britain to avoid the German bombing campaign.[24]

Back on *Sourabaya* and back to reality, Plante was discouraged to find that because of the number of passengers they would carry on their return to England he had to share a cabin with the second radio officer again. After his few days away, he found the company of his shipmates even more tedious than before. "These fellows think because they have their cabin floor covered with cigarette ends and some half filled beer cans that they are tough. I've had about enough of this ship . . . [and] unless they can give me a cabin to myself I think I'll make a change at the end of this trip." Apparently, it was the Scotsmen who bothered him most. They "seem so dour and pick on every little remark or joke and want to turn it into an argument. . . . When I meet men from other ships they are entirely different."[25]

On Friday, 27 June, Plante enjoyed one final day in New York. He had already visited the Museum of Modern Art and the New York Public Library so this day he made for the Metropolitan Museum, which he found "impressive," particularly their "magnificent" collection of early European paintings. After strolling through Central Park he took the subway up to Harlem where he did not see another white person beside himself. Taking in a show at the Apollo Theater, he found it "rather fun" with "the usual wonderful tap dancers and blues singers." The colored illustrations of Harlem they had seen in England "certainly don't exaggerate. They wear green suits, purple shirts, hats with fancy bands, and invariably the brim at the front is turned up. A great fashion with the young bloods is to wear their shirttails outside their trousers." On subsequent trips, after dinner with friends, instead of going back to the ship Plante often went up to Harlem "to listen to the most exciting jazz imaginable." Although "being the only white face did make me a little bit conspicuous," he never felt unwelcome. On the contrary, he got the impression that people were happy to talk to somebody interested in their music and who knew so much about the musicians who played it.[26]

By 31 June (according to Plante, who clearly had forgotten that June has only thirty days) *Sourabaya* was on the first leg of the journey home. The ship had moved from the Brooklyn Navy Yard to Bayonne, New Jersey, that, as far as Plante was concerned, richly earned its nickname—"the Back of Bayonne." To get to Manhattan from there required taking a ferry, a bus, another ferry, and then the subway, and since he was broke he stayed on board. From Bayonne they would move back to Manhattan and then to Halifax and home, taking the same route as on the trip over. In addition to a dozen or so other passengers they also had quartered below decks quite a number of those Distressed British Seamen.[27]

At sea on 3 July Plante wrote a letter to be posted in Halifax—so quite definitely the last letter from him for this trip, he told his wife. He still did not know their port of arrival in Britain (though the cargo and passenger report tells us he was destined for Liverpool) and hoped that maybe Salvesen, the shipping company, would let Evelyn know. In addition to the usual fuel oil, they carried with them five airplanes, two motorboats, and four ambulances. The passengers—seven American Red Cross nurses, a Frenchman, a Dutchman, an Englishman with his Japanese wife, and a woman from China—proved to be amusing company, but in two to three weeks he expected to be seeing Evelyn and he could not wait. "New York surely has the most attractive girls in the world but—someday I'm going to take you over there and my wife will be the most charming of them all." Apparently, a quick turnaround was planned for *Sourabaya* in the UK, so they might not have much time together but at least it would be enough for a brief reunion.[28]

According to the Cargo and Passenger Reports issued in New York, *Sourabaya* continued a grueling schedule of crossings for the rest of the year. During 1941 the German U-boat fleet grew from 80 to more than 250 and Plante's first nine months at sea corresponded with this growth. During this phase of the Battle of the Atlantic, however, the U-boats moved their operations gradually to the west, in part to operate beyond the reach of British aircraft. The problem in this for the Germans was that the vast area of operations now made it increasingly difficult for their submarine packs to locate convoys. In addition, the longer transit times from their bases meant they had less time on station, which resulted in fewer ships sunk. From January to March 1941, before Plante was on *Sourabaya*, sinkings averaged about 300,000 tons monthly, but from then on they fell to about 120,000 tons. During this same time the British were producing more escorts and were using intelligence to better effect. They were also aided by the growing, if unofficial, help from the United States Navy with convoy escort efforts.[29]

Sourabaya was back in New York from Liverpool on 19 August, in ballast and with no passengers listed on the manifest, although there may have been some who disembarked in Halifax. In New York the ship's regular berth now was on the Hudson River just at the bottom of 57th Street. This was Pier 54, the famous Cunard pier, where their majestic liners had docked for years, setting sail for England again with festive bands, champagne, and streamers. The scene was very different in wartime. Now the ships were painted a drab battleship grey and they sailed away at night, attracting as little attention as possible. For Plante, though, Pier 54 was an "incredibly convenient location that suited me perfectly. I could walk to wherever I wanted to be. Only the Plaza Hotel could have been better!"[30]

On this second visit Plante had barely a week in New York before *Sourabaya* set off again for Liverpool on 25 August with twelve passengers and a cargo of fuel oil, fuselages, and wing boxes. As usual, the services and supplies in New York had been procured with requisition orders from the British Ministry of War Transport based on their allotment from the lend-lease program. While he was briefly home in September, Plante heard that the warehouse in London where he and Evelyn had stored all their belongings had been destroyed during the devastating bombing of the city. This happened again later in the war giving him a lifelong sense of detachment from material possessions.[31]

On 9 October 1941 *Sourabaya* again docked in New York. As usual, some repairs were required after the battering it had taken in the North Atlantic, this time general deck, engine, and tank repairs. Each time he returned, Plante wrote that it was "like arriving in Paradise. Total strangers treated me with overwhelming kindness and generosity." He had a cousin, Charlotte Pasman, who lived with her husband in Sutton Place, next door to the silent movie actress Lillian Gish. With his cousins he met all kinds of celebrities and dined at all the places in vogue: Sherman Billingsly's Stork Club, the 21 Club, the Copacabana,

Sardi's, and more. Through his cousins he became close friends with Russell Patterson, the illustrator/designer for the Ziegfeld Follies, and through Patterson he met all kinds of people in show business, the music business, and the fringes of the art world. He was thrown right into the heady social life of prewar New York.[32]

Of course, not everyone he met was rich or famous. One night at Jack Dempsey's bar on Broadway he was talking with some firemen and having a great time. Suddenly he realized he had to get back to *Sourabaya*, which was about to sail. He had cut it a bit close but the firemen solved the problem by "taking me back at great speed with sirens wailing and lights flashing. It was a great thrill and impressed my shipmates immensely who had been convinced that this time I really wasn't going to make it."[33]

While at sea, Plante worked on more sketches and the next time he was in New York he took them to Russ Patterson who encouraged him to see the art director of Young & Rubicam (Y&R), a well-known advertising agency with offices on Madison Avenue. The art director liked what he saw and commissioned Plante to do some more drawings for them. Not only did this connection influence the course of his post-war life, but the dollars he earned enabled him to express, as he put it, "some small token of appreciation for some of the generous hospitality" he had been enjoying. In a later newspaper interview Plante reflected, "To the extent that the artist can portray only his own experiences, the war actually helped me."[34]

This was a particularly vulnerable time for Britain. Although the threat of a German invasion had diminished by May 1941 thanks to the failure of the Luftwaffe to secure control of the air, the bombing campaign had devastated London as well as major ports and industrial cities. By that time, Greece had also fallen to Germany and British forces had had to be evacuated from Crete. That June, Hitler turned his attention to an attack on the Soviet Union, finally ending any chance of an imminent of invasion of Britain. In North Africa that fall, though, Rommel's Afrika Korps was menacing Egypt, and the desperate struggle to keep Britain supplied across the Atlantic continued.

During his October 1941 turnaround in New York, Plante's artwork was brought to the attention of Jan Juta. Juta ran the Exhibition Section of the British Library of Information, part of the British Information Services (BIS), the New York–based information department of the British consulate in New York. When it was established early in 1941 BIS enlisted many famous British authors including C. S. Forrester, Graham Greene, T. S. Eliot, Somerset Maugham, and A. A. Milne to quietly encourage support for Britain in the United States.[35]

It was clear to BIS that an aggressive publicity campaign was risky as many Americans still blamed British propagandists for dragging them into World War I. The United States had been profoundly isolationist since the end of that war and many Americans remained determined never to get entangled in European conflicts again. September 1940 had seen the launch of the noninterventionist America First committee, which soon leaned heavily toward the xenophobic nativism, anti-Semitism, and pro-Nazi sentiment of many of its members. It was also given dangerous prestige by Charles Lindbergh's support. A year later Lindbergh was still asserting that "the three most important groups . . . pressing the country toward war are the British, the Jews and the Roosevelt administration."[36]

In light of this, the BIS recruited Juta, a South African–born painter and muralist, to organize a discreet pro-British effort similar to the literary one but through the visual arts. One result of his work was an exhibition featuring paintings and sketches of Britain at war held in Manhattan's Museum of Modern Art, including the works of such well-known British artists as Henry Moore, Edward Ardizzone, Paul Nash, and Feliks Topolski.[37]

Juta's immediate assignment for Plante, however, was not to commission paintings. Rather, he enlisted Plante to do a couple of radio interviews about the Battle of the Atlantic at a time when losses to U-boats seemed unending and Britain's survival depended on American war credit. As Plante saw it, the American government was already helping Britain in many ways, but he clearly understood that "not all of the people were convinced that the United States should be involved." Still, he was uncomfortable about being presented as some kind of war hero and he hoped that none of his shipmates would hear the interviews. None did, but on his return to Britain he was amazed to find that some of his friends had picked them up on the BBC overseas service.[38]

After Plante's successful radio appearances, Juta tasked him to paint pictures of the Battle of the Atlantic that BIS could use to help urge American intervention in the war. It was clear that winning over American public opinion was the key to unlocking essential resources. As a result, Plante came to fight his war less and less as radio operator and more and more as the creator of stark and often gripping images of the struggle at sea. Because he was in the right place and had the right skills and inclinations he became a small stone in the intricate mosaic that made up the British propaganda structure in America.

Juta's BIS headquarters was located in the administrative offices of Britain's Ministry of Information in Rockefeller Center on Fifth Avenue in New York City. There, BIS worked closely with its Rockefeller Center neighbor, the British Security Coordination (BSC). Under the direction of the Canadian, Bill (later Sir William) Stephenson, BSC was at the heart of the U.S. operations of British intelligence. A man of few words, Stephenson, known as "the Quiet Canadian," has since the war become better known by his wartime telegraphic address, "Intrepid."[39]

When Stephenson set up shop in New York City in the summer of 1940, Churchill's assignment for him had been to secure American participation in the war—by whatever means possible. Eventually, Stephenson controlled a virtual empire of British secret organizations in the Americas and the Caribbean representing the intelligence agencies MI5 (Military Intelligence, Section 5), MI6 (Secret Intelligence Service), the Special Operations Executive (SOE), and the Political Warfare Executive (PWE). He employed an army of agents engaged in subversion, propaganda, and political warfare of all sorts. Stephenson's clandestine operation was by all accounts remarkably successful in weakening isolationist forces in America and encouraging intervention in the war on the side of Britain.[40]

A crew of colorful amateurs assisted BSC in the work of encouraging—as unobtrusively as possible—U.S. support for and—better still—actual participation in the struggle against fascism. A group of these volunteers was known as the "Baker Street Irregulars" (so called in honor of the street urchins enlisted by Sherlock Holmes). Among the well-connected young men recruited were Roald Dahl, Noel Coward, Ian Fleming, and David Ogilvy. Dahl, an RAF officer, was assistant air attaché at the British embassy in Washington. Ian Fleming, RNVR, was in the Naval Intelligence Department (NID) in London but visited New York and Washington as liaison with other British intelligence organizations and as personal assistant to Rear Admiral John Godfrey, the director of Naval Intelligence. David Ogilvy, Noel Coward, and Ivar Bryce were civilians. But whatever their official positions, they all ran in top social, political, media, and financial circles which they assiduously culled for information of great use to Stephenson's secret intelligence gathering and influence shaping.[41]

These men constituted what one historian aptly referred to as Churchill's underground army in America. In addition to passing on insider information to Stephenson, they "planted propaganda in American newspapers, radio stations and wire services; co-opted leading columnists . . . ; harassed prominent isolationists and anti-New Dealers; exposed Nazi sympathizers and fifth columnists; and plotted against corporations that were working against British interests." The more recently created BIS, while it shared a similar propaganda imperative with BSC, was engaged strictly in white, or open, propaganda.[42]

Juta was instrumental in the BIS effort to use the arts to change minds without inflaming what one historian referred to as America's "propaganda phobia," particularly with regard to perfidious Albion. As John Reith, the former director-general of the BBC and for five months in 1940 the minister of information, put it with approval, "it is impossible to say where cultural activities end and propaganda begins." Significantly, this British campaign also made use of American commercial expertise, hiring the advertising agency J. Walter Thompson, to help avoid arousing American anti-propaganda sensibilities. The intersection of propaganda and advertising was a natural one and one that quite naturally appealed to Plante.[43]

From then on Plante's work was affected by the needs of the Ministry of Information, the British Information Services, and the British Security Coordination, and eventually also by the American Office of Strategic Services (OSS) and the American equivalent of the BIS, the Office of War Information (OWI). According to historian Nicholas Cull, the effort to enlist American support was critical. "No component in sending that aid—let alone the role of British propaganda—can be dismissed." Without American aid, Cull maintains, "1941 would have brought a British defeat."[44]

On 17 October *Sourabaya* set sail again from New York with the usual oil for Britain as well as a consignment of airplanes.

As Plante recalled, they never felt that their protective naval escort was nearly adequate, and it was not. Still, it was comforting to see the destroyers and corvettes hovering in the distance, even one of the fifty-year-old American destroyers Roosevelt had given Britain in September 1940 in exchange for leases of some British naval and air bases in the Caribbean, the Bahamas, Newfoundland, and elsewhere. "We felt better when one of these funny, old-fashioned looking ships with its four tall skinny smoke stacks appeared off what we called 'Hell's Corner,' the forward starboard point of the convoy. It did a lot for our confidence to hear the deep rumble and bang of an exploding depth charge and to see the great splash gurgle up into the sky. We rarely knew at the time what the outcome was, but the 'galley wireless' kept us in touch with the latest gossip and rumors." It was also at about this time that U.S. Navy vessels were finally authorized to fire at U-boats on sight, although a technical neutrality was preserved for another couple of months.[45]

On the quiet days, Plante remembered, "I could look out over the sea and enjoy the changing colors and think how fortunate I was to be experiencing this and not marching up and down on some battlefield with a pack on my back." Sometimes a big seagull would join him, riding alongside in the slipstream only a foot or so away from the rail of the flying bridge. Other little land birds would surprisingly drop out of the sky a thousand miles from shore and hitch a ride for a little while and then disappear. "Where they came from and where they went was a mystery." It was always too soon when inevitably the war would intrude again on such peaceful interludes. On this trip, not long after sailing, they heard that the American destroyer USS *Kearny* had been attacked by U-boats and suffered great damage and loss of life. Surely this would force the United States into the war, they thought. But it did not.[46]

On 22 October *Sourabaya* left Halifax for Liverpool with convoy HX156, bound for Britain. It was dark and the visibility poor near Iceland on the night of 31 October when the convoy "was suddenly lit up and exposed to the world with bursting star shells. Something strange and most unusual was happening," Plante recalled.

> Normally, the darker the night, the safer we felt. It was as if someone had removed all of our clothes and we were left stark-naked in a spotlight. It was normal practice for destroyers to use star shells when hunting submarines at night, but never close to a convoy. Whatever was going on we did not care for it. When all the lights went out and we were safely in the dark again there was a hell of an explosion just off our port side. We were all lit up again, but this time it was from the flames of a blazing ship. It looked like a destroyer had been hit amidships. The convoy kept ploughing along and the burning ship dropped astern.[47]

It is a general rule in convoys that all but a pre-designated rescue ship continue on course so they could not stop to see what finally happened to the destroyer and its crew. Later, they heard that the ship was the USS *Reuben James,* the first American warship to be sunk in the war with only 45 survivors of the ship's complement of 160. "If my turn comes," Plante was quoted as saying in a newspaper interview he gave in 1942, "I'd prefer a torpedo to a mine. A mine often explodes directly under a ship and rips the whole bottom out. A torpedo tears a nasty hole in the ship's side but does not always sink the ship." Still, even the attack on *Reuben James* was not sufficient cause to bring the United States into the war.[48]

CHAPTER FOUR

"I am not seeking financial gain or desirous of leaving the sea."

On 3 December 1941 *Sourabaya* docked in the Hudson once again. Although few knew it at the time, most fully operational U-boats had been withdrawn from the North Atlantic in late November and sent to the Mediterranean and the Gibraltar area so the passage had been relatively uneventful. Arrangements had already been made to have *Sourabaya* undergo the usual deck and engine repairs and alterations needed to permit deeper loading and more effective "convoy operating measures." These measures included the installation of two machine gun emplacements, two Oerlikon anti-aircraft guns, and a "kite attachment to 16 Ready-use 4" Shell Racks," greatly increasing the defensive power of the vessel. Since it took time to make these changes, Plante was in New York on 7 December 1941 and heard the president's declaration that America was now at war with the Empire of Japan.[1]

With the nation now on a war footing, the work was completed in haste and after only one week in port, *Sourabaya* sailed for Britain on 10 December with aniline oil and fuel oil on board, as well as forty-five motorboats. Paradoxically, the full engagement of the United States in the war at sea, rather than bringing relief to the convoys as the merchant sailors hoped, heralded especially harrowing months for the Allies. This was because Germany's declaration of war on the United States on 11 December freed the U-boats to operate against previously out-of-bounds shipping in the waters off the Atlantic coast of North America. The Germans were already poised to strike. Twelve type VIIC U-boats arrived off the Newfoundland Grand Banks on 8 January 1942 and Operation Paukenschlag (also called Operation Drumbeat) began the very next day with the sinking of a freighter off Nova Scotia. Five larger type IXC U-boats followed the first twelve across the Atlantic a few days later en route for the Caribbean.[2]

The tale of the slaughter of unescorted ships, especially tankers, sailing close to shore in those months is a familiar one. Some 260 ships were sunk in American waters between January and April 1942. The disaster has often been blamed on Admiral Ernest King, the newly appointed commander in chief, U.S. Fleet, who focused his efforts on the Pacific rather than the Atlantic. Additionally, King's well-known Anglophobia is said to have prevented him from taking the advice of the more experienced British and Canadian counselors and he failed to immediately institute convoying and to provide adequate escorts.[3]

It is true that in the complex world of international cooperation in wartime, personal antipathies sometimes played a significant role. In the case of King, however, the naval historian Clay Blair demonstrated that King, perhaps more than any other American naval officer, understood the need for convoying but was handicapped by serious deficiencies, among them the desperate shortage of escort vessels. Blair contends that King was working assiduously to improve the situation and to prepare as quickly as possible for convoying in U.S. coastal waters. Moreover, the initial slaughter had been made all the easier by a factor beyond King's control—the initial refusal of coastal cities to institute blackouts. Ships sailing by were silhouetted against the cities' bright lights making perfect targets for lurking U-boats. In March 1942, in addition to holding the operational command of all fleet units, Admiral King became chief of naval operations gaining control of all navy bureaus. Two months later he began the process of instituting convoying between Florida and Maine.[4]

Meanwhile, *Sourabaya's* Atlantic commute continued into the spring of 1942, facing the greatly increased dangers of U-boat attacks close to the North American mainland. In January 1942 blackout switches were installed while the ship was in New York, and in February two more machine gun emplacements were added to *Sourabaya's* arsenal to increase its defenses. In April *Sourabaya* was at Pier 24 in Brooklyn having five hundred boiler tubes and additional, unspecified, "Defense Equipment" installed. What is notable here is that the Lend-Lease Act—engineered by President Roosevelt to help fund Britain's war effort—worked so smoothly, relying largely on trust between allies. In spite of the opposition of some, many people at many levels nurtured this trust.[5]

Outward bound in ballast, *Sourabaya* crossed to New York from Liverpool or sometimes from the Gareloch, a sea loch about thirteen miles northwest of Glasgow where there was a large naval base. The ship then took a northerly course up through the Irish Sea and the Minches off Scotland, zigzagging across the Atlantic to the Newfoundland Grand Banks. After a brief stop in Halifax *Sourabaya* hugged the American coast down to New York. Inward bound, usually to Liverpool, *Sourabaya's* tanks were always fully loaded with evil-smelling fuel oil. On the deck there might be fighter planes, armored vehicles, tanks, landing craft, or railway locomotives. They might also be shipping drums of chemicals as well as other kinds of oil—from grapefruit oil to lubricating oil. There often were passengers on board, almost all of whom were European. Unlike most ships, *Sourabaya* also carried an artist, hard at work recording the drama unfolding before them.[6]

One aspect of this life that Plante enjoyed immensely was the running battle of wits with the customs officers back in Britain. He admitted that they were always very generous, but he and his fellow sailors always wanted more—not for themselves, of course—they had plenty—but to give to family and friends. As soon as they anchored in Liverpool or the Gareloch, the customs launch would arrive alongside. While watering the customs officers with plenty of Scotch, the crew filed past showing whatever it was they wanted to declare. After they had processed the crew the customs men donned overalls and searched the ship from top to bottom. If they suspected anything out of the ordinary they would turn things upside-down, even going so far as to remove cabin panels. Their ingenuity was matched by that of the crew and sometimes one side won, sometimes the other.[7]

Sailors filled water jugs with gin and suspended cartons of cigarettes down into the water tanks. They emptied the sand out of fire buckets, placed bottles of booze or nylon stockings in the bottom and then replaced the sand. Once Plante was sitting at a green felt-covered table in the salon while the customs officers were checking the crew. He tried to look calm and nonchalant while knowing full well that "the underside of the table was solidly covered with cartons of cigarettes and plugs of tobacco taped to it." Fortunately for Plante they were not discovered. Besides all the contraband, sailors also staggered ashore with suitcases and cartons filled with canned fruits, chocolate, bananas, and onions. They were allowed to take home twenty-five pounds of rationed food each. "It was fun to walk down the corridor of a darkened train, open the door of a compartment and watch people who had been sitting in the gloom light up when we tossed in a banana or a few onions. Packets of Edgeworth tobacco were very effective in persuading engine drivers to make every effort to reach their destination a minute or two early," when Plante had tight connections.[8]

Perhaps Plante's most nerve-wracking coup was when he scrounged a ride ashore on a customs launch. He had his usual heavy load of canned fruits as well as huge cardboard cartons roped up for easy carrying. The customs officers kindly helped him load all this onto the launch, then onto the dock, and finally into a taxi. They read the captions on the cartons saying something like "10,000 Lucky Strikes." "Wouldn't it be funny if they actually were full of cigarettes?" they laughed. Plante agreed and they all smiled as he got on his way as fast as he could. In fact, the cartons were "completely and totally packed with cigarettes, thousands and thousands of them. Plante was a nonsmoker, and as he noted, "my friends love me for it."[9]

On 9 February 1942, after a frigid crossing and a few days leave ashore in New York, Plante returned to Pier 54 on the Hudson River in Manhattan to find *Sourabaya* missing. The huge former French luxury passenger liner *Normandie*, which had been in the next berth, was now "lying on its side like a gigantic wounded whale. It was a sad spectacle to see the burned out hulk of the half-submerged queen of the ocean on its side filling the whole dock." On the outbreak of war *Normandie* had been interned in New York and after Pearl Harbor the U.S. government began to convert the ship to a troop transport. While this work was going on, the ship caught fire. Sabotage was suspected (perhaps even by the Mafia) but never proved and the vast amounts of water pumped into it to put out the blaze caused it to capsize. *Sourabaya* had been towed quickly out of danger into the Hudson and later moved to a distant berth on Staten Island. Plante's easy access to Manhattan was over for this visit.[10]

In part owing to his own initiative, Plante's life soon improved immensely. In March, following Jan Juta's advice, he wrote to artist E. M. O'R. Dickey, secretary of the War Artists Advisory Committee of the Ministry of Information, to secure official support for time at sea to spend sketching and painting. Kenneth Clark, the director of the National Gallery and a dominant figure in the British art world, chaired the WAAC. The committee was Clark's brainchild and he was largely responsible for getting it established within the MOI in 1939. Its mission was to compile, "through commissions and purchases, a documentary and artistic history" of Britain during World War II.[11]

Brian Foss, a historian of the WAAC, has written of the war's enormous impact on the production and consumption of art noting that the committee "played a dominant role in the sustenance and promotion of art," in that it helped "to articulate national values and beliefs when they were most needed." Equally important was the conviction that a photographic record, as opposed to an artistic one, had significant limitations. "The camera cannot interpret, and a war so epic in its scope by land, sea and air, and so detailed and complex in its mechanism, requires interpreting as well as recording." Clark's view that painters and sculptors "differed from photographers because they could produce visual records that combined historical documentation with the subjective 'feel' of the war" was central to the work the WAAC commissioned.[12]

Clark's vision was to support the production of high-quality art that expressed the liberal cultural values of the British in contrast to the tightly controlled and heavily censored art produced by the Nazi state. The committee provided different levels of support and in a number of different ways. It employed some British artists on contract while it commissioned others to produce specific works. It also purchased works from independent artists "many of them in active service, and permits were given to enable them to work in restricted areas." Eventually, the art collection put together by the committee included some six thousand items in various different mediums and styles, representing a very broad range of subject matter. More than four hundred artists—some of them famous, others unknown—created the works. There were some obvious limitations in the collection, among them a lack of geographic diversity. Few Scottish artists were represented, particularly from the Edinburgh School, arousing the indignation of the Scottish Royal Academy. Women artists, too, were very poorly represented. Nevertheless, without the WAAC, one commentator observed, "many [artists] would have lacked the opportunity to make any significant contribution to the Allied effort."[13]

Against the odds, Plante benefited from the support of the committee. The first phase of what was to become his unusual contribution to the Allied war effort was quickly getting under way, although even after the United States entered the war propaganda was still considered a somewhat tainted word and Plante had to tread carefully. As Kenneth Clark realized, "in order to preserve truth for posterity, one must pickle it in style." That is what Plante now received official encouragement to do.[14]

Plante's bold letter to Dickey urging the inclusion of the Merchant Navy in works sponsored by the WAAC clearly helped him gain both recognition and support. "Though the various services such as the RAF, Navy, and Army have official artists, I'm unaware of any such appointment in regard to the Merchant Navy which is admittedly one of our most vital war efforts." In fact, of the thirty-seven salaried artists of the WAAC, six were assigned to the Admiralty, none of them specifically to the Merchant Navy, although they did cover some Merchant Navy activities. The War Office employed eleven artists and the Air Ministry seven.

"At this point," Plante's letter continued,

> I must make it quite clear that I am not seeking financial gain or desirous of leaving the sea. But I am of the very definite opinion that some kind of official recognition or endorsement would assist me considerably in my work. It would afford me some protection from the inherent suspicion that the name "Artist" seems to arouse in a real old "sea dog." Your department's blessing and a word or letter to the appropriate quarter is all that would appear necessary. And of course the grant of a permit for sketching.[15]

Plante was hardly alone in believing that his fellow mariners did not have much time to waste on artists and many on the front lines everywhere probably shared the sailors' views. A year later, when the well-known British artist, Michael Rothenstein, was giving a lecture to a group of soldiers they let him know quite candidly that they thought it was pointless to record the war in art because photography could do a much more effective job.[16]

Plante felt it important in making his case to Dickey to emphasize that he had already made a substantial contribution to the war effort by encouraging American appreciation for Britain's role in the conflict. By way of explanation he enclosed the newspaper clipping from the *Canton Repository* with the headline about a visiting British radio officer who had been in the thick of the dangerous Battle of the Atlantic. He also mentioned that some of his paintings—for example, "Bombers for Britain" and "British Raider in Brooklyn"—were to be exhibited in an upcoming show at the American British Art Center. He noted that the center had promised him a show for all of his work, and that he had been told that his paintings would be of great interest to the Artist's Advisory Committee. He further informed Dickey that the quality of his work would be vouched for by a Mrs. Storey at the

Art Center and that "Sir Kenneth Clark and Mr. Jack Beddington will uphold Mrs. Storey's qualifications as judge." Plante could scarcely cite better references than Clark and Jack Beddington, the latter the advertising executive who took over the chairmanship of the MOI Films Division from Clark.

Any questions about his personal integrity, Plante noted in his letter, could be answered by Lieutenant Robert Harling, RNVR, Naval Intelligence, late of Everetts Advertising where the two had worked up to September 1939. Plante assured Dickey that he would continue to perform the "useful duties of a Radio Officer" adding, most empathically, he did "*not* suffer from sea sickness." In his response, Dickey noted that it would be extremely difficult to secure the support Plante wished for unless he could show examples of his work to the WAAC "whose responsibility it is to advise on matters relating to artistic war records."[17]

In April, Jan Juta got into the act with a letter to Mr. Dickey addressed to the American Division of the MOI in London in which he explained his connection to Plante. "Despite our deep concern with the war we are doing all we possibly can to keep up an interest in British Art on this side of the world and furthering the interests of British artists wherever possible." Artists, he argued, provided "not only a living record, but an interpretation through the artists' eyes of the whole progress of the war." He had seen Plante's paintings, he wrote, and found them "both of real interest and value," and he was hopeful that the American-British Art Centre in New York would hold a one-man show for him. He urged Dickey to give further consideration to Plante's "application for some sort of 'official' opportunity to record the story of the Merchant Marine." Juta noted, too, that in recommending Plante he was merely passing on the verdict of "several whose opinion is of far greater importance than my own." For himself, he found Plante "obviously sincere, anxious, and a good painter and seems in the fortunate position of being able to combine his services to his country with his art."[18]

On 29 April Dickey replied, saying, "Sir Kenneth Clark and his Committee will be interested to hear what you have told me about Plante and that they will be grateful, as I am, for the trouble you have taken in writing on his behalf." He also reiterated that he very much hoped they would soon have an opportunity to see some of Plante's work and that photographs "would suffice." In the event, Plante immediately sent some photographs. Later, he provided the WAAC with his painting of the shipment of tanks leaving New York. On the basis of that, the WAAC wrote to the Marconi Company—the larger employer of Radio Officers—on Plante's behalf. They also notified Salvesen, the owner of *Sourabaya*, who agreed to give Plante "facilities for painting war subjects at sea."[19]

This minimally documented arrangement organized by the WAAC, which was typical of many of their unsystematic appointments, meant a dramatic change to Plante's life. From then on he was relieved of many of his responsibilities on board ship and was able to, as he put it, "get on with my life as an artist once again." Won over by his official status as a real artist, the crew now tiptoed around him when he was sketching or painting, not wanting to disturb his concentration.[20]

Pearl Harbor had not ended the need for positive British publicity in America. In fact it was seen as essential to ensure the smooth running of the alliance and it continued until the war's end. Pro-British publicity was also important to support the "Europe First" strategy agreed upon by Roosevelt and Churchill. American anger at the Japanese sneak attack at first forced the Roosevelt administration to concentrate attention and resources on the Pacific and the balance did not shift back to Europe until the landings in North Africa as part of Operation Torch in November 1942.

That June, the American-British Art Centre on West 56th Street in New York City mounted an exhibition of about one hundred watercolors and drawings by British artists. It displayed twenty of Plante's paintings and a photograph of one—"Tanker in Dry Dock"—appeared in the *New York Times*. The accompanying review noted that "in an unusually attractive show," several of the paintings were "vigorous marine subjects by George Plante, who is serving as a transport radio officer. Henry Moore, Paul Nash, Rowland Suddaby and Michael Rothenstein are others well represented." Plante was much amused by the priority of his name over some of the greatest contemporary names in British art. Clearly, the reviewer did not know much about who was who in the British art world. The exhibition later went on tour around the United States. And when, in the following year, the WAAC bought one of his paintings for twenty-one pounds sterling, Plante officially joined the ranks of artists whose work provided a memorable record of a devastating global war. [21]

In the meantime, Plante continued to make trans-Atlantic crossings, mostly uneventful. Of course the term uneventful is a relative one when speaking of the war at sea. In 1942, "in the single month of March, 94 ships were sunk; in May 125; in June 144—nearly five a day: the appalling rate of loss continued around the 100 mark, every month for the rest of the year." Even if not attacked by U-boats, convoys always had to contend with "the weather, which was the most violent enemy of all." The combination of rising tanker losses to U-boats and battering by the weather led to increasing dependence by Britain on U.S. repair yards, a costly but necessary way to maintain the delivery of fuel to keep the RAF in the air.[22]

Consequently, when Plante arrived once again in New York, on 8 June 1942 he barely had time to visit the gallery on Madison Avenue where two of his paintings were on show. The woman who worked at the gallery told him that his paintings had been much admired, and one of his sketches of New York had been sold. Thirteen galleries had contributed art for the show at the American-British Art Centre to be held the following week and the proceeds were to go to purchase war bonds. Plante was disappointed that he would miss the opening, not least because of all of the "important people who would be there." He thought he would be lucky if he even got to see the show at all.[23]

That was because *Sourabaya's* course had just taken a dramatically different turn. "When we arrived here we were told that if we wanted to load up with oil we would have to go down to the Gulf [of Mexico] and collect it ourselves." At a secret strategy meeting with Roosevelt in mid-June, Winston Churchill deplored the "heavy sinkings" of merchant ships in American waters occurring in spite of the fact that convoying had been instituted in bits and pieces down the coast southward since May. Churchill urged Roosevelt to "do everything possible to hasten the extension of the convoy network into the Gulf of Mexico and the Caribbean." Admiral Ernest King responded to Roosevelt that his goal was "to get every ship under escort," although he admitted that due to lack of escort vessels "there are no regular convoys at present to Gulf of Mexico ports."[24]

This largely unprotected route was a stunning omission. Japan had cut off oil reserves to Britain from Borneo and the Dutch East Indies, and Japanese submarines and German surface raiders attacked supplies from the Persian Gulf sailing through the Indian Ocean. Britain had come to rely on oil from the refineries of Aruba, Curacao, Mexico, Trinidad, Venezuela, and Texas oil from U.S. gulf ports, in a tanker pipeline through the Caribbean and up the East Coast. But during the first six months of 1942, sixty-eight British tankers had been sunk, sixteen off the U.S. East Coast and seventeen in the Caribbean, while in the same months twenty-five American tankers were lost off the Eastern seaboard. It was in this dangerous situation, with the shortage of oil and oil products reaching New York, that *Sourabaya* was sent to the Gulf to pick up its own load.[25]

About to embark on this hazardous route, *Sourabaya* waited in the narrows for the signal that would send it out to join a convoy heading south. The "Darken Ship" signal was piped at sunset as it was every day and from then on not a glimmer of light could appear on any ship, merchant or escort. The faintest gleam could give away their presence to the lurking U-boats. "The code word arrived at midnight and we raised anchor and set sail for the rendezvous off the New Jersey coast." Later, by then off Virginia, Plante observed that apparently time was no object in their present circumstances.

> We are making our way South in easy stages down inland waterways we just dodge in and out anchoring overnight. The weather, of course, is very warm and will become much more so as we get further south. We are wearing whites (if anything) and at night I sleep with a fan directed at my nude tummy. It serves two purposes, cools and chases away mosquitoes. They come at you droning and swerving like dive-bombers. Soon we'll be fitting up our insect nets. As we came up to the Delaware (I didn't notice Washington crossing it) the water was a fawn colour with a clear blue sky dotted with white puffs of cloud, and the sailors were hard at work putting up awnings over the bridges, etc.[26]

As he always did, Plante took advantage of quiet times to write long, evocative, often amusing, and sharply perceptive letters to his wife. "My mad rush around New York seems somewhat like a dream now," he wrote from "somewhere off the Virginia coast."

> While in Russell [Patterson]'s studio I received two lovely presents. The first was the most magnificent carrying case for my sketches. If it could have been bought it would have cost pounds but it was especially made for the Wallace Silver Company, with two others. They were presented to Russell who insisted on my having one. The second, from Ruth [Russell's wife], was her album of records I had admired. Evelyn darling, you've no idea of the hospitality and friendliness I have met in America, it is really staggering and a continual sorrow to me that you haven't experienced this with me. Someday you will meet my friends in America, you'll simply have to. I've told them all how lovely and charming you are and I can't disappoint them now. How lucky I am to have a wife that makes me feel that way.[27]

By Tuesday 16 June they had been lying at anchor awaiting another convoy since the previous Saturday. This was no hardship at all as far as Plante was concerned. He found it rather like staying in a hotel on the French Riviera. "Permanent sunshine, bathing over the ship's side (amongst fish with [brightly colored stripes that made them look as if they had] football jerseys on) and just waiting for the bell to ring for meals. Some of the fellows are pretty fed up but I rather enjoy it—because I read a great deal and keep painting. In the evening we play darts on the deck. We've fitted a light over the board and enjoy music from the radio."

Apparently, the heat somewhat slowed the consumption of alcohol but there were still some pretty wild parties. Ironically, Plante, the most abstemious of the crew, was the only one who almost fell overboard. Wandering out on deck for some air before turning in one night he "chose to lean on the bit of rail that wasn't there. It had been removed for the gangway." Fortunately, he caught hold of a cable to stop himself just before plunging over the side.[28]

Later on that day they were on the move again, joining a convoy that "in this part of the world was rather a comic affair after the smart efficiency and seamanship we have been accustomed to. No doubt, experience makes all the difference." Convoys organized by the United States had only been operating for a month at this point and there was still a lot to learn. When U-boats were reported in the vicinity the convoy had to take immediate evasive action. "The normal procedure," Plante explained years later, "would be for the whole convoy to make a concerted turn as ordered and change course together." But that is not what happened:

> The ships on the nearside decided that they would be far safer on the far side and took the shortest route to get there. Ships bore down on us from every direction. They crossed our bows and our stern. It was chaotic and highly dangerous. When the order to scatter came, we were already scattered all over the sea. From then on we were on our own, every ship for itself. We did everything we could to get down south to the Gulf without going out into the Atlantic. We went up waterways, up rivers and through canals. If we could have fitted wheels and gone overland we would have done so. We sailed up the Delaware and squeezed through the canal and into Chesapeake Bay. We went where no big ships had ever been before. Our worries changed from U-boats to running aground and knocking down bridges.[29]

That first day out there was plenty of excitement, which Plante "rather enjoyed," in spite of his belief in the futility and waste of war. Perhaps, he admitted, this was because "the blueness of the sea and sky and the warmth of the sun . . . made the grimmer side rather unreal. It is pretty exciting to see an airship, a plane, a destroyer and a sub chaser going around tossing depth charges. Probably all brought about by a shoal of fish." He concluded pragmatically, "We are the luckiest ship on the seas." Although Admiral King was making every effort to "get every ship that sails under constant close protection," the protective net was far from complete. Plante might well have felt even luckier at their escape had he known that just the day before he wrote those words to his wife U-701 had planted mines in the mouth of the Chesapeake Bay and then turned to patrol the waters off Cape Hatteras. Four other U-boats converging on the Cape Hatteras area were also very busy during the last ten days of June.[30]

On this trip Plante had taken to addressing his letters home to "My dearest Evelyn, and Oscar or Judy" acknowledging his wife's pregnancy, which she had told him about his last time home, and his pleasure at the thought. Since the baby was due in September, this would probably be his last trip for a while as he had asked to be relieved from the ship, or temporarily transferred ashore, so he could be with his wife for the birth. He was confident that everything could be arranged. That is, if he could get home safely.[31]

For three weeks, between 20 June and 13 July, U-67 patrolled the Gulf Coast between Florida and Texas attacking six tankers of which four were sunk and two damaged. *Sourabaya* was lucky to slip through unscathed as it rounded the tip of Florida and sailed west across the Gulf toward Texas City, Texas, on the coast near the mouth of Galveston Bay. Texas City had greatly expanded recently and its oil refineries were working around the clock to supply the war effort.[32]

Plante found Texas City a very small and not very attractive town that looked as though it had been built out of huge oil containers on the edge of the desert. But the inhabitants were very friendly and completely corroborated his preconceived notions about Texans. "The men were lean, bronzed, wore high heeled boots and ten-gallon hats," he wrote. "Their legs were bowed and their toes turned in and they spoke exactly like a western film. It was so like the movies that I instinctively ducked to avoid the squirt of tobacco juice that should have followed." The town itself was divided into two sections, "white," and "colored and Mexican," and the social life centered around the Long Horn Bar, which—to his disappointment—merely turned the lights off at closing time instead of shooting them out. The local hoosegow did not disappoint, though, with its barred window looking out onto the main street. "Sailors from our ship could be observed peering out rather forlornly at any time during our stay."[33]

By 2 July, after spending two days in Texas City, *Sourabaya*, now loaded with oil, sailed east and steamed up the coffee-colored Mississippi through the flat lands of the delta. It was scheduled to reach New Orleans the next day to take on a deck cargo of landing craft. New Orleans was the home of Higgins Industries, a small boat company that, during the course of the war, turned out thousands of landing craft and other small boats. What had been planned as a short stop in New Orleans turned into a considerably longer stay, much to Plante's delight. When it was time to sail home they found that *Sourabaya's* boilers needed some work done. Although this was soon taken care of they then discovered that U-boats had trapped them again. "Joy of joy," Plante recalled in his memoir, "we couldn't get out of the Mississippi. We had to stay in New Orleans."[34]

Writing from New Orleans on 10 July Plante could not help enthusing about the women. "Down here, the French influence in the girls is very noticeable, and coupled with the American background, the result is pretty devastating. Yes, the girls here are even more stunning than the girls in New York." One wonders what Evelyn felt reading his frequent descriptions of beautiful women, although he always added that, of course, they just succeeded in making him yearn for her.

The women may have been beautiful, but the climate in New Orleans was not. Indeed, Plante found it rather unhealthy. The torrential tropical rains poured down day after day and the heat was stifling. There was "a continual dampness from the swamps and the tropical vegetation makes it smell exactly like the greenhouses in Kew Gardens," Plante informed his wife in the cold and distant Orkneys. "On the river bank there are some old shacks, sort of hillbilly places, just over from where we are lying at anchor." One of the shacks was particularly dilapidated but outside in the yard there was, "of all things a magnificent shining electric washing machine. This would make a pretty good *New Yorker* cover, eh?" Plante continued,

> All the dwelling houses are made of wood, with colourful chairs on their porches. As you ride into town on the tram (sitting in the section reserved for "whites") you run along wide avenues with grass and flowers and palms planted between the tracks. This is a real old part of the States and the wooden houses in the coloured section are pretty dilapidated. Little pot-bellied black children pop in and out through the holes in the walls while their coal black mammas—of shapes larger and more grotesque than Epstein [the sculptor] has thought of yet—take occasional swipes at them with broomsticks, while papa just sits around.[35]

Of course Plante went ashore on his own to explore the city and "inevitably," as he put it, reached the French Quarter. He admired its narrow streets, the French colonial architecture with its wrought iron-work, and strolled along Bourbon Street from "dive to dive," enjoying the "negro pianists and bawdy female vocalists." The blatancy of the "rackets" in these "clip joints" especially amused him. He sketched the scene:

> As you enter a girl sits down beside you and says "Hello! Would you like to buy me a drink?" If you say yes she has swallowed about three before you have even sipped your beer. The beer costs 15 cents, her drink, which is always Scotch or brandy, costs 65 cents. Of course she *really* drinks cold tea and gets fifty per-cent commission. But—if you refuse they don't trouble you. I had no trouble because when they approached me I countered by saying "That's funny, I was just going to ask you the same thing!"

Plante recalled that while "there were plenty of bars, and maybe a few naughty ladies, . . . people went to listen to the music." He also found some very fine restaurants that served "magnificent Southern dishes with the inevitable watermelon to follow." In the South, as in Ohio, Plante felt sure he had seen "the real America," which he found "without doubt the most livable place in the world." Contrary to what she may have imagined, Plante wrote Evelyn, the people were courteous, drug stores were clean, friendly places, every kind of service was efficient, and clothes were "smart and colourful."[36]

While in New Orleans Plante received a letter from "the M. of I., New York," telling him that if he could get ashore on his return to the city he would be interviewed and "given a 'write up' in *Life* or some similar publication—that is assured." Plante was enthusiastic. "So it appears that I have at last achieved one of my aims, eh? Yes, now that I've had my show, which incidentally I've no news of except from the MOI who said it looked 'grand' and managed to have the paintings and sketches reproduced, the time is just right for me to relax for a few weeks and then plan my next offensive!"[37]

The art Plante produced as a result of the leisure he had been afforded by the intervention of the WAAC aptly buttressed Kenneth Clark's contention that "fine art made its strongest contribution to . . . wartime propaganda by refusing to compromise its status as the ultimate symbol of individual and creative freedom, and as the visual expression of innately British character traits."[38]

Sourabaya finally departed New Orleans for New York on 11 July, loaded with fuel oil from Texas City and landing craft from New Orleans. Then, as had happened on the way south, they had to spend a day or so at anchor, this time in the Gulf of Mexico. The sun shone continuously as it had done for weeks, the flying fish played, and the sea was so clear and blue that swimming seemed irresistible. The crew were warned, however, that the waters were shark infested so instead of swimming a few of them took a lifeboat out for a sail. Plante understood that big ship sailors do not know much about sailing small sailing boats but he thought he would risk it anyway. At first he was in heaven: "Just like a boy's dream, there were even sharks in the seas and pelicans in the sky—and I was being paid for it!" Then came the anticlimax. After sailing for several miles they were becalmed and no matter what they tried, they just kept drifting farther and farther away.[39]

Eventually, there was nothing for it but to row back to the ship in temperatures topping 105 in the shade. They were all pretty tanned and were wearing sun helmets, but they had forgotten all about their feet. That night a few of them, Plante included, were totally crippled with severely sunburned feet. "Agonizing as it was," Plante remembered with feeling almost fifty years later, "I was determined to stand—or perhaps sit—my watch." So he struggled to the surgery where he had seen a pair of crutches tucked away in a corner. "Imagine my surprise," he recalled, when he opened the surgery door to find he could hardly squeeze inside because instead of the one pair of crutches he had seen, "there were crutches stacked all over the place." Nobody could say how they got there. The only possible explanation was that when they had taken stores on board in New York there had been an order from the ship for crutches—the sailor's name for oarlocks. Perhaps some new boy at the ship chandler had delivered the wrong thing. In the rush of loading, someone had looked at them, checked them off without too much thought, and put them where he thought they belonged—in the surgery.[40]

In spite of this delay, the trip back north was somewhat less dangerous. Allied antisubmarine measures were steadily improving and while there was still plenty of danger, convoying in the Gulf had begun to frustrate the work of the hunters. On 20 July *Sourabaya* was again somewhere off Florida. While he was happy to be heading in the right direction, Plante also noted that he would be sad to be seeing Ruth and Russell Patterson "for the last time for goodness knows how long. This side of the world seems more to me like home now than Britain, and I won't rest, dear, until I can revisit it with you." Of course he was also concerned about his pregnant wife. "I'm not exactly worried," he wrote, "because when I saw you, you were taking all this so well. But I do get a bit anxious at times, just to know how you are. . . . By the way, what do you think of Beverly for a girl's name? I think it's rather cute."[41]

On Wednesday, 29 July, Plante wrote his wife from the Chesapeake Bay where, together with many other ships, they were trapped by U-boats. At least they could swim without fear of sharks. "This swimming business has been providing us with a bit of diversion," he wrote. "Two evenings ago, a sailor who was a strong swimmer, was carried away with the current and three men dived in as he drifted by a Dutch ship and they caught him. A coast guard cutter returned him complete with a new pair of shorts." As a reward, the crew of *Sourabaya* sent down three bottles of Scotch to the Dutchmen. In spite of these diversions, Plante told his wife that he was, "of course" also continuing to paint.[42]

In 1942 forty-three tankers were lost off the Eastern seaboard and another ninety-nine were sunk in the Gulf of Mexico, the Caribbean, and around Trinidad. *Sourabaya* successfully evaded the lurking sea wolves on the way south and again on the way north finally docking in New York on 31 July after a return journey that with all the precautions and delays took twenty days. Eventually, improved convoying and convoy diversion measures as well as improved air coverage made it too expensive for U-boats to operate in U.S. coastal waters and in the Caribbean and the Gulf of Mexico. By the end of that summer Admiral Dönitz diverted his hunters back to the safer North Atlantic.[43]

Meanwhile, *Sourabaya* was "in transit" in New York for a week for repairs. Plante was able to dash off a quick note to his wife telling her that *Life* magazine was "definitely doing my story, but of course it will not be in for a few weeks. Right now they are trying to arrange for photographs aboard, but whether the permission will come through in time is doubtful."[44]

While Plante was in New York, Jan Juta took him to dinner at the St. Regis and then to see Ray Bolger in "Oh! Jupiter," a new Broadway show, after which Plante took Juta to the "Gay 90s," an 1890s-themed café and piano bar. "He really is a very fine fellow," Plante wrote of Juta, "and very, very enthusiastic about my work." The next day Plante was off to *Life* to fix final details. So far, he had made $75 on the sale of a sketch, which covered the framing of his paintings and a bit to spare. At that time his works were on show at Bar Harbor, Maine, and he had been told that "great things" were expected. He thought he would be with Evelyn in about four weeks, he ended, and was bringing baby gifts "in both colours" from his friends.[45]

On 7 August *Sourabaya* finally sailed for home, fully loaded with fuel oil and with forty-eight jeeps on deck for the U.S. Army. Plante anticipated he would arrive close to his wife's due date, "that is, if you keep to the schedule. Anyhow, we should have two or three weeks together, and Evelyn, I can't express in words how much that means to me. Being this much in love with one's wife makes life awfully sweet." In the event, Plante arrived back in Scotland in good time for the birth of his son on 22 September, and he and Evelyn decided to call the baby not Oscar, but Derek Charles. For the first time in a year and a half the sailor artist spent a few quiet weeks away from the turmoil of the war at sea.[46]

CHAPTER FIVE

"I didn't feel panicked so much as angry that this should happen to me when I had so much I wanted to do."

While Plante was basking in domestic bliss with his wife and newborn baby in Scotland there was no rest for *Sourabaya*. After returning to America, *Sourabaya* left New York City again on 16 October 1942. It soon joined the forty-five vessels of convoy HX 212 bound for Liverpool. For the first time since May 1941, the ship was sailing without Third Radio Officer Plante. The convoy was better protected than in the past—by Escort Group A3 with the large U.S. Coast Guard cutter *Campbell*, the old four-stack destroyer *Badger*, and six supporting corvettes, five Canadian (*Rosthern*, *Trillium*, *Alberni*, *Summerside*, and *Ville de Quebec*) and one British (*Dianthus*). On the night of 27 October, southeast of Cape Farewell off the southern tip of Greenland, the convoy came under attack by U-boats from wolfpack Puma. After firing a torpedo that damaged the 7,400-ton Norwegian tanker *Frontenac*, U-436 fired a spread of three torpedoes, one of which struck and sank *Sourabaya*. The fifth torpedo from U-436 damaged the 8,200-ton American tanker *Gurney E. Newlin*. According to the U-436 war diary, "A feeble dark red flame is observed amidships in the second freighter; and the same is seen forward in a third ship. A glowing red flame plume about 200m high rises roughly amidships in the large tanker. A large smoke mushroom sits above it."[1]

More attacks on the convoy followed the next night until on the 29th the convoy was close enough to Iceland to get support from B-24 bombers based there, forcing the U-boats to break away. In all, the

12-boat Puma group sank six ships from HX 212, including four tankers, while an additional tanker was damaged, inflicting "the heaviest damage . . . on a Halifax convoy since the attack on Halifax 133 sixteen months earlier." Tankers were always a special target because without the oil they supplied there could be no bomber offensive against German industry, or against the German U-boat pens in western France, nor could the planes of Coastal Command attack U-boats in the Atlantic. Britain required the cargoes of at least 4 large tankers every day to launch any military campaigns overseas. With a total of 447 tankers lost between September and November 1942—the fourth highest three-month loss rate between December 1941 and May 1944—the situation facing Britain was very grave.[2]

The loss of trained tankermen was also bitterly high, in part due to the "high percentage of loaded tankers [that] went up in flames." Of *Sourabaya*'s 158-man crew, 77 died while 81 were picked up and survived. As he did not write any letters while at home with his wife there is no information on how this news affected George Plante. We only know that it did not keep him ashore.[3]

Southern Princess, another Salvesen & Co. converted whaler, had followed a pattern very similar to that of *Sourabaya* since June 1941, with North Atlantic crossings punctuated by stops in New York for repairs, dry docking, degaussing, the addition of defensive armament, and conversion of quarters for the use of troops. As they had been on *Sourabaya*, two Oerlikon antiaircraft batteries were added to *Southern Princess*' defensive armament as well as wooden ramps in the twin machine-gun emplacements and two lockers for their ammunition. In January 1942, the ship required dry docking for general deck and engine repairs, the addition of convoy-operating equipment, as well as repairs to areas of fire damage.[4]

In May, *Southern Princess* had been "destined to pass through the Cape Cod Canal and proceed to New York." Unfortunately, because her masts were too high to clear bridges, the ship was "ordered to Boston where it is planned to reduce the height of the masts as much as is necessary with due regard to the use of the mast in dealing with deck cargo and in regard to the wireless aerial. As for reasons of safety it is necessary for this vessel to proceed through the canal, we believe that this work should be considered as a necessary safety measure, and therefore request that repairs and convoy operating measures on the above whaler be handled under the Lease Lend Act at Boston."[5]

Whether George Plante was with *Southern Princess* for the crossing reaching New York on 23 December 1942 is not clear but he was certainly on board on 24 February 1943 when the ship arrived in New York from Greenock, Scotland. During that crossing there were several large wolf packs of up to eleven U-boats each on station in the North Atlantic. They formed long patrol lines aimed at crossing the path of oncoming convoys whose routes were revealed by their wireless transmissions picked up by the B-dienst, the German naval intelligence cryptanalysis department.

Despite the fact that merchant ships were increasingly subject to attack, Plante had signed on to a tanker again. Nicholas Monsarrat has written of the "unstinting admiration" felt by the crew of every escort that crossed the Atlantic for the men who sailed in tankers. "They lived for an entire voyage of three or four weeks as a man living on top of a powder keg: the stuff they carried—the lifeblood of the whole war—was the most treacherous cargo of all; a single torpedo, a single small bomb, even a stray shot from a machine-gun could transform their ship into a torch." And yet these men "seemed to display not the slightest hesitation at the prospect of signing on again, for the same job, as soon as they reached harbour."[6]

Interviewed some months later about the strange life of an artist afloat on a perilous ocean in wartime Plante, as was his nature, told an amusing story at his own expense about the time he had been most frightened when faced with a torpedo attack. When in New York the last time he and some of his friends had visited a show featuring a man who called himself a "half man half woman." Half of the man's face was shaved and the other half was bearded. Half of his body was dressed as a man, in pants, and the other half was in a skirt. Just when the ship was approaching New York Plante decided to take "leave of his splendid beard and moustache" that he had been growing for a number of weeks. It occurred to him to have some fun and amuse his friends by imitating the man in the show. He did a fine job of it and just when half his face was "as cleanly shaved as a hamburger there was a bang, and what a bang! I thought that this time it was the end. But the idea of my dying did not trouble me half as much as the idea of arriving in New York as a 'half man half woman' survivor. I almost wept when I reached the deck." As it turned out the bang was not a torpedo but just a particularly heavy depth charge dropped by mistake. "My colleagues all had a good laugh at my expense," Plante concluded, "and they still laugh every time they meet me."[7]

When asked how he could paint in the midst of action Plante responded that it was of course impossible, "to fix on canvas everything you see at such moments." So he took notes in a language he had developed for himself to fix in his memory everything he saw. He invented new words with which he was able to record not only impressions but even shapes and shades and colors. Then, during quiet times, he put it all on canvas. "The most difficult thing is to avoid exaggeration. You are bound to see things during a battle with different eyes, and in addition there is always the danger that memory will remove the scene even farther from reality." As he was well aware, the danger was especially real for those sailing in tankers. Plante remembered seeing a tanker carrying a cargo of benzene struck by a torpedo. The effect was complete and instantaneous "with a great blossom of flame as the torpedo and benzene exploded together. There were no survivors," he recalled.[8]

On 8 March, *Southern Princess* departed New York with the forty-ship convoy HX 229. Bound for Liverpool, the tanker was loaded with petroleum, 4 locomotives, 139 drums of phenol, 31 drums of peppermint oil, and 4 landing craft. The thought of the heavy iron locomotives cutting loose and careening around the deck made them all pray for a calm crossing. Whatever the weather this would be a difficult trip, especially because the Germans seemed to be winning the

Battle of the Atlantic and the convoy link between North America and Britain appeared in danger of being cut.[9]

It was impossible to hide the growing carnage—especially as those seamen lucky enough to survive a sinking were repatriated in other merchant vessels. In fact, twenty-nine of them were hitching a ride home on *Southern Princess*. Rumor had it that nearly one hundred ships had been lost in the previous few weeks and, as Plante noted, everyone believed (correctly) that the number of U-boats was increasingly dramatically. At the same time, however, resistance to the U-boat attacks was much stiffer than before. The convergence of more numerous defensive forces and the greater offensive capabilities of large U-boat wolf packs led to ferocious mid-Atlantic battles.[10]

Traveling northeastward from New York, *Southern Princess* was followed the next day by the twenty-seven ship extra convoy HX 229A. A slow convoy, SC 122 (fifty-two ships), left for Britain some days earlier and was traveling ahead. Although SC 122 struggled against a fierce storm, by the time the two HX convoys appeared they only had to contend with spring fogs and snow. Three days later, after passing off Halifax without incident, HX 229 and HX 229A were in position due east of Newfoundland where ocean escorts took over from the mostly Canadian local escorts that had been protecting them. While there are differing accounts of the total number of ships involved, and additional escorts joined the convoys later, at the outset something like thirteen total escorts were divided between the eighty-some ships of the two fast convoys, with only six escorts—four destroyers and two corvettes—assigned to HX 229. By this time the ships had traveled almost a third of the way from New York to Britain, but they still had as far to go as the distance between New York and Los Angeles. The speed of even the fastest convoys was not much faster than that of someone riding a bicycle at a steady pace.[11]

By 16 March the three convoys ploughing their way through another succession of spring storms were perilously close together creating a concentrated target of some 131 ships. Eighty-one of the ships were British and 29 were American, although they flew the flags of ten different nations. Between them they carried 920,000 tons of cargo including frozen meat, tobacco, grain, lumber, minerals, steel, aircraft, and tanks in addition to *Southern Princess*' oil, landing craft and locomotives. By then, acting on good signals intelligence, there were 44 U-boats organized into three large wolf packs gathering at the edge of the mid-Atlantic air gap northeast of Newfoundland. For almost a year from July 1942 until June 1943, Admiral Dönitz's codebreakers had been able to provide U-boats with "an extraordinary wealth of information about convoy movements," enabling them to successfully converge on convoys just beyond the range of Allied land-based aircraft. Now, the greatest ever concentration of submarines was ready to pounce on the eastbound convoys without fear of attack from the air.[12]

The atrocious weather conditions further hampered convoy defensive measures with storms now reaching force eleven and fog, ice, and forty-foot waves. Indeed, the weather finally forced the diversion of SC 122 to the south bringing it to within one hundred miles of HX 229. The Royal Navy's Submarine Tracking Room was responsible for rerouting convoys according to the most up-to-date appreciation of U-boat positions but the sheer numbers of submarines deployed at this time made it impossible, in spite of intelligence about German positions, to effectively evade U-boat patrol lines.

Because of German confusion about the separate locations and identities of the three target convoys, and some miscommunication on both sides, the U-boats were initially directed against only one convoy, HX 229 and *Southern Princess* sailing in it. Had all the sleek hunters arrived at the same time the convoy's escorts would surely have been completely overwhelmed.[13]

The attacks on HX 229 began shortly before 10 p.m. on the night of 16 March. Eventually, thirteen ships were sunk in what was the single biggest convoy battle of the entire war. The American freighter *Irénée du Pont* and the British refrigerated ship *Nariva* were among the last ships to be hit by U-600 that night, shortly before 3 a.m. Ensign Frank

Pilling, an American naval officer taking passage to England on *Irénée du Pont* gave a vivid account of what happened next.

> I was not surprised when we were hit, for suddenly I saw, deep under the surface, two streaks of greasy light, parallel, moving fast, coming in at an angle. There was no time to shout a warning; in one instant there were the tracks, in another a great shattering crash. Holding onto the rail I was not thrown down but seeing what appeared to be flying metal in the air, I rushed towards the opposite side of the ship. The second torpedo shook the *Irénée* with amazing violence. She quivered and staggered so wildly for a moment that I lost my footing and lurched crazily before running forward to the port ladder. Passing the captain I heard him say, "well, this is it!" Then I joined the mad rush of humanity on the ladder.[14]

Nariva, the second ship hit "was torpedoed with an ear-shattering roar," remembered G. D. Williams, the Second Officer.

> The deck bucked and heaved violently under my feet. A huge tower of black smoke, tons of water and debris was flung into the air just forward of the bridge. Captain Dodds came out on the port wing of the bridge when I remembered the adage that what goes up must just as assuredly come down and, without ceremony, I pushed the "old-man" back into the wheel-house and not a second too soon for tons of water and debris fell on the bridge with a crunch and a clatter.[15]

As the crew of *Nariva* prepared to abandon ship, another explosion erupted from the column of ships to starboard. A torpedo from U-600, the same U-boat that hit the other two vessels, slammed into *Southern Princess*, the largest ship in the convoy, and it was quickly engulfed in flames.[16]

Until then, "it had all seemed so quiet, just the regular thudding of the engines and the swish of the wake." Although it was obvious their escorts were hunting U-boats and dropping depth charges, "it was too far away from our ship to see anything or have any real information about what was actually happening," but it was evident "from all the zigzagging and course changes going on that it was nothing trivial." Though it was Plante's watch, the chief R/O had taken over the earphones, so Plante was able to be on the bridge. There was nothing he could do except to look as though he were ready to be busy if their time came and to make sure his life jacket was securely fastened. "That night nobody undressed. We all walked around with our lifebelts on, expecting to jump for it and then to swim for it at any moment."[17]

By this time it was clear to everyone that the convoy was in acute distress. "Ships were being picked off," Plante remembered vividly fifty years later.

> An explosion would shatter the silence and flames light the night. Some were far, some nearer. There was no pattern. Cargo ships would burn and tankers explode. The most spectacular displays happened when a benzene tanker caught it. Sometimes we could tell which ship it was from its position in the convoy. Much of the time, we just had to take a guess. Ships were disappearing, blazing astern, and it was almost a matter of waiting until our number came up. There was absolutely nothing we could do about it as we plowed our way through the night.[18]

As the action moved closer "it was hell around us," Plante told a newspaper reporter some months later. "Every few minutes new explosions from depth charges shook our boat." According to the convoy commodore's report on HX 229, "when the third attack came, at 0259/17, only two destroyers of the escort were present and the U-boat was not detected." Although it was not unexpected when the torpedo struck, it was still "a hell of a shock," Plante remembered. "We heard a terrific bang and we knew at once that this was the real thing." One torpedo had hit *Southern Princess* on the starboard side under the bridge. The resulting explosion broke down the bulkheads separating the cargo tanks and the crew accommodations and oil quickly gushed out of the torpedo hole and onto the surface of the sea. The explosion had ignited the gas in one of the cargo tanks so the oil in the holds soon caught fire creating a huge, towering blaze "so intense that paintwork on a ship in the next column was blistered."[19]

In an interview reported in the *New York Times* the following month, Plante noted that he had just returned to the radio cabin and was looking at his watch when the torpedo hit, exactly on the hour. The force of the explosion threw him across the cabin, which was located high in the ship just aft of the bridge. Although very shaken he was not injured. He managed to send out SOS calls before grabbing a photograph of his wife and trying to leave. "All the lights were out," he recalled,

> and the deck was tilted at a bit of an angle that disoriented me somewhat. The door had slammed shut but wasn't jammed. It was just a bit hard to open because of the tilt. I got out on the boat deck but it must have taken me longer than I realized. The last boat was being lowered. Everything was brilliantly lit by the fire, which was raging amidships. It was all very dramatic, but I didn't feel panicked so much as angry that this should happen to me when I had so much I wanted to do.[20]

It was a sad coincidence that *Southern Princess*, previously named *San Patricio*, should be destroyed on St. Patrick's Day.

Plante did not hear any loud agonizing screams from his shipmates, although one account of that night says there were some. Perhaps he was in a state of shock, or too preoccupied with his own safety, to hear anything. The signal to abandon ship had been given and most of the crew was already off by the time he got on deck. Because of the heavy list to starboard they had not been able to lower the lifeboats on the port side and many of the other lifeboats had washed overboard. This had slowed the evacuation, somewhat disrupting their well-practiced procedures.[21]

Plante recalled that he was about to get into the last lifeboat when he remembered that one of his duties was to take the emergency transmitter with him. By the time he returned to the wireless cabin and dragged the transmitter on deck the last boat was already in the water. Concerned that the ship would explode or roll over and suck him under he realized he would have to jump. He took his shoes off and set them neatly side by side on the deck. Even as he did so he thought it was "a pretty damned silly thing to be doing," but force of habit was strong. The drop from the boat deck into the water was a long one, and a cold one in March, but "When flames are attacking your rear it isn't difficult to jump into the middle of the Atlantic at three o'clock in the morning." Although they all knew the chances of surviving in the frigid waters were very slight, he never even felt the cold. The transmitter remained behind on the deck with his shoes.[22]

Plante soon forgot any fears he had about being sucked under by the ship as it drifted farther and farther off into the night. It seemed to be still under way, all on its own, and going in a huge circle. In the water he rose and fell on the waves, getting an occasional glimpse of lifeboat lights bobbing up and down in the distance and men swimming all around with little red lights on their shoulders. He saw the convoy slowly disappearing in the darkness and thought of his wife and son and worried about how they would manage without him. He also thought of all the things left unfinished to be completed on his next visit to New York, most especially seeing the *Life* magazine people to discuss the feature they were doing on his paintings.

Plante had no idea how long he had been in the water, but it could not have been very long when from the top of a wave he spotted a nearby lifeboat. He got their attention and was hauled on board. By then the lifeboat was packed with some of his own shipmates as well as men from *Irénée du Pont* that had been struck nearby.[23]

By great good fortune that night was one of the calmest of the trip, but still there was a heavy swell. It was wet and very dark and "those of us who could get our hands on the huge oars hung on and rowed as hard as we could. Obviously we didn't have anywhere to go."

> We were just trying to keep our minds and bodies busy . . . to keep the circulation going any way that we could. Though I was soaked in oil and sitting in water, I don't remember feeling cold.

> We all did all the things that people do when they are under stress. We became hysterically witty and sang songs like "Roll Out the Barrel," and "I belong to Glasgow." We picked up another sailor out of the water who, bobbing up and down in the black sea a thousand miles from land hailed us with "Taxi!"[24]
>
> When I called out to the Chief Officer, "Where are we rowing to?" a calm voice came back from out of the darkness, "We're rowin' straight to Glasgie, and we bain't stoppin' at Greenock nayther!"[25]

They all knew that their chances of survival were not good, especially as no rescue ships of any kind had been available to sail with the convoy. Suddenly, out of the darkness loomed the bow of a huge black mass of a ship bearing down on their lifeboat. Thinking they were about to be run down by one of their own ships they rowed frantically to get out of the way with no success. They quickly realized the large ship now looming above them was stationary. It was just lying there, all alone and exposed in the glare of the burning *Southern Princess* that lit up the night sky. The ship was a sitting duck for any U-boat in the vicinity. When Plante yelled up to find out if they had been torpedoed the reply came down, "No, but we damned well will be if you don't hurry up and get aboard!"[26]

Plante and his fellow survivors managed to tuck their small boat in on the leeside of *Tekoa*, a New Zealand Shipping Company refrigerated ship that had stopped to pick up crewmen from *Irénée du Pont* and *Nariva* as well as *Southern Princess*. Though *Tekoa* lowered cargo nets and rope ladders and the scene was lit up by the blazing *Princess*, the huge swell made getting on board a challenge. Their lifeboat rose to the top of the swell and then suddenly dropped like a stone about twenty feet. The men had to poise themselves and leap when it looked as if they were at the peak of the swell, before they dropped to the bottom. If they jumped too soon or too late they could be crushed against the side of the ship. Two or three men from other ships were killed that way and some were badly injured. The flickering light from the tanker did not make it any easier. Plante got it right and remembers holding onto the rope ladder tighter than he had ever held onto anything in his life. Amazingly, of the one hundred men on board *Southern Princess* only four were lost in the blazing inferno, two crew-members and two Distressed British Seamen hitching a ride home. *Irénée du Pont* lost twelve men and *Nariva* none at all.[27]

At about the same time as Plante had begun his radio training, increasing losses to Merchant Navy crews led to a series of measures aimed at improving lifesaving. Red battery-powered lifejacket lights were first introduced in the fall of 1940 and became compulsory the following March. From then on all cabins had to be equipped with portholes to enable escape when doorways were blocked. New and better-equipped lifesaving rafts were developed and distributed starting in the fall of 1941. In addition, and perhaps most important for the crew of *Southern Princess*, new metal lifeboats were introduced for tankers instead of the customary wooden ones that were susceptible to fire.[28]

As *Southern Princess* continued to blaze, the ammunition from its guns started to explode "spitting out shells like a giant fireworks display." For a while after clambering on board *Tekoa*, Plante and the rest of the survivors just lay on the ship's cold wet deck. Many were covered in fuel oil and had to be hosed down. Their clothes were thrown overboard and someone gave Plante a raincoat that was to be his total wardrobe for the rest of the trip. "The ship's radio officer took good care of me," he recalled, "and after a couple of glasses of rum I felt able to get a pen and paper and make some sketches of the survivors. I also made some sketches on deck as dawn broke for a painting of a burning, sinking ship."[29]

According to British records, after being torpedoed *Southern Princess* soon sank at 50.3 degrees north, 34.30 degrees west. Summing up the reasons for the calamitous results of HX 229, the commodore cited: "A. Small size of surface escort during critical period, B. Lack of rescue ship which resulted in escorts being absent from convoy picking up survivors, C. Inability of shore based aircraft to provide cover during period of action."[30]

Meanwhile, one of the other U-boat wolf packs, closing fast, had run into SC 122. The battle against convoys HX 229 (including HX 229A) and SC 122 lasted four days until the U-boats were forced to break off the attacks on 20 March. The struggle pitted forty-some U-boats against two convoys totaling more than eighty merchant ships. *Southern Princess* was sunk along with twenty-one others: sixteen cargo ships, five refrigerated ships and one tanker, representing 20 percent of the vessels involved. Of the 1,494 crew and passengers, 360 crewmembers and 12 passengers lost their lives. No escorts were sunk. The Germans lost only one U-boat in the engagement, with 47 men on board. Fifteen of the vessels lost from HX 229 and SC 122 were sunk in a twenty-four hour period when the convoys were beyond the reach of air cover. The heavy loss of ships, cargoes, and personnel helped convince the Allies to finally allocate sufficient resources to close the air gap and to provide more support groups to go to the aid of threatened convoys.[31]

Tekoa was the first command of Albert Hocken, the New Zealander captain. In convoys with no rescue ships the procedure was that if a merchant ship was torpedoed, the last ship in that column was to stop and act as rescue ship. This perilous maneuver, which had been ordered in New York before the convoys departed, was extremely unpopular with the ships' masters and, in fact, had been ignored. The designated rescue ships at the end of two adjacent columns sailed on, not stopping for survivors.

Captain Hocken, however, had decided he could not just leave all those men in the water and stopped without any obligation to do so. In the end, he succeeded in rescuing 146 men, mostly from *Irénée du Pont* and *Southern Princess*. "Tekoa," a Maori word meaning "good luck," surely held for those fortunate seamen. Although numerous awards were made to those who had distinguished themselves in this convoy action, to the disgust of many he had rescued, Albert Hocken only received letters of commendation. By the time *Tekoa* got under way four hours later, by then in daylight, the convoy was far ahead. Fortunately, the ship's luck persisted as she steamed on for another three days to the nearest landfall. Sailing up the Mersey, *Tekoa* arrived in Liverpool eighteen days after weighing anchor in New York.[32]

The ship tied up at the Cunard pier where in happier times fashionable passengers disembarked from luxury liners. Anxious not to adversely affect the morale on the home front by the sight of bedraggled shipwrecked sailors—the public had been told they were winning the Battle of the Atlantic—Plante and the others were hustled down the gangway at five o'clock in the morning. Greeted by officials from the Merchant Navy headquarters in the Liver Building, they were taken to the public baths or to the hospital if they needed medical attention.[33]

As he stepped down from the gangway, naked except for his borrowed raincoat, Plante was welcomed by "my natural enemy, the customs' officers solemnly asking me if I had anything to declare. I opened my raincoat wide and invited them to search me, and if they found anything I told them they could keep it." As he passed through the sheds to board the bus for the baths, Plante was amused to hear a group of recently rescued sailors shouting at a harassed representative of the Ministry of War Transport who they had pinned against a wall. "We'll be having our rights, we'll be having our rights. We don't know what they are, but we demand them!"[34]

A short time later, luxuriating in a great big hot bath immersed in soothing soapsuds up to his chin, Plante was glad to be alive and anticipating being reunited with family and friends. After cleaning up, he and the rest of the survivors were taken to a large store where they were completely outfitted from underwear to suits to gloves and handkerchiefs, "We entered the store in rags and we left it a bunch of capitalists straight from Savile Row." They all then received rail tickets and money to get them home for their allotted two weeks survivors' leave. After that, they were expected to do it all over again.[35]

The Battle of the Atlantic was the longest-running battle of the war. It began on the very first day, 3 September 1939, with the sinking of the British ocean liner SS *Athenia* bound for Canada with men, women, and children on board and ended with the surrender of Germany in May 1945. Plante had survived the toughest two years of the six-year campaign at sea.

❖ ❖ ❖

By the spring of 1943 the German U-boats had come the closest they would ever come to throttling the trans-Atlantic supply lines. They sank 108 ships in March alone, but just at that point all the Allied antisubmarine measures began to come together effectively. These included centimetric radar, shipborne high-frequency direction finding, air cover by long-range land-based aircraft, air cover by carrier escorts acting in concert with support and hunter-killer groups, more and better escort vessels, new weapons, new tactics, and the successful use of radio intelligence known as "Ultra." The tide had turned against the U-boats and there was a dramatic drop in the number of cargo ship sinkings and a corresponding rise in the loss of submarines. April and May 1943 were two of the least successful months of the whole U-boat campaign. In May forty-one U-boats were lost in exchange for only fifty merchant ships sunk. On 24 May Admiral Dönitz withdrew his submarines from the North Atlantic for a time and sent them in search of easier targets to the south. In his memoirs, Dönitz concluded that after these spring 1943 actions,

> Wolf-pack operations against the convoys in the North Atlantic, the main theatre of operations, were no longer possible. They could only be resumed if we succeeded in radically increasing the fighting power of the U-boats. This was the logical conclusion to which I came. . . . We had lost the Battle of the Atlantic.[36]

Indeed, the struggle for HX 229 and SC 122 proved to be the last of the U-boats' great convoy successes. Naval historian W. J. R. Gardner has described this phase of the war at sea as "climactic. . . .

Before it, U-boats enjoyed their greatest success; afterwards they scrambled for fragments." As another historian put it, "Finally [Allied] tactical superiority triumphed."[37]

The terrible campaign in the Atlantic was fought with unflagging determination at a total cost of almost 2,500 Allied and neutral merchant ships. By one estimate the British Merchant Navy alone lost 30,248 men, most of them in the Atlantic. But between 1940 and 1943, 84,109,000 tons of petroleum of all sorts was successfully imported into the United Kingdom. After the sinking of the *Southern Princess*, the war at sea went on for another two years. More ships were sunk and more sailors lost their lives before peace was restored, but from now on without George Plante. A few hours after his wife and mother were notified of the sinking of *Southern Princess* and that he was missing at sea, Plante arrived home in Edinburgh. Soon after, his survivor's shore leave was cut short. His military career now took a far different turn.[38]

CHAPTER SIX

"[I was] helping to undermine the enemy in the Middle East and the Balkans."

Few people know that the first British air drops over Germany in September 1939 were not bombs but leaflets. From the very outset Britain waged what became an enormous airborne paper campaign as part of a relentless propaganda war against the Nazis and their allies. It was in this murky endeavor that George Plante now found himself.[1]

On shore leave and expecting his next ship assignment Plante was surprised when, out of the blue, he was summoned back to London with instructions to report to the Political Intelligence Department (PID) of the Foreign Office. Plante arrived at the Foreign Office where he was met by an army brigadier. Although he did not identify the general in his postwar account of these events, this must have been Brigadier William F. Jeffries, deputy to Paul Vellacott, the man Plante was there to meet. Vellacott was at the Foreign Office on leave from his position as master of Peterhouse, one of the colleges of Cambridge University. During World War I, Vellacott received the Distinguished Service Order (DSO), an award ranking just below the Victoria Cross and had risen to brigadier. Now he had been persuaded to contribute to his country's new war effort by working in the shadowy Political Intelligence Department. The PID had recently been revived as a temporary war department of the Foreign Office and was ostensibly tasked to provide confidential reports on foreign affairs. In reality, the PID was a cover for the clandestine Political Warfare Executive.[2]

When Plante was recruited to the PWE, Jeffries was also the head of the military wing of PWE Middle East. As with so many of the other colorful characters in this story, Jeffries had an interesting intelligence background. Educated at Trinity College, Cambridge, he was wounded twice while serving with the Royal Irish Fusiliers in France in World War I where he too was awarded the DSO. After the war he served in Rome, on the army's intelligence staff in Dublin, and with the army intelligence staff at the Horse Guards in London. Following four years in Nigeria he joined the army general staff as commandant of the Intelligence Corps before being assigned to the PWE. His army colleagues thought he had been a member of the "Cairo Gang," a group of British intelligence agents operating against the IRA during the Irish War of Independence.[3]

Also accompanying Vellacott at the meeting with Plante was Commander Ian Fleming, personal assistant to the new head of the Naval Intelligence Department, Commodore E. G. N. Rushbrooke. Fleming was working in his capacity as Admiralty liaison with the PWE. Fluent in German and fascinated by propaganda, Fleming had done some radio work for the BBC's German Service through the PWE. He also had assisted his friend Sefton Delmer's black propaganda operations for the PWE making broadcasts designed to lure U-boats away from Allied convoys. Fleming's flair for intelligence planning and his wit and charm made him an eminently suitable representative of naval intelligence to the other numerous and often competing intelligence organizations that flourished during the war.[4]

Brushing aside formalities and with few preliminaries, Vellacott and Fleming asked Plante if he were willing to undertake a confidential mission about which they could say nothing except that it meant leaving for Cairo at once. It all sounded too good to be true and Plante had to ask himself, "Why me?"

"I have no qualifications for desert warfare," he said. "I have never even seen a desert." But they seemed to know more about him than he did about himself and assured him that although they could tell him nothing further they were confident he was well qualified for the job they had in mind that, as he would soon learn, had nothing to do with desert warfare.[5]

Having just experienced the frigid North Atlantic, Plante thought anything was preferable to returning to sea. Indeed, he had nothing to lose. His family was safely ensconced in the distant Orkney Islands, he had lost everything on board when *Southern Princess* sank, and all his belongings that were in storage in a London warehouse had again been destroyed when it was bombed. A stint in a nice, hot, dry desert certainly was inviting, particularly as Erwin Rommel's Afrika Korps no longer threatened Cairo. In fact, the Germans had been pushed out of Egypt altogether.[6]

Quickly running through this mental calculus Plante eagerly agreed to the proposition but felt obliged to mention that he was due to report back to the Merchant Navy. Vellacott and Fleming told him not to worry about that but to go along to the Ministry of War Transport that controlled Merchant Navy policy and request his discharge. Knowing this was highly irregular in wartime, and wondering what reason he could possibly give, Plante followed instructions with some trepidation. But all went smoothly. He was much amused to see that on his official discharge papers the only reason given for his release from the Merchant Navy was "At Own Request." The photograph in his Continuous Certificate of Discharge reveals the same receding hairline as when he had joined the Merchant Navy two years earlier, while the physical description also still listed his eyes as brown. In later life Plante's eyes were certainly blue, but the change was clearly not due to his time spent gazing at the sea and the sky from the decks of tankers. Another good story regrettably proved untrue.[7]

Back at the Foreign Office Plante had been "issued with a couple of books of clothing coupons and sent down to Austin Reed's in Regent Street to be outfitted in tropical civilian suits for life in Cairo." His whereabouts over the next couple of months is hazy. Years later, as he told his family, he had been put on a train to a large manor in the countryside which served as a school for spies. Probably this was the Duke of Bedford's estate at Woburn Abbey where the PID was training intelligence agents and propagandists. Plante's new job was to provide cartoons and drawings for anti-Nazi leaflets to be dropped on German-occupied countries in eastern and southern Europe and to do this he needed a degree of familiarity with the military, political, social, and economic situations in the region. It is likely that he spent several months acquiring this knowledge from the experts employed by the PID. The next time Plante surfaced, he was in Cairo.[8]

One of the mysteries surrounding Plante's enlistment by Vellacott and Fleming was how they had heard about him in the first place. In later years Plante used to amuse his family by claiming he had been stopped in the street in London by Ian Fleming and recruited on the spot. By then, of course, Fleming was famous for his James Bond novels, and though the real story was mysterious enough, the Fleming touch added an even greater glamour. Since it was originally the Ministry of Information that had authorized, supported, and publicized Plante's war art as valuable propaganda, it is possible that Jan Juta passed on his name to Vellacott and Fleming. Ian Fleming may even have heard of Plante's work for the MOI in the United States through his contacts with the British Security Coordination on one of his trips to New York. As Vellacott and Fleming needed artists for their work in Cairo, it is also possible that Plante's name came up through his connection with the War Artists Advisory Committee.

Still, there is an even clearer and more direct connection between Fleming and Plante. In his March 1942 letter to E. M. O'R. Dickey of the WAAC, Plante had given the name of a Lieutenant Robert Harling, NID, as a personal reference. Harling, an expert typographer, worked with Plante at Everetts Advertising before the war and they knew each other well. Once war was declared Harling, a keen sailor, joined the RNVR and spent a year at sea on a corvette on convoy duty in the Western Approaches. Then, in 1941, Ian Fleming, who had met Harling just before the outbreak of war and who had commissioned him to redesign the Admiralty's weekly intelligence report, pulled him away from the war at sea to join NID. Harling remained there until the end of the war, eventually working in Fleming's audacious Special

Intelligence Unit—also known as 30 Commando and (after 1943) 30 Assault Unit. Harling operated on the front lines on a variety of memorable and successful assignments for Fleming including a meeting with General George Patton and a dash across Germany to round up German scientists.[9]

It seems highly probable that Fleming told his colleague Harling about the need for artists in PWE's new organization and that Harling suggested Plante, with whose work he was very familiar. It is also quite possible that the WAAC contacted Harling as a reference for Plante, that Harling was aware of Plante's war art, and even that he knew Plante's tanker had been sunk and that he was on shore leave. Many appointments in Britain, and not only in wartime, hung on personal recommendations through the Old Boys network. Fleming was recruited to NID though this clubby network, he recruited Harling, and it seems logical that Harling was responsible for Fleming's recruitment of Plante for PWE. Plante's first-hand experience of action, moreover, as well as his familiarity with Germany and Germans, would have been attractive to Vellacott and to Fleming.[10]

Over the years, when interviewed for various publications, Plante referred to this next phase of his life in discreet and vague ways. In one brief biography he said that after losing two ships he "was sent to work with the Foreign Office Political Intelligence Unit in the Middle East and engaged in some frantically unusual activities with the OSS and the OWI around Egypt, Italy, Greece and the Balkans." At other times he said that he had worked in Cairo "at the Office of Political Intelligence of the Foreign Office on a unique—but unspecified—mission," or that he had been in the Middle East "working in the underground with the Political Warfare Executive arm of the British Foreign Service," or that "he was involved with political intelligence for the Foreign Office," or that after his merchant navy days "he was dispatched to Cairo where he focused his talents in other directions, helping to undermine the enemy in the Middle East and the Balkans." These descriptions add a certain James Bond mystique to Plante's post-Atlantic activities. His letters home were far tamer—as both censorship and secrecy required.[11]

Plante quickly learned that the Political Intelligence Department was a cover for the Political Warfare Executive, a clandestine body created in 1941 to coordinate the production and dissemination of British propaganda to enemy and enemy-occupied countries, mainly in the form of radio broadcasts, leaflets, and other printed materials. The MOI, for its part, was in charge of propaganda for home, Allied, and neutral territory. The PWE's objective, working in cooperation with Allied strategic and military needs, was to undermine enemy morale and boost that of the peoples of territories occupied by the Axis. Paul Vellacott, based in Cairo, was director of PWE's political warfare unit in the Middle East. Under Vellacott, Cairo became the launching ground for propaganda to Italy and to other German allied and occupied areas in the Balkans. In addition to Brigadier Jeffries, Vellacott depended in these complex dealings on the help of Ralph Murray. Murray, a journalist and diplomat with international credentials and fluency in French, German, Italian, Spanish, Greek, and some Russian, was invaluable as Vellacott's political adviser and deputy. After the war, his experience in PWE ME served him well when he was appointed British minister in Cairo during the Suez Crisis.[12]

After the end of World War II, following its own freewheeling and quixotic bent, the leadership of the PWE chose David Garnett, PWE's director of training, to write the organizations' official history. Perhaps predictably from a left-leaning pacifist and a successful novelist in the bohemian tradition of the time, Garnett wrote in such an uninhibited way that his history was not published until 2002. Far from being a bland official account, Garnett's work freely criticized the many shortcomings, the interdepartmental squabbles, and the personal rivalries that characterized the "wasteful pointlessness of British propaganda in the early part of the war." Not surprisingly, his draft history was quickly buried in an obscure bureaucratic file. When it was unearthed in 1952 it was found to contain such incisive judgments of people still prominent in public life that it was classified "Secret—for Official Use Only" and disappeared from view for another fifty years.[13]

The PWE had been created from elements of the European Services of the BBC, the Foreign Publicity Department of the Ministry of Information, and Special Operations 1 (part of the Special Operations Executive under the Ministry of Economic Warfare). PWE was given the political warfare side of the work of the Special Operations Executive while the SOE continued to control the operational aspects of clandestine warfare, often referred to disparagingly as the "dirty works" section. On the other hand, PWE personnel were derisively known as the "Peewees," somewhat diminishing the organization's "high-sounding and baffling title."[14]

In 1942, the Ministry of Information had taken over responsibility for the administration of the PWE while policy came under the Foreign Office, a dual ministerial oversight that was hard to manage and often caused problems. Fortunately, the very able R. H. "Jock" Bruce Lockhart was named director-general of the PWE, establishing its headquarters in Bush House in London, directly above the European Service of the BBC. Lockhart developed a remarkably cordial and effective relationship with both his bosses—the foreign secretary, Anthony Eden, and Brendan Bracken, the minister of information—that stood the PWE in good stead throughout the remainder of the war. Eden, Bracken, and Lockhart were also among those who had early formed a pro-American bloc within the British elite and this, too, was to be profoundly important for the PWE in its work supporting coalition warfare.[15]

A career diplomat with experience as an agent for the Secret Intelligence Service (MI6) in Russia during World War I, Lockhart had been a vocal critic of the passivity of Neville Chamberlain's government in the early days of the war, maintaining that the capital was suffering from "gangrene of the soul." Among his many other qualifications this endeared him to Churchill's circle and helped him establish a good working relationship with the prime minister himself, although as Lockhart candidly confessed, Churchill "took only a spasmodic interest in propaganda," and was frequently heard to growl "This is a war of deeds, and not of words." Still, much of the credit for the effective operation of the PWE was due to Lockhart's leadership.[16]

In the late 1930s, after many years serving overseas for the Foreign Office and then as a journalist, Bruce Lockhart had retired to his native Scotland to write. On the outbreak of the war, however, his knowledge of central Europe and the Balkans made him an essential recruit to the Political Intelligence Department. After service with the PID at their Woburn Abbey headquarters and then in London as British representative with the Provisional Czechoslovak government, Lockhart's extensive contacts in government, his close relationship with many exiled European leaders, his deep understanding of the workings of Whitehall, and his experience in journalism made him a natural choice to head the newly created PWE. He already had some experience with propaganda because while with the PID he had attended policy meetings of the propaganda organization dealing with enemy and enemy-occupied countries. He quickly grasped the essentials of his new trade that he aptly referred to as "wordy warfare."[17]

The implementation of psychological warfare was, in part, a result of advances in the field of psychology in the 1920s and '30s. The term "psychological warfare" was originally a Nazi term for the scientific application of propaganda to assist in victory over the enemy. The British—who called it "political warfare"—had reservations about its unconventional methods but soon adopted the example of the Germans while seeking to avoid their malignant perversions of the truth. Still, it took some time for military leaders to embrace what many eventually came to regard as the "fourth fighting arm." When the Americans entered the conflict in 1941 they were equally inexperienced with this kind of subversive warfare, and to many it seemed undemocratic and un-American. They soon began to borrow heavily from British experience.[18]

Thinking back on those years, Lockhart noted that political warfare was "neither an exact science nor a separate art." Rather, it was "the handmaid of official policy and of military strategy, dependent on the calculations and errors of government." It also needed to be "supple, with an instinctive feeling for the element of chance in human affairs. Above all, it must on occasion act with great speed in order to kill an enemy lie which otherwise might do great harm." To be able to react quickly to rapidly developing situations political warfare had to "take its directives not only from ministers and chiefs of staff who are not always readily available but also from the incidence of time and events." The propagandists at ground level, whether at PWE headquarters in London or overseas—as, for example, in Cairo with Plante—had to dance to the tune of these various masters, trusted to align their output as best they could with the strongest imperatives of the moment, and always to keep in step with military progress whenever and wherever British and Allied troops were engaged.[19]

Like Vellacott, Lockhart was greatly assisted in directing this task of balancing competing initiatives by having a military man as deputy. Lockhart's deputy, Brigadier (later General) Dallas Brooks of the Royal Marines, was the head of the Military Wing of the Department of Enemy Propaganda. As with so many in leadership positions during the Second World War, Brooks had distinguished himself in World War I, being the recipient of a DSO. In addition to being "pleasant in manner, always good-tempered, and at his best in a crisis," Brooks was a most valuable asset because he enjoyed the confidence of the Chiefs of Staff Organization. Coupled with Lockhart's close contacts in the Foreign Office, the combination enabled the two men to know "nearly everything" of importance going on the capital and to ensure that their propaganda reflected the government's political, diplomatic, and military aims.[20]

Bruce Lockhart argued that the truest definition of political warfare was that it "practices every form of overt and covert attack which can be called political as distinct from military." It seeks "both to counter and by intelligent anticipation to forestall the political offensives of the enemy." This political warfare "demands a highly specialized intelligence service of its own and, above all, an accurate estimate of the enemy's intentions." It relies not only on "open and truthful propaganda," but also "on a whole series of secret or 'black' operations which can suitably be classified under the headings of subversion and deception."[21]

In spite of the eventual recognition of its significant role, the British propaganda apparatus continued to suffer from a lack of centralized structure and planning throughout the war. Over the years it underwent many transformations, only partly explained by the need to keep pace with the changing war situation. In the early years of the war a large part of the problem was "ignorance of the subject," both in Whitehall and among the military. Overlapping authorities, conflicting agendas, and internal turf wars involving the Foreign Office, various ministries, the BBC, and the military—as well as the need to coordinate with the Americans—further ensured a level of confusion that taxed even Bruce Lockhart's considerable diplomatic skills. Indeed, Lockhart found himself in charge of an organization that combined, by one account, "breathtaking incompetence and inspired brilliance in its attempts to undermine an adversary by means of psychological warfare."[22]

This turmoil was endemic in North Africa. Writing to the foreign secretary, Anthony Eden, in 1944, Paul Vellacott recapped the history of PWE Cairo, noting that when he was appointed director of political warfare in the Middle East in 1942 he had been entrusted

> with a charter to set up a Mission for the conduct of political warfare into enemy and enemy-occupied countries in South-Eastern Europe. This PWE mission was, not without dust and heat, established with its headquarters in Cairo, and until May of this year it applied itself, to the best of such ability as could be secured for it, to its task in conformity with the policy of His Majesty's Government.[23]

As if dealing with the complex and kaleidoscopic enemy situation was not challenge enough, much of Vellacott's correspondence with Bruce Lockhart in London was dominated by disputes over areas of responsibility and control within the British administrative structure itself. This included friction with military commanders and with the Special Operations Executive, much of which Garnett lays bare in his history of the PWE.[24]

The commanders of the naval, air, and military forces at first made little effort to conceal their "instinctive hostility" to political (or, in American terms, psychological) warfare. In the beginning, overlapping responsibilities also involved Vellacott in considerable political wrangling with Christopher Tennant, Lord Glenconner, head of Special Operations Executive in Cairo, which was already active in the area. Tellingly, Glenconner was known to many simply as "God." While Vellacott was solely responsible for the policy of the PWE in the Middle East and for the collection of propaganda intelligence material, these various constituencies he had to work with added to the delicacy of his task.[25]

As the war developed causing frequent reorganizations of the intelligence and propaganda apparatus, internal frictions nevertheless continued. "It seems to me quite shocking," Vellacott wrote Bruce Lockhart from Cairo at the end of November 1942, "that out here the energies of individuals and of two organisations should be consumed to a large extent in a fight with each other." Another insider wrote, "Nobody who did not experience it can possibly imagine the atmosphere of jealousy, suspicion, and intrigue, which embittered the relations between the various secret and semi-secret departments in Cairo." Eventually, however, by all accounts Vellacott was eminently successful, and the good relationships he painstakingly cultivated with both the diplomats and the military leaders made possible the effective work of the PWE ME. While Plante could mention none of this in his letters from Cairo, the uncertainties these rivalries heaped on an already chaotic situation made his work there that much more difficult.[26]

Of more significance for the effectiveness of his propaganda art than his ability to steer clear of the hazards of internal politics, however, was that Plante had a good grasp of the tangled politics of the region covered by PWE ME. He understood the thrust of the message the Allies were sending that day, or week, or month, and he appreciated to whom the message was aimed so that he could provide apt illustrations. As his paintings of the Battle of the Atlantic had already shown, he had a sure touch when depicting the high drama of war. The realism and immediacy of his art—whether in pen-and-ink sketches or full-color paintings—and his grasp of the nuanced and carefully calibrated messages he illustrated made him a natural propagandist.

Much of PWE Middle East's vast production of printed propaganda and artwork has been meticulously preserved at Britain's National Archives at Kew alongside the production of other PWE units. The political and military aims the propaganda was designed to support—laid out in weekly reports of Cairo's political warfare activities sent by Vellacott to Bruce Lockhart in London—are also carefully preserved. Much of the artwork is anonymous, although a number of quite distinctive styles emerge and some of the art is signed. After the war Plante took back to England—probably against regulations—quite a number from among the many leaflets, pamphlets, posters, newssheets, magazines, and miniature booklets he had illustrated. He kept none in English translation; all the materials he took home with him were in their original languages. These he kept until his death in 1995 leaving a partial but vivid record that, when seen against the backdrop of PWE ME's total output, makes clear his valuable contribution to the propaganda war of printed words and images.[27]

By the time Vellacott arrived in Egypt, and well before Plante got there, it looked as though the war in North Africa had finally begun to turn in Britain's favor for good freeing PWE ME to focus propaganda efforts on southern and eastern Europe. British general Bernard Montgomery had taken over the Eighth Army and was about to break the Axis lines at El Alamein preventing a German advance into Egypt and beginning General Erwin Rommel's long retreat west to Tunisia. The so-called Benghazi Stakes—the frantic to and fro of British forces against Rommel's tanks fought across eastern Libya and western

Egypt—was over, leaving Britain in control of access to its Middle East oil supplies and, through the Suez Canal, to its empire in Asia.[28]

On 8 November 1942, the Americans under the command of General Dwight Eisenhower entered the fray with Operation Torch, a series of joint U.S.-British landings in French Morocco and Algeria and the first combined Allied military operation of the war. Torch set the stage for the situation in Cairo that greeted Plante on his arrival and that determined the conditions and the relationships defining his work for the rest of the war. The operation was America's first venture across the Atlantic and its green military had much to learn. Rommel was only too happy to teach them, orchestrating a humiliating, if temporary, setback at Kasserine Pass in Tunisia in February. Miffed by what many British troops felt was the undue credit given the Americans for the successful Torch landings, they quipped "How Green Was My Ally," a play on the popular novel *How Green Was My Valley*. Some even referred to the Americans as "our Italians." Eisenhower bore the brunt of the criticism, much from the highest levels. General Alan Brooke, chief of the Imperial General Staff at this time wrote in his diary that "Eisenhower as a general is hopeless."[29]

While it certainly aroused many strong personal reactions, the advent of American influence in the Mediterranean area had much more specific repercussions. PWE's focus on Greece reflected Britain's long and close relationship with the Hellenes, romantically reflected in Lord Byron's ill-fated support for the Greek struggle for independence from Turkey in the nineteenth century. Historian Antony Beevor pointed out that once the Americans landed in North Africa, their soon-dominant influence shifted the focus to Italy. During Plante's tenure in Cairo, PWE was inexorably drawn into the American orbit.[30]

Eisenhower set up his Allied Force Headquarters (AFHQ) in Algiers with Robert Murphy as his American political adviser and French North Africa remained an American sphere of influence. Churchill sent Harold Macmillan to Algiers as minister resident to represent British political interests there, while Egypt continued to be a predominantly British sphere. It was in large part due to Eisenhower's leadership, and the good working relationship developed between Murphy and Macmillan, that the two nations continued their successful collaboration against the Axis. This was not always easy, particularly in view of American determination to bring the British Empire to an end. This sentiment was widespread, stretching across the American political spectrum and reflecting motives as varied as the desire to penetrate closed British colonial markets, support for international free trade and for national self-determination, and anti-British hostility in the Irish-American community.[31]

Elsewhere, personal animosities led to tensions. Bernard Montgomery, for example, the prickly British general who successfully led the Eighth Army as it pushed the Germans out of Egypt and through Libya, had a reputation for ill-concealed anti-American sentiment. At the time of the Kasserine debacle, his boss (and from February 1943 Eisenhower's deputy while Ike was supreme commander), General Harold Alexander (later Field-Marshal Earl Alexander) thought the American troops had proved to be "soft, green and quite untrained." Soon, though, he was much more conciliatory, writing of the Americans that "we must take the line that we are comrades and brothers in arms, and our only wish is for them to share the honours and war (and the handicaps) and reap the fruits of victory together." Alexander wrote of Eisenhower that he was a "nice chap and could not be more frank, friendly and helpful." Alexander's "gift for making divergent personalities work together harmoniously" proved invaluable in smoothing out the inevitable wrinkles in the alliance, an alliance that historian David French aptly called "cooperation competition." On the other hand, American general George S. Patton, "Old Blood and Guts," was a well-known Anglophobe who flouted efforts at cooperation. Patton commanded the Western Task Force during the Torch landing and subsequent operations. On 6 March 1943, following the U.S. defeat at Kasserine Pass, Eisenhower made Patton commanding general of II Corps.[32]

In spite of all the opportunities for internal dissension in the Allied camp the alliance held, in part reflecting the strenuous efforts at joint strategic planning that had begun before Pearl Harbor—particularly the secret Anglo-American staff talks held in Washington, D.C., in early 1941. As a result of successful collaboration, by the end of February 1943 the Axis position in North Africa was hopeless. With Monty's forces advancing from the east, and Ike from the west, Rommel was caught between the two. His unenviable position was exacerbated by the fact that he was physically ailing, so he was recalled to Germany. The Germans finally surrendered Tunisia on 13 May 1943 and Rommel was eventually sent to fortify France against an expected Allied invasion.[33]

After Torch, when American organizations were added to the already complex propaganda mix, many of Vellacott's problems were compounded by the additional opportunities for misunderstanding presented by the need to work with allies. In order to bring some structure to Allied political warfare efforts, PWE Cairo had to work in tandem with the newly created Psychological Warfare Branch (PWB). PWB was established as an integrated joint Anglo-American civilian-military team operating under the direction of Allied Force Headquarters in Algiers and as the center of political warfare against enemy forces in Italy. An American colonel, Charles B. Hazeltine, was put in charge of the PWB in Algiers, assisted by British PWE personnel as well as personnel from the U.S. Office of War Information and the Office of Strategic Services. In August 1945 Colonel Donald F. Hall, then American military director of PWB, AFHQ in Italy, wrote a comprehensive review for the War Department of the role of the U.S. Army in the development of psychological warfare in the Mediterranean theater. His report gives valuable insights into the evolution of PWB.[34]

Hall notes that the relationship between PWE Cairo and PWB Algiers was not always clear. While PWE had some influence over PWB policy, there was little joint planning and the British contribution was mainly one of experience. Although PWE printed all propaganda materials, some friction was almost inevitable between competing U.S. and British national objectives as well as civilian versus military priorities. Indeed, some on both sides thought that Colonel Hazeltine was an impediment rather than an asset to cooperation. In his official history of PWE, David Garnett referred to Hazeltine as an "ignoramus." As was so often the case, whether things ran smoothly or not had more to do with the people involved than with what everyone agreed was the byzantine structure of the propaganda apparatus and the many constituencies to which it was beholden.[35]

In addition to establishing machinery for the creation and dissemination of both radio and leaflet propaganda to Nazi-occupied areas, Vellacott's brief included maintaining constant liaison with Harold Macmillan who took up his post as British minister resident in Algiers in January 1943. Churchill himself had selected Macmillan for the critical cabinet-rank position representing the British government at Allied Force Headquarters. Like Winston Churchill, Macmillan had an American mother and from the outset was well disposed to his allies. Macmillan not only mediated early disagreements between Roosevelt and Churchill, but thanks to his perfect French, helped to handle the supremely prickly Charles De Gaulle as well.

Macmillan accepted the post of minister resident though he suspected it would be "political Siberia." In the event, it afforded him his first taste of independent power and a chance to use his substantial administrative gifts. Most importantly, the critical Anglo-American alliance was first put to the test in North Africa. Macmillan quickly gained the respect and confidence of General Eisenhower and other American officials, smoothing away many of the difficulties inherent in a multinational endeavor. Macmillan had "a clear, logical mind"; he "knew what he wanted, and had a talent for getting it in a tactful way." Lockhart understood and appreciated Macmillan's role in keeping the peace among the Allies in the Mediterranean and in facilitating their effective collaboration in the production and dissemination of propaganda.[36]

The importance of Macmillan's position in Algiers rested on the fact that the command structure of the British and American forces and the staff at Eisenhower's AFHQ were—like the PWB—completely integrated, with officers from both nations serving as members of a single team. While there were also political officers from each nation embedded in this joint structure, Macmillan's appointment was outside it, giving Churchill both "stronger representation and a responsible source of information." Roger Makins, Macmillan's adviser and deputy in Algiers, was particularly influential in helping negotiate Macmillan's successful dealings with the Americans.[37]

The American civilian team with whom Macmillan and Makins had to deal was led by Robert Murphy, Roosevelt's special envoy, who was well versed in the region and its politics. Since Eisenhower delegated most day-to-day political and economic decisions to Murphy, Macmillan and Makins were able to exercise influence through successfully cultivating a good relationship with the two Americans. It is difficult to recognize the importance to the successful prosecution of the war in North Africa and then in Italy, without understanding the role of the hard work and good will of men from both nations.[38]

Since most PWE paper materials for all regions were disseminated by air it was also essential to establish smooth working relationships with the various available air units. By agreement in London, Bomber Command had been involved regularly in leaflet distribution throughout PWE's areas of responsibility but Air Marshall Arthur Harris, heading Bomber Command, remained unconvinced of the value of propaganda. While he did not oppose the dropping of leaflets he did object to exposing his bomber crews to additional danger in order to deliver what he called "pieces of bumph." He did promise the PWE all possible aid but insisted on the development of a mechanical dropping device. This was eventually created, although it took months to do so. Until then, the arrangements for dropping leaflets were both primitive and dangerous. The tail gunner had to leave his position in order to release the leaflets, exposing the plane to the German fighters in the area of operations.[39]

With American forces established in North Africa at the end of 1942, it suddenly seemed feasible to bomb shaky Italy out of the war. American aircraft joined the RAF in a campaign to bomb Italian cities from bases in Egypt and Algeria, interspersing this effort with what historian Richard Overy has called "massive leaflet drops" of sixty-four million items in the first eight months of 1943. According to the PWB, the purpose of the leaflets was to "harden Italian opposition to Mussolini, to Germany and the war." When Plante arrived in Cairo he joined this ongoing effort.[40]

Before leaflets could be dropped, however, propaganda materials had to be conceived, composed, laid out, and illustrated. Plante's paintings of the Battle of the Atlantic had been part of the British "white" (overt and acknowledged) propaganda effort to create public support in America for intervention in Europe. With his move to the PWE and to Cairo he moved, too, from positive to negative, from white to gray propaganda, from boosting the British position to undermining that of the Axis. He also moved from the sea arm to what Lockhart called the "hot-air arm." Plante relished the new challenge, learning to create images to fit simple and often aggressive texts and to work within demanding time constraints. "This extraordinary body," as one historian wrote of the PWE, "recruited some of the most exceptional, unusual and talented people of the nine [British] secret organisations of the Second World War." Plante was clearly a good fit for what historian David Welch described as the "bohemian and experimental nature of PWE." Indeed, Plante's talents were well suited to the promising new social science research about "engineering consent" that was beginning to fuel the fledgling advertising industry. As David Garnett noted puckishly in the introduction to his history of the PWE, "Americans believe in Psychological Warfare, if only as a variety of advertising."[41]

CHAPTER SEVEN

"No one dare interrupt during this job. Time is so valuable for this short period each day the pressure is tremendous."

After Operation Torch, the American leadership wanted to prepare for the invasion of France, but the British disagreed. They believed it was vital to continue to weaken Germany at the periphery before attempting a cross-Channel attack. In January 1943 the Allied leaders assembled at the Casablanca Conference finally agreed to the British proposal and the next attack was planned for Sicily preparatory to an invasion of the Italian mainland. The strategic aim was to bring about a speedy Italian collapse, knocking Germany's main ally out of the war. In propaganda terms this was to be accomplished by warning Italians of what was in store, and that Benito Mussolini and his Fascist government were to blame for the hopelessness of their position. Every effort was to be made to aggravate Italy's internal disruption, to encourage passive resistance as well as sabotage, and to drive a wedge of distrust between the Italians and the Germans ultimately detaching Italy from Germany. The Allies were to be presented as liberators not conquerors.[1]

The invasion of Sicily—Operation Husky—was launched in July 1943 with General Bernard Montgomery heading British forces and General George Patton leading the Americans. Despite the rivalry between these two difficult leaders the successful progress of the campaign on the island hastened Mussolini's overthrow on 24 July. The following day Marshal Pietro Badoglio, retired chief of the Italian general staff, was named head of a new non-Fascist government. King Victor Emmanuel III, Marshal Badoglio, and other elements of the Italian leadership opened negotiations with the Allies. Churchill sent the ever-accommodating Harold Macmillan from North Africa to Italy to help negotiate terms, eventually resulting in an armistice that was announced publicly on 8 September. The next day Operation Avalanche—the Allied landings on the Italian mainland began.[2]

Over the next year-and-a-half, Macmillan helped frame Allied policy for occupied Italy aimed at establishing a new, more liberal and democratic regime. He was appointed UK high commissioner to the Advisory Council for Italy while also continuing as resident minister to Allied Headquarters in Algiers. In his diary in November 1943 Macmillan wrote of what he had already accomplished that he might "even win the next election at Stockton as the man who drove Fascism out of North Africa and dethroned King Victor Emmanuel in Italy!" Less plausibly, Plante wrote to his wife from Cairo not to count on his speedy return home because "now that I have brought about the downfall of Mussolini you can't expect me to stop at this stage!"[3]

Even before the overthrow of Mussolini, German forces had been poised to seize control of Italy. On receiving news of the Italian armistice, Hitler rushed his troops down from the north, unwilling to cede the strategically important peninsula to the Allies. With sixteen new divisions in Italy he intended to prevent the Allies from establishing airbases within striking distance of southern German cities and close to Germany's primary oil supplies in Romania. Following the armistice, the Italian state became a co-belligerent of the Allies, although German troops still occupied two thirds of the Italian peninsula where they installed a puppet government—the Italian Social Republic—nominally under Mussolini. German forces moved to disarm and intern Italian troops in the areas under their control. Some units surrendered to them without a fight, some deserted and went home, others fought fiercely against them and still others continued to fight alongside them against the Allies. Italy was in a civil war pitting those who were pro-Allies against those who were pro-Axis, although the role of the Italian partisans provided formidable assistance to the Allies eventually neutralizing seven German divisions. At the same time, German forces moved to take control of Italian-occupied areas outside the country.[4]

Bruce Lockhart recorded that for PWE this "was the most trying period of the war because of the difficulty of coordinating propaganda policy between London and Washington and General Eisenhower's headquarters." In general, he noted, the military regarded propaganda as solely an adjunct to their operations. They approved of anything the propagandists did to lessen Italian resistance and they were willing to back Badoglio or any Italian general who would provide them with military support. On the other hand, the British and American governments "although eager to facilitate the task of the soldiers, had to give consideration to the political consequences of military expediency."[5]

The many different factions in Italy complicated any line taken by Allied propaganda. Just as problematic were the official peace terms of unconditional surrender agreed to by the assembled leaders at Casablanca. In theory, those terms prevented holding out any carrot to would-be defectors. President Roosevelt had unexpectedly sprung the notion of unconditional surrender on Churchill, perhaps accounting for Churchill's uncharacteristically ready assent. Both the propagandists and the military understood that this grand pronouncement would, as American general Albert Wedemeyer warned, "unquestionably compel the Germans to fight to the very last." Realists wanted to see "a hope clause" included in the surrender terms for Germans in order to weaken their will to resist. But as Lockhart pointed out, "we were never allowed to make any promises in our propaganda." Although eventually the prohibition of promises was more or less ignored, the lack of any "hope clause" continued to be an asset to German propaganda minister Joseph Goebbels, who used the omission to prove that the Allies intended to destroy Germany.[6]

As Middle East regional director, Paul Vellacott was allowed considerable autonomy in framing PWE ME's propaganda messages. He was, however, guided by directives from PWE headquarters in London, by Allied Force Headquarters working on intelligence from the American Office of Strategic Services and the Office of War

Information, by the British Ministry of Information, and by other sources. Under Vellacott's watchful eye, and that of his political adviser and assistant deputy head, Ralph Murray, PWE ME produced two types of political warfare: radio broadcasts from clandestine stations known as RUs set up around the region (including in Jerusalem), and printed matter, including pamphlets, magazines, informational handbooks, and—most importantly—newssheets and leaflets.[7]

On his arrival in Cairo in the summer of 1943, Plante immediately set to work on the propaganda campaign designed to break down Italian opposition. As one of three artists assigned to the Production Section at the Kasr El Aini Press, he was responsible for the layout and illustration of a broad array of propaganda materials. The KA Press, as those who worked there called it, was named for its location on the prestigious street in the Garden City district of downtown Cairo that runs directly down to Tahrir Square. Special Operations Executive Cairo's headquarters was on the same street, in a nondescript building that, in spite of elaborate security precautions, was widely known to Cairo taxi drivers as "secret building." A Leaflet Dissemination and RAF Liaison Group, comprised of an air force major and his secretary, was attached to the PWE's Production Section. These two people, an essential part of the production team, arranged airdrops of materials the press had created. Sergeant J. H. Bruce was also assigned to the production team as an artist; he would serve as Plante's assistant. A Miss D. J. Bramble was also on the roster. Donald T. Ingles worked with them as an expert in layouts. Locally, linguists from each country section composed the text for the pamphlets and newssheets.[8]

With the beginning of Operation Avalanche, the chiefs of staff issued a directive to PWE ME to continue encouraging the Italians to resist the Germans in order to minimize military opposition. "We did our best to make the official line as acceptable as possible to the Italian people," Lockhart recalled after the war, "but our Italian section, being itself pro-Italian, was suspect to ministers and to the Foreign Office." One PWE approach to walking this tightrope was to put out a small (four by five inch) booklet capitalizing on the deeply felt cultural differences between the Germans and their Italian allies. Illustrated by Plante, this ten-page booklet was one of his first contributions to the PWE's propaganda war. By focusing on the fifteen centuries of enmity between Italians and Germans, the booklet emphasized the contrast of that hostility with the long friendship between Italians and Britons. Plante's painting for the multicolored cover of the booklet showed the nineteenth century Italian hero Giuseppe Garibaldi riding in to unify Italy. "Come Garibaldi. The Germans have returned!" it proclaimed.[9]

Inside the front cover of the booklet was a photograph of a vicious-looking storm trooper manning a machine gun. The translated text read:

> For fifteen centuries Germans have been the enemies of Italy. Whether they were called Visigoths, Vandals, Ostrogoths, Alemans, Burgundians, Lombards, Franks, Saxons, Swabians, Austrians or Nazis, they have always been looters, murderers and despots, always Germans. The treacherous Germans of Dante, the mad Germans of Petrarch, are the same today as they were ten or fifteen centuries ago. Instead, Great Britain has always been a friend, until Mussolini turned against her.

The rest of the booklet was filled with brief illustrated accounts of German attacks on Italy from 1176 through World War I, a photograph of Mussolini and Hitler riding in an open car together, and an account of Garibaldi's visit to London during the nineteenth-century Risorgimento when he proclaimed the freedom of all nations. On the back cover there was an illustration of the Garibaldi Legion's flag in Uruguay. In exile from Italy for his revolutionary activities until his return to his homeland to continue the struggle for unification in 1848, Garibaldi for many years commanded the Italian Legion in the Uruguayan civil war. Here his men were identified by their famous red shirts—later imported to Italy—and their black flag with a volcano erupting in flames symbolizing resistance to tyranny. Trading on this inspiring history the PWE booklet urged Italians to "Remember the tradition of Garibaldi. Be worthy, now and forever!"

Lockhart noted that such miniature booklets were a "special" feature of the work of the PWE. "Reduced to the size of a lady's handkerchief" they were "nevertheless so beautifully printed that the text could be read with ease and comfort with the naked eye." In fact, Lockhart proclaimed these miniatures "the best propaganda productions of any country." In addition to the Italian booklet, Plante helped to lay out and illustrate numbers of other miniatures, including six that he managed to keep at the end of the war. One was in French, two in Greek, one in Croatian, one—"The Dodecanese"—was in English, and one (dated 1945) was in Norwegian.[10]

At the time of the armistice many Italian troops were serving overseas as occupation forces, principally in Yugoslavia, but also in Albania, in parts of Greece—including Crete—and in the Italian-controlled Dodecanese. It was not at all clear to anyone whether these troops would remain loyal to the Fascists or to the king, how they would behave, and what would become of them. One way the PWE addressed this issue was with a flyer in Italian designed by Plante. At its head he had drawn a British crest with a lion and a unicorn holding a shield and the motto of the British monarch, Dieu et mon droit. In bold letters the flyer had the single word "Ordine" (Order) and under it "From the Allied Commander in Chief of the Middle East Force to all Italian troops in the Balkans and the Aegean."

"Your government has signed an armistice," the flyer announced to the officers, NCOs, and soldiers of the Italian armed forces. "The war between Italy and the United Nations is over. Any hostile act against the people of the country you are occupying must cease from this moment." The leaflet went on to urge rigid discipline and firm opposition to any attempt by the Germans or their allies to disarm or disperse Italian troops. At the same time, Italian forces in the Dodecanese were instructed to disarm any German troops who were there. Royal Italian Navy elements that were east of 17 degrees east (the line that passes through the heel of Italy, between Bari and Taranto) were instructed to sail immediately for Alexandria, while Italian air forces were instructed to fly to Cyprus, to Tobruk in Libya, or to Aden on the Arabian Peninsula. The Italian military was warned that any opposition to this or subsequent orders would be considered a violation of the terms of the armistice and would determine its future treatment. The order was signed by General H. M. Wilson, the commander in chief of the Middle East Force, a post Wilson had held since January 1943.[11]

According to Antony Beevor, a historian who documented the many faces of the World War II campaigns in Crete, "Stories of friction between the Axis allies [on Crete] were not new. There had been fights between Italian and German soldiers: on one occasion an Italian threw a grenade at a group of Germans killing one and wounding two others." PWE's task was to exacerbate these existing animosities and to undermine any residual opposition to the armistice from the overseas Italians. Plante's contribution to this effort was a large (14 by 21 inches) yellow, black, and white poster showing an Italian soldier unloading a large wooden packing crate from the back of a truck. Playing on the homesickness of Italian troops, the message was as simple and clear as the drawing itself: "To return home . . . help the English."[12]

Following the announcement of the armistice, General Angelo (Angelico) Carta, "a short plump officer with a monocle and a mistress," did just that. He was the Italian commanding officer of the Siena Division in Crete and a Royalist, not a Fascist. Not wishing to surrender to the Germans who occupied the majority of Crete, nor to be associated with the "ghastly experience of the Cretans under German occupation," Carta fled into hiding. Anticipating an Italian collapse he had already made contact with SOE agents on the island who now smuggled him and several of his staff to Egypt where they turned themselves over to the British.[13]

In Cairo, a PWE staff member interviewed Carta and sent a résumé of the general's views to London. Carta testified to the efficacy of PWE's propaganda efforts, explaining that their leaflets were "read by all Italian troops and the majority of German troops." He noted the interchange of leaflets between Crete and the Greek mainland and maintained that "both Germans and Italians sent leaflets home." Carta told his PWE interviewer that when leaflets were dropped on Crete during the night, his orderly would collect piles of them and lay them out on the breakfast table for Carta to read. The same PWE ME situation report that outlined Carta's views also pointed out, with regard to their own radio activities, that Badoglio's speeches broadcast from the southeastern Italian city of Bari were "fully reported," and that listeners were "constantly informed of the existence of Radio Italiana, the pro-Allied Italian government's official broadcasting station." According to Carta, however, one of the first things the Germans did after the armistice was to confiscate all radios from Italian troops. Carta warned that future propaganda would have to consist almost entirely of leaflets.[14]

Part of PWE's response to the uncertainties of Italian loyalties was to conduct a "re-moralisation" campaign aimed at Italian troops, particularly on the Greek islands of the Dodecanese. With this objective in mind, in addition to leaflets dropped on Crete they also dropped leaflets on the Dodecanese islands of Rhodes, Skarpanto (Karpathos) and Cos (Kos). The Kingdom of Italy had occupied the twelve major islands of the Dodecanese in the southeast Aegean Sea since the Italo-Turkish war of 1912. After the surrender of Italy in September 1943 the Allies attempted to capture the Italian-held Dodecanese but were thwarted by a concerted German effort to occupy the islands, causing problems for the Cairo propagandists. German successes on Kos, for example, made it hard to raise the morale of Italian troops on other islands.[15]

Many overseas Italians wanted to change sides and fight with the Allies, while others just wanted to surrender and go home. Germans were already known to be executing Italians in the Aegean and on the mainland. The Italian language leaflets capitalized on this by emphasizing the brutality of the Germans. Among the illustrations Plante produced on this theme were several stark drawings with equally stark messages. One showed a woman in tears, on her knees, holding a black-bordered letter. Her young daughter, also crying, was kneeling next to her mother, clasping her around the waist. The translated caption reads: "How much longer will the German war cause Italian tears?" On the reverse side Plante sketched an Italian soldier lying on the ground on his back, with his helmet beside him, obviously dead. Hovering above him was a vicious looking vulture, talons outstretched, with a large swastika on its chest. "Will you be the last victim?" the caption asked. General Carta himself composed the text for at least one of these leaflets printed and disseminated by the PWE to Italian troops overseas.[16]

Paul Vellacott's annexes to the weekly situation reports often spelled out in detail the tactical situation giving rise to the development of particular leaflets. In his report of 9 October he wrote regarding the German campaign to replace Anglo-Italian influence in the Dodecanese. Because the island of Simi (Symi) was close to Rhodes and only held a small number of British troops, in order to support them "Simi had for some time past been a target of PWE leaflet raids." Twenty-four hours after the news that the Anglo-Italian forces there had repelled a German attack, "congratulatory leaflets were dropped on the Italian garrison at Simi." This turned out to be premature as the Nazis successfully occupied Simi on 12 October. Within two months the British effort to control the Dodecanese ended in a bloody shambles. The Germans succeeded in their campaign to conquer the islands and they continued to occupy them until the end of the war.[17]

As Vellacott well knew, the need was acute for trained staff to produce effective propaganda in this complex and fast-changing political and military environment. That same October he complained to Bruce Lockhart that "we have had to struggle along as a poor set of amateurs . . . in an amateurish fashion to the best of our ability."[18]

The situation was not much different in London where Lockhart noted that the composition of PWE was "extraordinarily varied" including a handful of professional soldiers and civil servants, journalists, business men, advertisers, teachers, authors, farmers, lawyers, stockbrokers, psychologists, and one landscape gardener. Of these Lockhart found that journalists were "the best exponents of propaganda in part because they understood the value of words and also because they were used to urgency" although they were often frustrated by the "hampering necessity of consistency." Apparently, "the advertising men were generally a disappointment, the professors tended to resent criticism, and the theoretical analysis of the psychologists was still too untested in war 'to justify any firm conclusion.'"[19]

Plante had a similar critical view of those producing the propaganda for PWE in Cairo. "I'm right on top of the work," he was already writing his wife in September, "and have had considerable praise. You see, the standard was so dreadfully low that Don [his colleague and his flat-mate] and I have had tremendous effect." In this they were handicapped by a lack of equipment. Ten months earlier, when the Ministry of Information began discussing setting up bases in Egypt for producing and disseminating printed propaganda, it had recognized the need to supply them with "paper, type, printers, block making equipment and more—as well as with qualified personnel." But these requirements were not easy to fulfill in wartime Egypt and shortages continued to present challenges. As Vellacott confirmed to his boss in London, at the time Plante arrived PWE Cairo still lacked "paper, printing facilities and the like."[20]

Demanding deadlines were an additional, and ongoing, problem for the artists. Still, except for missing his wife and son—"Little Chief One-Year-Old"—Plante professed himself "very happy out here." He and Don had found an apartment on Sharia Soliman Pasha, a street near the Midan, one of the city's most prominent squares. At this point all was "work, good food, and rest periods in between." Even though Plante claimed that late nights out were impossible as work started so early in the morning, the arrival of a radio soon made "life sweeter." Listening to his favorite music was always important to his sense of well-being.[21]

As he had been in New York, Plante was keenly interested in discovering what Cairo had to offer. Leaving behind the rationing, the drab greyness, and the air raid shelters of London, he had been thrown into an entirely different world. Here, on dusty streets, ancient buses spewing noxious fumes fought for road space with men in gallibayas riding scrawny donkeys, their feet dangling inches from the ground, looking like something straight out of the Old Testament. Carts heavily loaded with produce jostled people and animals, dodging perilously in and out of the incessant traffic of small European cars and endless streams of military vehicles.[22]

Unlike much of the rest of the city though, Plante found the bazaar—the Mousky—quite fascinating, especially "the quaint old places with antiques and old jewelry and metal work. Here there are all kinds of treasures to be found among the junk," he wrote.

> Lovely pieces of Greek, Roman and Persian, to say nothing of Egyptian pottery. There are cheap imitations of all of them, of course. But there is plenty of the genuine article. All these people have at some time or other in the past been in Egypt and left their mark. The locals themselves have no appreciation and are thieves. With the result that it has often been possible for people who really know their subject to purchase in the streets for a few coppers priceless articles from the tombs, etc. that have been stolen by the guards and looters at the museums.[23]

Plante himself, ever the collector of fine things, eventually shipped home an old Egyptian mask, some intricately carved "harem doors," some lovely pieces of pottery, and a small stone Greek sculpture, among other treasures. "Now I can see behind the smells and the dirt," he wrote, "to the real attraction of Egypt. This is absolutely the *only* attraction though."[24]

Plante, as was his nature, took full advantage of his time in Cairo and soon acquired an international group of friends. This was made all the easier as the coordination of the work of PWE with the American-headed equivalent, the PWB, became smoother. For Plante, one of the big advantages of the joint PWE/PWB propaganda effort was that he was able to continue his close professional as well as personal association with Americans. The Americans "are a pleasant bunch," he wrote

Evelyn in September, "but apart from Pike (my opposite number) they are not nearly as efficient as we are." John Pike served in the PWB in Egypt and then later, like Plante, in Italy. When Plante met him in Cairo, Pike already had a solid reputation. "This fellow . . . is considered one of the best watercolor artists in the US," Plante explained to his wife. "His illustrations are certainly very good, sound stuff. He himself is a most likeable fellow who comes from near Boston. Like myself, he saw war service before this job. He was a pilot."[25]

Plante's friendship with Pike strengthened his conviction of the many advantages of life in America. Always fastidious and a natty dresser, he "couldn't help but notice the difference in grooming between the Americans and the British. . . . They were all very immaculate and well manicured, etc." In this, as in other respects, Plante had a greater affinity for Americans than for his own compatriots. "Our fellows were clean and smart enough, but their suits hadn't had the same cleaning and pressing. Don looked as though he had slept in his suit." To Don's disbelief, Plante changed into shorts every day as soon as he arrived at the studio to work, hanging his suit up until he left again.[26]

"The more I meet these people," Plante continued his letter to Evelyn, "and understand and realize the standard of living they enjoy, the more I am determined to take you to America. I do think that with my contacts I shouldn't have any great difficulties achieving this. After that, our future will mold itself."[27]

In the meantime, there was more for the KA artists to deal with than propaganda to Italy and Italians. Political warfare aimed at the other Mediterranean and Balkan areas under direct Axis control or the control of their sympathetic satellites, presented a formidable challenge to Vellacott's team, in large part because of the confused and highly volatile history of the region. Italians had exercised considerable sway over Albania since the late 1920s and Mussolini's quick and successful invasion in April 1939 only served to formalize a longstanding dependency. The Albanian king was forced to abdicate and Albania became a part of the Italian Empire under the Italian crown.

Mussolini's invasion of Greece in the fall of 1940 was less successful. His campaign stalled the following April in face of fierce Greek resistance. The Greeks not only stopped the invasion but also launched a successful counteroffensive into Albania. Confronted by this humiliation, Hitler sent in his German forces to bail out the Italians. Although a staunch supporter of Greece, Britain was besieged at home and the best it could manage was to send a small—and as it turned out inadequate—force including British, Australians, and New Zealanders to assist the Greeks. The Germans, invading through Bulgaria, quickly overran Greece. By the end of April resistance ended, leaving Germans, Italians, and Bulgarians in occupation. Driven off the Greek mainland, British and Dominion forces retreated to the island of Crete where they and their Greek allies were routed a month later by a successful German airborne attack. By 1 June, Crete had fallen to the Germans and surviving British and Dominion troops were evacuated to Egypt.

Vellacott had organized specialized country sections for propaganda to the five Balkan states for which he was responsible (Albania, Bulgaria, Greece, Romania, and Yugoslavia) as well as for Italy and Germany. Printed matter was assigned a country code and the target country or forces were identified on most documents by small printed letters and a number. Leaflets for Greece or for Greeks serving overseas, for example, bore the notation "Gr"; those for Italy an "I." Leaflets printed in more than one language might have more than one letter of identification, such as "YC" for Yugoslavia (meaning Serbia) and Croatia.[28]

The Italian armistice on 8 September had encouraged anti-German resistance movements in Greece, as well as in Yugoslavia and Albania, resulting in Cairo's increased emphasis on propaganda to those guerrilla forces. One issue of the *Daily News*, a Greek flyer, dated 29 October 1943 and laid out by Plante, stated that this was "The Journal of the Alliance for the Friends of Greece." This *Daily News* issue featured resounding British naval successes in the Aegean. It also described disastrous German losses, including news of the German retreat in Italy, and noted triumphantly that the eastern front campaign on the Dnieper River had become a slaughterhouse for Germans. On the reverse side of the flyer were bombastic quotes from Hitler from 1942 and 1943. This flyer was dropped extensively over Greece and Bulgaria, aimed at demonstrating how Germany was losing the war and encouraging continued resistance.[29]

In order to be credible, leaflets conveying real news had to be current, putting great time demands on those producing them as they responded to day-to-day changes in the political and military situation. When, for example, information was received that part of the German garrison at Skarpanto "consisted of rather older men between 35 and 45, of low morale with young officers and a high percentage of Austrians, Yugoslavs, etc. in their ranks," a special leaflet was hastily written to drop on "this excellent political warfare target." No wonder Plante wrote to his wife that at times his work was quite stressful. Still, he claimed it didn't worry him, and that he had everything under control. In his memoirs Lockhart was absolutely clear about the constraints that determined the effectiveness of their propaganda. "I could see that, as usual, uncertainty would prevail almost to the last minute and that we should be given little time to prepare [our materials for dissemination]."[30]

As the Allies pushed farther into Italy, the PWE followed, leading to Plante's speculation to his wife that a transfer was always possible. Plante told Evelyn that he might be moved from Cairo, but probably not for some time yet. He knew he could well be transferred to anywhere under the command of the Middle East Force, an area that expanded and contracted but which at various times for the PWE included—in addition to Egypt—the Middle East, the Balkans, Italy, and Germany. He had already been sent to the Middle East at least once as confirmed in an interview he gave in Jerusalem for the *Palestine Illustrated News*. Acknowledging that Plante worked for the "Silent Service," the interviewer could not ask anything about Plante's present job but instead told the tale of his adventures against U-boats in the Atlantic. In any case, Plante thought wherever he went would be of interest and would definitely be "beneficial to my study of art."[31]

In late September 1943 Bari, in southeastern Italy, was captured by the Allies. Soon after that the British embassy in Cairo forwarded to the Foreign Office in London–to the attention of Bruce Lockhart—preliminary plans for the establishment of a PWE sub-mission in Bari, a major port on the Adriatic. PWB made similar plans. Proximity to the fighting offered obvious advantages over North Africa so PWE Mission Cairo and PWB Algiers agreed to share Bari's excellent transmission and printing facilities. The distribution of leaflets, however, was described as a "most complicated problem owing to great uncertainty at present as to the movements and location of aircraft we depend on."[32]

Eventually, Plante would indeed be transferred to Bari, which became the major staging area for most of the Allies' covert missions into the Balkans, but in the meantime he was kept busy in Cairo. In addition to all the graphics, Plante and the other Kasr El Aini artists produced the designs, layouts, and fonts for everything they published. Many of the leaflets, such as *H Epithesis* (The Attacks) in Greek, and *Soldaten-Nachrichten* (News for Soldiers) in German, were produced and distributed every week and the pressure to churn out large quantities of propaganda continued until the end of the war. *Notizie del Soldato*, an Italian language daily newssheet aimed at Italian soldiers was typical of the overt propaganda Plante was engaged in. There was no attempt to disguise the origin or purpose of the leaflet; the notification that it was distributed by the RAF and the USAAF (United States Army Air Forces) appeared prominently on the masthead. Right next to the name of the newssheet was a small box with a notice in Greek, Serbian, and Albanian asking whoever found the leaflet to pass it on to the Italians.[33]

The lead headline of the 2 October issue of *Notizie del Soldato*, "L'Italia contro i Tedeschi," or "Italy against the Germans," included pieces about the fighting in the suburbs of Naples, Russia's headlong advance 650 kilometers westward, and a great Japanese defeat at Wewak in New Guinea. The reverse side of the newssheet, with Plante's layout and line drawings, made its case in a typically straightforward way. Under the heading *Perché l'Italia combatte* (Why Italy fights) Plante drew two clouds, one labeled "The Italy of Today," and the other, "The Italy of Tomorrow." Quoted under the "Today" cloud were Hitler's orders to the German forces occupying Italy to treat the entire population of the country as traitors to the Axis. Badoglio, Roosevelt, and Churchill were each quoted under "Tomorrow's" cloud, Churchill affirming that "As the Anglo-American armies advance, the Italian people will be freed and Italy will once again take its rightful place among free democracies."[34]

Unfortunately, it was not until the end of the war in Europe that the Allies gained complete possession of the entire Italian peninsula. This was due in no small measure to continued support for the Axis among numbers of Italians. When Mussolini was rescued by the Germans and set up as the head of the Italian Social Republic, many Italians had rallied to the Axis cause. Other than what is suggested by anecdotal evidence there is no way of knowing definitively how many Italians were swayed in the Allies' favor by their propaganda. What is clear is that Plante and his colleagues had a hard sell ahead of them.

Naturally, Plante barely mentioned the work he was engaged in to anyone at home and wrote nothing at all specific about it. Apparently, however, his organization was not secret since he addressed his letters from PWE, GHQ (General Headquarters), MEF (Middle East Force), Cairo. Instead of filling his letters with shoptalk he often wrote about his infant son and how, for example, he had bought him a pair of shoes in the Mousky. "They probably won't fit and might make him have turned-up toes if they did," he told Evelyn. "But they amused me and I think they'll make you laugh too."[35]

Careful not to reveal anything that would catch the censor's eye, Plante's letters from Cairo to his wife sometimes read more like travelogues than war stories and he was not at all reticent about his views on life in Egypt. "Having seen the Egyptians at work it is a wonder that any mail ever gets anywhere. I'm certain that if the postman was a bit tired, he would think nothing of throwing the whole lot in the Nile." He also wrote frequently of the heat, the filth, and the squalor of Cairo. Fleeing the German invasion of Greece, British writer Lawrence Durrell escaped to Cairo in the spring of 1941. There he witnessed ". . . cripples, deformities, ophthalmia, goiter, amputations, lice, flies. In the streets you see horses cut in half by careless drivers or obscene dead black men with flies hanging like a curtain over their wounds."[36]

Egypt was legally neutral for much of the war and many Egyptians deeply resented the British occupation. In fact, British forces had been stationed in Egypt since the Anglo-Egyptian war of 1882 and remained there until 1956. Although the relationship of the two countries changed frequently—through protectorate status, revolution, monarchy, and independence—for Britain the one compelling imperative was to keep troops there to protect the Suez Canal and the route to India. Many Egyptians, including King Farouk, harbored pro-German and pro-Italian sentiments. The king, it has been said, had even written to Hitler suggesting an invasion of Egypt, and Farouk was far from alone in his anti-British attitude. Both Gamal Abdel Nasser and Anwar Sadat had been part of a military conspiracy planning to rise up and aid the German invaders. When it had looked as though Rommel's forces might break through to Cairo from Libya some former patriots even joked that their erstwhile Egyptian friends were taking crash courses in German.[37]

Nevertheless, by the time Plante arrived in Cairo that particular danger was well over and he was soon introduced to another side of life there that he greatly enjoyed. This centered on the vibrant, cultured, mostly Jewish, expatriate community. In the late nineteenth and early twentieth centuries many Jews had fled to Cairo to escape pogroms in Russia and Eastern Europe, while other waves had arrived in the 1920s and '30s in response to rising anti-Semitism all over Europe.

On Sunday 29 August Plante had set out to visit the Maison des Artistes, which he had heard was a famous meeting place for Egyptian and foreign artists. Labib Tadros, an Egyptian artist whose ambition was to create a whole district where artists could work and meet and exchange ideas as they did in Paris, had rented a studio in an old Mameluke house in the Citadel area of the city. Plante wound his way through "the usual smells etc. of the native part up to the Citadel," that "stands away up on a hill in the centre of Cairo, somewhat like the Sacre Coeur in Paris, and is surrounded by a squalid but colorful quarter like Montmartre. After some seeking," he wrote, "I at last found the house tucked in an alley. The approach was grim, but inside it was well worth the effort." Tadros, who had founded the Maison des Artistes in the 1920s, had died tragically just a few weeks before Plante arrived in Cairo but his studio had been taken over by a Russian Jew, " a Mr. Miloslavsky."[38]

Miloslavsky was "not a painter but a musician and an author of several books on music, and his house," Plante noted, "is apparently the focal point for all people interested in the arts. At one time the idea was to have a kind of club, but apparently there is not a great circle in Cairo—and the heat as a rule makes most people lethargic." Miloslavsky and Plante "sat chatting in a kind of roof garden. There were various tropical plants and huge iron lanterns. On the white-washed walls were many old Egyptian masks, and all the while doves flew around. We sat in the shade! The whole was intriguing and very old."[39]

While Plante and his host were talking several people arrived—young arty types—and it was really very difficult to say what nationality they all were. "Some Jewish blood, French and German seem to be the main ingredients. Cairo is like that," Plante observed. Later a young Polish RAF officer arrived who shared a sort of studio across the street with another Pole who produced a large art publication, similar to *Picture Post,* called *Parade.* He was a soldier and *Parade* was the Polish army's officers' publication. "Any day now," Plante noted of the second Pole, "he will be released and will become a civilian with a similar status to myself." The second Pole spoke no

Left: George Plante, Radio Officer, Merchant Navy, 1941. *Photo courtesy George Plante Papers*

Below: Sketch of the galley of the coaster *Amelia* in the North Sea off Scotland, March 1941. *Courtesy Imperial War Museum, London*

Sketch of oil tanker *Sourabaya*'s chart room—somewhere in the Atlantic, May 1941. *Courtesy Imperial War Museum, London*

Sketch of *Sourabaya*'s radio cabin, Battle of the Atlantic, spring 1941. *Courtesy Imperial War Museum, London*

Gouache painting of the wheelhouse on *Sourabaya*, Battle of the Atlantic, 1941. *Courtesy Imperial War Museum, London*

Gouache painting of raising signal flags on *Sourabaya*, Battle of the Atlantic, date unknown. *Courtesy Imperial War Museum, London*

Gouache painting of ship in dry dock in New York, summer 1941. *Courtesy Imperial War Museum, London*

Gouache painting of *Sourabaya* in convoy, Battle of the Atlantic, summer 1941. *Courtesy Imperial War Museum, London*

Gouache painting of airplanes on *Sourabaya*, 1942. *Courtesy Imperial War Museum, London*

Gouache painting of destroyer dropping depth charge, Battle of the Atlantic, 1942. *Courtesy Kathleen Broome Williams*

Gouache painting of tanks on *Sourabaya*, heading out of New York for Britain, 1942. *Courtesy Imperial War Museum, London*

Gouache painting of landing craft on *Sourabaya*, heading out of New Orleans for New York and then Britain, summer 1942. *Courtesy Imperial War Museum, London*

Sketch of radio cabin on the New Zealand rescue ship *Tekoa,* Battle of the Atlantic, March 1943. *Courtesy Imperial War Museum, London*

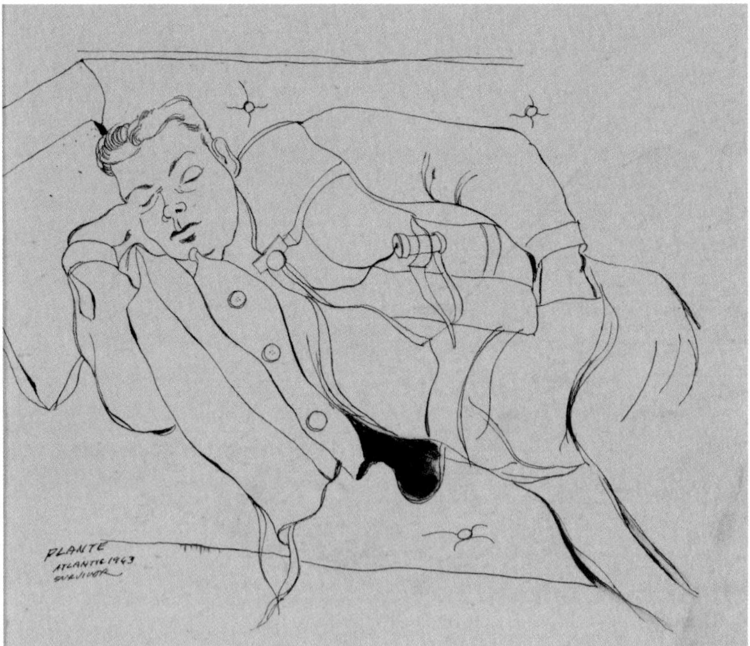

Sketch of survivor on the New Zealand rescue ship *Tekoa,* Battle of the Atlantic, March 1943. *Courtesy Imperial War Museum, London*

Gouache painting of burning, sinking tanker *Southern Princess*, Battle of the Atlantic, March 1943. *Courtesy Imperial War Museum, London*

Plante and PWE colleague visit pyramids outside Cairo, Egypt, 1943. *Photo courtesy George Plante Papers*

Right: "Will you be the last victim?" Political Warfare Executive leaflet aimed at Italian troops overseas, October 1943. *Courtesy George Plante Papers*

Left: Photograph of a Plante illustration of a Greek in a helmet, designed to encourage a united front in Greece against the Germans, fall 1943. *Courtesy George Plante Papers*

Illustration of a German soldier attacked by two-headed eagles, the national symbol of Albania, for a leaflet aimed at reassuring Albanians of Allied support, October 1943. *Courtesy George Plante Papers*

Pen-and-ink sketch of a vast armada of U.S. and British bombers for a leaflet, Y/121, aimed at bolstering the morale of all Yugoslavs who resisted the Nazis, November 1943. *Courtesy George Plante Papers*

Cover of the magazine, *Glas Pobede*, *Broj 13*, of March 1945, aimed at Yugoslavia. *Courtesy George Plante Papers*

Pen-and-ink sketch of a Murmansk convoy for *Heute* (Today), a magazine aimed at explaining the Allied victory to the German people, summer 1945. *Courtesy George Plante Papers*

Satirical sketch, "The Art Director," for *Advertiser's Weekly*, December 1951. *Courtesy George Plante Papers*

Oil painting of a Greek church, 1982. *Courtesy Kathleen Broome Williams*

Photograph of George Plante from the front cover of the *Beaufort and South Carolina Low Country* magazine, summer 1995. *Courtesy George Plante Papers*

English so conversation was limited, but when Plante went across the street with him to visit his studio he found he was "a very clever artist. His drawings are not in the least disciplined for publication, like mine. But he shares the same interest in line and they are very, very similar to Brodzky's." Horace Brodzky was an Australian artist of Polish descent who studied and worked in London where he sometimes exhibited at the Redfern Gallery, one of Plante's favorite London haunts.[40]

Pronouncing the Pole "very good indeed," Plante arranged to meet him a few days later to draw from a model that the Pole would produce and they would share the cost. "This is exactly what I was seeking," Plante enthused, "and I've found the right group. I want to use my spare time developing myself and drawing freely as relaxation and as stimulus to my other [discretely unnamed] work."[41]

With the help of new friends, including those he met at the Maison des Artistes, Plante began to enjoy an energetic social life, much of it centered on cocktail parties at the historic Shepheard's Hotel. Often, there were visiting entertainers, such as Noel Coward, who ostensibly was there to promote the sale of war bonds. Plante told Evelyn that the shape of Shepheard's Hotel was "like the North British Station Hotel in Edinburgh. In the big circular lounge there is a piano although only very accomplished pianists dare to sit and play." Coward "put on a wonderful show the other evening. He was really grand, singing his own songs for three quarters of an hour. Boy was he dirty though. Some of his songs would make you blush."[42]

In Cairo, Plante's career hovered yet again at the very edge of a fascinating web of clandestine wartime Anglo-American activities. Noel Coward—with Ian Fleming, David Ogilvy, and others—was one of that small group of well-connected Britons who had worked for the British Security Coordination secretly advancing the British cause. After the United States entered the war, they continued helping to cement the Anglo-American alliance by working to disarm American suspicion of British imperialist sentiment. Coward's name crops up frequently in accounts of activities—some open, some clandestine—supporting this effort. From time to time he lent his considerable and purposefully flamboyant talents to the PWE and in 1943 he was active in Cairo.[43]

Given the volume of paper propaganda produced in Cairo, it is surprising that Plante had time for any extracurricular adventures. The PWE printed 13,700,400 leaflets in the few days between 26 September and 2 October 1943. In the whole month of September they created 115 separate leaflets for a total print run of 59,482,200. These included, for Greece, the weekly newspaper *H Epithesis,* several issues of which Plante kept after the war. On the masthead, next to the Greek flag and the RAF bull's-eye logo, appeared the attribution that this was "the newspaper of the British for their Greek allies." Undated edition No. 24 included photographs of a bombed-out Sicilian street, one of General Montgomery and British tanks in the desert, and another of a bomber flying over a Romanian Ploesti oil refinery that was engulfed in smoke and flames, an unmistakable message that the Allies were winning the war. Plante's contribution to this issue was a cartoon of King Boris of Bulgaria, Germany's ally, talking to a Nazi officer (complete with monocle and Knight's Cross) while a portrait on the wall behind the king shows Herman Goering, Hitler's air chief, coming under bombing attack.[44]

Also produced for Greek consumption was the illustrated *Fortnightly Epithesis*, aimed especially at members of the Resistance. The local situation in Greece was complicated by the prospect of civil war between those loyal to the Greek king (George II) in exile in Britain and leftist and Communist forces. Noting the contradictions inherent in Britain's avowed policy to support anyone who would fight the Germans, Macmillan observed that "it is difficult to be a Communist in Yugoslavia and a Royalist in Greece."[45]

Indeed, Cairo had been grappling with the issue of internal dissension in Greece since Plante's arrival. A leaflet aimed at the leftist partisans of the Resistance group ELAS, or National Popular Liberation Army, informed them that the German high command was short of men and had only one way to hold down "brave Greece." That was to "divide you Greeks and to make you fight amongst yourselves. Man, don't be misled," the leaflet warned. "Don't allow any superior officer to order you to fight another Greek. The Germans alone can gain by this." When Greece is free again, the leaflet promised, such "traitors" who serve as "German tools" will "meet the fate of all traitors." The ELAS warriors were exhorted to "Think, man, before you kill a fellow Greek for the benefit of your main enemy—the Germans!" The fellow Greeks to whom ELAS was opposed were enrolled in various centrist and rightist groups, principally EDES (the National Republican Greek League) led by former army officers.[46]

Among the other examples of his work for PWE that Plante managed to take home with him at the end of the war were two postcard-size photographs of illustrations designed to encourage a united front in Greece. One shows a Greek flag flying over two clasped hands, the arms encircled by bracelets made of strings of Allied flags. The caption reads: "United Nations." The other photograph shows a man's head in an ancient Greek helmet, the plume replaced by a Greek flag. Three white doves flutter next to the helmet and underneath, in tatters, is a flag bearing a swastika. The helmeted warrior's mouth is open wide as he shouts "Freedom for Greece, Freedom for the Greeks!" On the back of each photograph Plante noted that he had been responsible for both the design and the artwork for these illustrations.[47]

Although the propagandists customarily worked very quickly to deadlines, much of what they produced soon became routine. In late September, already seeking "relief from the monotony" of what he discretely referred to as his "other work" Plante had taken on a number of independent projects. "I have just opened a branch of Everetts Advertising in Cairo," he told his wife, "in as much as I am handling all the advertising for the 'House of Seddy' beauty preparations." Plante had a friend, Kearly (in the surviving letters he gave no other name or identification for him), who had introduced him to Seddy, a Hungarian Jew, and her fiancé Max, also Jewish, from Berlin, and he was soon "going full swing designing packs and press ads" for the Seddy beauty products. Seddy's previous packs were "pretty poorly designed" and the ads prepared by the local press were "awful," according to Plante. In this work he met with innumerable snags including having to deal with unreliable Egyptian labor. He also had to learn to make allowance for the differences in taste, "But as you know," he assured Evelyn, "I can enjoy this type of work." He also recognized what an insight into advertising he had acquired in his travels. His New York experience, in particular, now stood him "in good stead."[48]

Whether or not the Seddy deal turned out to be lucrative financially, Plante was beginning to have fun. He was "doing six finished drawings for press ads and plenty more to follow. All their packs and labels have to be redesigned," he wrote, and "apart from technical difficulties in this part of the world, which have made necessary certain restrictions, and also wartime shortages of ink, type, etc., it is encouraging to be so appreciated. Seddy was squealing with excitement" when she saw Plante's sketches, he told his wife. "Oh boy, would her competition be shaken," she had exalted. Of course Kearly would have to have his cut for the introduction and the slogans he had already thought up, but Seddy and Max were "really charming people, and now I am experiencing a similar life, in a way, to what I had in New York." Noting that Seddy and Max were "terribly thrilled" with his work, Plante said they made rather a fuss of him with the result that he had seen a very different side of Cairo in the past few days. "It has been colourful," he acknowledged, "but I still prefer London and New York and that will never alter as far as Cairo is concerned."[49]

By this time also, Plante had become quite friendly with "Milo" Miloslavsky, that "pillar of the Jewish diaspora," whose apartment was where "all the arty crafty people meet and have a cocktail and talk mainly rubbish—in a nice way. It is interesting and most international." After dinner one evening, Plante's friends whisked him away in Max's Buick through the "camel manure and filth of Cairo" out into the countryside to an exclusive club. There he saw yet another side of Cairo—not the filth or squalor, nor yet the "officer infested smart bars," but the "real Egyptian society club." The club was out of bounds for military officers because, as Plante explained to Evelyn, one or two of the very best places had been reserved solely for civilians. While technically a civilian himself, he had been admitted only as a special guest.

It was a lovely night, and all the trees of the club had been sprayed white and illuminated as people sat at tables around the pool. An "American dance band (from the Army) was playing grand music" and all the men (except Plante) wore white dinner jackets and black ties. The women wore light colored evening dresses that showed off their fine figures and "beautiful brown backs and arms. . . . In no other place in the world is there such a contrast between poverty, filth and squalor and luxury," wrote Plante with all the savoir faire of someone who had recently celebrated his twenty-ninth birthday and who had traveled somewhat more than many of his contemporaries. Luxury was much in evidence, both homegrown and imported. "I understand there are more Egyptian millionaires than any other," Plante continued. In addition, during the war Cairo had become a refuge for many of the Balkan monarchs-in-exile whose Fascist-occupied countries were the target of Plante's propaganda. "[And] yet, the natives are the most degenerate in the world," Plante ended.[50]

That evening, after the first club the whole party went on to the Hunting Club, which was similar to the first, but more informal. Plante nearly committed a faux pas by sitting at King Farouk's table, although, as he said in his defense, it looked like all the others ("no gold knobs or anything"). Unlike most nights, the king was not actually there. The apparent simplicity of the king's table, if true, was uncharacteristic. Farouk was well known for his extravagance and lavish lifestyle even during the war at a time of deprivation and hardship for most of his people. This made him deeply unpopular and helped to ensure his forced abdication in 1952. That evening, Plante and his friends lingered at the Hunting Club until about 2 a.m., Plante and Max talking about Europe and the war. "I danced with Seddy once," Plante admitted to Evelyn, but quickly reassured her that "I just can't be bothered dancing unless it is with my wife."[51]

Plante's aesthetic sensibilities and his attraction to those who shared them set him apart from many of his colleagues. As he explained to Evelyn,

> The G. H. Q. crowd and the Graphic Grenadiers and Cairo Commandos just don't interest me at all. And the Gezira Shooting Club is just awful. Completely English, all officers with brushed up moustaches, all "shooting a line." God, it's awful and yet they love it. One young captain who spends all his time there said seriously to me that "one meets such frightfully nice people there."!

Plante was not alone in his views, of course, and the GHQ staff officers in their well-tailored uniforms who thronged the Gezira Sporting Club were laughingly known to many as the "gaberdine swine." Britisher Freya Stark, who was in Cairo in 1940 and 1941, already noted that the "colour of khaki grew in the streets," becoming a veritable torrent in which "Shepheards and the Continental and their immediate neighbourhood were first submerged." The torrent spread on to the quarter where GHQ "gradually gathered itself out of a labyrinth of villas into one huge edifice built with grey pillars as if to house a Sphinx."[52]

While recognizing that Plante could write little about his official assignment, it still seems from reading his letters as though all his time was taken up by outings with friends and by his work for the House of Seddy Beauty Products. On 30 September he was again enthusing that as soon as Seddy, Max, and Kearly saw his designs they wanted to scrap all current labels and boxes and "they are only using up what they have on hand." They even paid for Plante to spend two days in Alexandria to instruct their printers on how to obtain the best possible results. As Seddy told him, "never before have they seen such work in Egypt." Plante agreed that competition was very weak and noted that they "seriously" wanted him to join their staff as soon as possible to handle all their publicity.[53]

"What a pity such an opportunity has to arise in Cairo," he reflected. "Anywhere else would have been a chance in a million. Big money and tremendous scope. But I wouldn't consider for a moment settling in Egypt for all the pounds that there are grains of sand! And I certainly wouldn't ask you and Derek to live out here." Still, he knew he was very lucky, and whenever the war did end he would have added another job to his list of opportunities for peacetime. The chance "to make headway with my work and the good reception it receives makes me very optimistic about the future."[54]

Only on very rare occasions did Plante's real occupation creep into his letters. Once he explained to his wife that his official work was on a very tight schedule. Daily, around eleven a.m., just when mail arrived from home, he could not stop to read it, eager though he was to hear from Evelyn. That was because "come what may, for an hour and a half I do a certain job at intense speed. No one dare interrupt during this job. Time is so valuable for this short period each day the pressure is tremendous," and he could not possibly stop "until this layout is completed."[55]

At one point Plante even admitted to his wife that holding down two jobs took its toll and since every waking hour was devoted to work he was pretty tired. "But I'm lucky getting this opportunity [working with Seddy]," he told her "and I'll mail you home proofs as they appear." In fact, he had been working late one night, the radio playing softly, "when it happened! There was actually rain in Cairo." Don had been asleep and Plante was tempted to wake him for the extraordinary event. The next day Don told him that of course he should have. "He would have stuck his head out the window and cooled and soothed. 'Rain, beautiful rain,' Don had sighed."[56]

CHAPTER EIGHT

"In political warfare we achieved combined staffs long before the armed forces thought of doing so."

Between September and October 1943, PWE's propaganda campaign was reaching its stride. In addition to Italian and Greek materials, PWE Cairo also produced leaflets and flyers for the Balkans. They had in preparation an illustrated version of the Yugoslav newspaper *Pobeda* (Victory) put out in cooperation with the American Office of War Information with several maps and drawings by Plante. They also produced an airplane insignia recognition leaflet for the Yugoslavs; an Italian "Diary of Resistance"; a German version of the pamphlet "Total War"; a Romanian leaflet on "Big Bombs"; versions of the leaflet entitled "To Save Time" in Serbian, Greek, and Bulgarian; a message to the Slovenes; a booklet on "Fourth Year of War, First Year of Victory" in Serbian, Slovene, Croat, and Albanian; a weekly issue of *H Epithesis*; and a fortnightly illustrated issue of *Epithesis*. According to Colonel Donald Hall's report on psychological warfare in this theater, from among all types of propaganda materials it was the leaflets and newspapers giving a factual picture of the war's development that seem to have been the most valuable.[1]

A major complication faced by PWE ME in the creation of this propaganda was the many languages, ethnicities, and religions of the countries in the region, their internal political differences, and their centuries of intense and intertwined histories. The three vernacular tongues in Yugoslavia alone required care and subtlety in how information was framed. The war was moving fast and the effectiveness of the propaganda depended on how good the leaflets were—linguistically, artistically, politically, socially, and historically—as well as on their prompt delivery.

Until March 1941, Bulgaria had remained neutral, hoping for a bloodless recovery of territory it had lost in World War I. However, the threat of a German invasion that month induced the Bulgarian government to join a tripartite pact with Germany and Italy. The decision was made reluctantly, in part to avoid the threatened German invasion and in part persuaded by the promise of acquiring territories in both Yugoslavia and Greece. While it did not participate in the invasion of Yugoslavia or Greece, Bulgaria—now an Axis power with interests in those areas—occupied parts of both countries. In June 1941, largely due to opposition from its strong pro-Russian element, Bulgaria did not join Germany in the invasion of the Soviet Union. Bulgaria had gained its independence from the Ottomans with Russian help in 1877–78 and the two Slav nations shared close religious, cultural, and linguistic ties. These sentiments, and an internal Communist resistance movement against the pro-Nazi Bulgarian government, induced the government to hedge its bets by maintaining diplomatic relations with the Soviet Union throughout the war. Unable to straddle all fences, however, Bulgaria was forced to declare war on Britain and the United States that December, eventually resulting in the Allied bombing of the capital, Sofia.

Romania also presented a rapidly changing picture. At the outbreak of war in 1939 Romania, under King Carol II, remained neutral. Like Bulgaria, however, it was soon forced to take sides. In the summer of 1940 pro-Fascist elements staged a coup, creating a Fascist dictatorship and in September King Carol was forced to abdicate in favor of his son Michael. Romania officially joined the Axis alliance in November 1940, supported Germany in its invasion of the Soviet Union in June 1941, and supplied large numbers of troops to the Eastern Front. From 1943 (when Plante arrived in Egypt) onward, Romania—like Bulgaria—became subject to Allied bombing attacks.[2]

In the case of Yugoslavia, the Royal Yugoslav Army collapsed when the Germans invaded in April 1941 and the country quickly fell, giving rise to a number of separate resistance groups. But history was against a united opposition. In her account of her travels in Yugoslavia as World War II approached, author Rebecca West described in detail the striking and seemingly irreconcilable differences that had long existed among the Slavs of the different regions. Indeed, in addition to modern political rivalries, age-old intransigent animosities divided the competing Yugoslav resistance groups, fatally weakening their effectiveness.[3]

A civil war looked likely upon German withdrawal from Yugoslavia and for much of 1943 it was not clear to PWE whether His Majesty's government would choose to side with the pro-Royalist Četnik militia of the Serb general, Drâza Mihailović, or with the Communist partisan forces led by the Serbo-Croatian, Josip Broz Tito. Bruce Lockhart noted that in an effort to support any group that would fight the Germans, British agents were instructed to supply money to both Mihailović and Tito as they did to ELAS and EDES in Greece. However, at their conference in Teheran in December 1943, Roosevelt, Churchill, and Stalin agreed to support Tito and the partisans although the United States insisted also on keeping a military mission with Mihailović and his Četnik forces. Other groups further muddying the waters were the Croatian nationalist Ustaše, the Home Guard, and the Slovene Home Guard Troops. The vacillations of British and American policy with regard to Yugoslavia added to the difficulties of creating a coherent propaganda campaign.[4]

One way PWE addressed this dilemma was to encourage resistance to German occupation in as generic a form as possible and Plante designed a flyer along those lines. Printed in Croatian, the flyer was headed by four banners labeled "Harmony," "Discipline," "Endurance," and "Caution." The lead caption read "Europe against the Germans." "Throughout Europe," it maintained, "determined patriotic individuals struggle for freedom. Throughout Europe they are fighting against the Axis, preventing its plans, attacking its operations, tying up a large number of its troops. Germans and other occupying troops know they are sitting on a barrel of gunpowder that can explode at any time." Inside the flyer—assuring Yugoslavs that "You're Not Alone"—were stirring examples of resistance measures undertaken in France, Czechoslovakia, Poland, Belgium, Norway, Occupied Russia, the Netherlands, Greece, and Albania—each illustrated by appropriate line drawings by Plante.[5]

Bulgarian occupation troops in Macedonia were another important target for PWE propaganda and by late October 1943 special leaflets were being prepared for them in an effort to shake them from adherence to the Nazis. One such leaflet headlined "America speaks to the Bulgarians," told them, "We know your government was forced into war with the United States against the wiser instincts of its people. Never was there less cause for conflict between two nations. In this crisis," the leaflet ended, "Bulgaria still has the opportunity to change its destiny. Once before, an alliance with Germany sucked it into a morass of defeat and devastation. The Bulgarian people must decide now whether they will follow the same path again." Leaflets aimed at Romania followed much the same approach.[6]

The propaganda task of the PWE with regard to these countries was also complicated by the need to address both Italian and German occupiers and, in the case of Slovenia, Hungarian occupiers as well. In general, resistance movements in the occupied countries were left leaning, opposed to the Nazi and Fascist occupiers and to their local collaborators. Indeed, many of the resistance groups were Communist inspired and led, presenting a growing challenge as the war progressed and as fears emerged about the role of the Soviet Union in the postwar world. While all resistance movements shared a determination to be rid of the Axis invaders they did not share the same vision for the future. The PWE had to tread lightly to avoid accentuating divisions among the rival groups, which might have the effect of strengthening those looking to Russia for their salvation.[7]

At PWE headquarters in England, Lockhart noted that many of his young colleagues were committed socialists who might be expected to sympathize with the left-leaning resistance groups on the continent. However he was surprised to observe "the easy zeal" with which they "discarded their principles and, in the fight for our existence, indulged with relish in perversions of the truth." Propaganda, he concluded, "is a modern evil; in war it becomes the most insidious and easily acquired of all vices." Or as Winston Churchill saw it, in war the truth needed to be protected by "a bodyguard of lies."[8]

While propaganda was produced for the entire region, it was the daily Italian and German bulletins printed in Cairo that helped to account for the high numbers put out during this period. An anti-Nazi political cartoon usually enlivened each issue of *Notizie del Soldato*, requiring unrelenting effort from the Kasr El Aini artists. The full-page cartoon in the 14 October issue showed Hitler propping up a large Mussolini scarecrow, while a diminutive Goebbels looked on in bewilderment. The caption read "Ormai non fa piu paura neanche al passeri" ("Now he doesn't even scare the sparrows"). The date of this particular issue is significant. On the previous day, 13 October 1943, Italy declared war on Germany. Badoglio had followed up on an agreement made at the time of the armistice and Italy had been identified as an Allied co-belligerent although Italian participation in ground combat alongside British forces began only in November 1944. Until then, Italian troops were used for labor and other rear area services. The major Italian assistance to the Allied cause came from the large number of partisans active in Central and Northern Italy.[9]

The German newssheet, *Soldaten-Nachrichten*, followed the same pattern as the Italian *Notizie del Soldato*, including noting that it was distributed by the RAF and the USAAF and with the same admonition in Greek, Serbian, and Albanian to pass the flyer on to the Germans. The 16 October issue had an all-caps headline: "Italy Declares War on Germany," with the news that Great Britain, the United States, and Russia had recognized Italy as an Allied power. It also quoted an address by Marshal Badoglio in which he declared that "Italy would not be free as long as a single German soldier remained on Italian soil."[10]

Meanwhile, Germany's hold on the Atlantic was also collapsing. Plante's handiwork on the reverse side of the 16 October issue of

Soldaten-Nachrichten was a map of the Atlantic under a quote from a speech by Churchill explaining that the Portuguese government had granted the British government the use of air bases in the Azores. The map showed Allied shipping routes between the United States and Europe with large overlapping circles demonstrating Allied air coverage of the entire area. The caption read: "The net is closing around the U-boats."[11]

Not only was the U-boat campaign floundering, but now Germany itself was subject to devastating air attacks. One leaflet dropped on Germans troops in Italy, Greece, and the Balkans gave a sobering account of the air raids on the Bavarian city of Schweinfurt with its heavy concentration of critical ball bearing factories. The leaflet pointed out that—according to the situation report's typically dry prose—"there are few areas [in Germany] safe from this daylight bombing and that whatever the losses [to the bombers], Allied air production can more than make them good." PWE's radio programs reinforced this line of propaganda, dramatically emphasizing the horrors of the air war, including a "realistic and gruesome" account of the heavy air raids on Hamburg under the heading "I Saw Hamburg Die." In fact, far from being the success touted by Allied propaganda, the Schweinfurt raid was a disaster for the Americans and deep raids into Germany were suspended. Only after long-range fighters became available in early 1944 to escort the bombers were such attacks renewed. On the other hand, the attack on Hamburg did inflict horrifying damage on the city. A firestorm destroyed most of the city center, incinerating tens of thousands of Germans. By December 1943, PWE was widely disseminating leaflets with the even more devastating news that according to information received from neutral Sweden, "In some parts of Berlin not a single building is left standing."[12]

Cairo's "Special Political Warfare Campaign against German Troops" in the fall of 1943 was particularly aimed at perceived points of weakness. These included a German division in Albania composed mostly of middle-aged Austrians and Bavarians as well as units from 999 Division—most of whom were political offenders—in the

Dodecanese. According to Vellacott's situation report these units provided "good material and good targets for a special overt and covert campaign against Austrian and South German elements as well as politically unsound German troops in the Balkans" who received an "extra special dose of leaflets."[13]

American-led PWB, headquartered in Algiers, and British-led PWE in Cairo were in general agreement on the goals for political warfare against Italy, Greece, and the Balkans, whether advanced by broadcasts from radio stations in Cairo and Jerusalem or by leaflets and posters. One already discussed goal was to foment anti-Axis feeling in order to keep as many Axis divisions as possible fully occupied. Leaflets aimed at Axis satellite nations such as Romania, Bulgaria, and Hungary were designed to make them less enthusiastic Axis supporters in an effort to get them to withdraw their forces from occupied territories. On 1 October 1943, the British Eighth Army liberated the southern Italian city of Foggia, which had served as a transportation hub for German troops opposing the Allied invasion. By mid-October PWE leaflets were already emphasizing the danger posed to Albania, Yugoslavia, Greece, Romania, and Bulgaria by Allied possession of the Foggia airfields and the inadequacy of their own air raid defense measures. As Vellacott reported to London the following week: "more frequent leaflet sorties over Sofia have enabled us to give more punch to our implied threats of Allied bombing."[14]

By this time considerable progress had been made in the art of dropping propaganda leaflets from the air. Although initially it was clear that USAAF pilots "preferred steel to paper," once their units became involved they worked with the RAF to develop several different methods for leaflet dissemination. These included U.S. parachute flares adapted for leaflet dropping. The chute compartment held sixteen thousand leaflets and a block and cordite pad placed just above the nose-fuse was set to eject the leaflets at a predetermined height. These devices were used mostly for beachhead dissemination, as in the landings in the south of France, and on several occasions over Germany. Smaller RAF parachute flares held eight thousand leaflets and needed no adaptation other than the substitution of the leaflets for the parachute. They were used extensively over targets in Romania and Hungary. Delayed action packages were made up of four packets of leaflets that split open when a timed fuse broke the string that bound them together. On occasion, the air forces dropped duffle bags with leaflets for agents and resistance groups to distribute. Officers of the PWE field units worked on the ground to supplement the messages contained in the leaflets.[15]

Lockhart, in his memoirs, notes how cooperative American Army Air Forces general Fred Anderson was to PWE "in providing airplanes for leaflets," as well as planes to experiment with the leaflet bomb, a bomb-shaped container that opened in mid-air dispensing tens of thousands of leaflets. The leaflet bomb revolutionized air propaganda warfare by making it possible to drop leaflets accurately on specific targets.[16]

While most leaflets were dropped in the vicinity of military targets, many others scattered due to drift, or the rate of fall. Additionally, when leaflet packages were loaded into bomb bays they were often jettisoned when pilots tested their bomb bay doors. The system was extremely inefficient and as a result vast numbers of leaflets had to be printed. Indeed, the whole system of dissemination by bombers was inherently flawed as PWE relied on leaflets being sent aloft with operational missions. Since missions were not necessarily planned for when and where the leaflets would be the most effective and since it was impossible to tell more than an hour or two in advance over which countries operations were to take place or from which airfields, the lack of advance information as to specific targets meant that all airfields had to be supplied with leaflets for all targets. This decentralization involved an extensive transport system as well as staffs for stock-keeping, briefing, loading, and reporting at various points. It also meant a considerable waste of leaflets—perhaps as many as 20 percent—as the strategic or tactical needs they were designed for might have passed, or changes in the military or political situation might make them obsolete before they could be delivered.[17]

Perhaps the greatest difficulty in the dissemination of leaflets by air, however, was overcoming the resistance of many flight crews. Understandably, they viewed this work as an additional burden on an already difficult and dangerous job. One of the most valuable innovations that helped break down this reluctance was to provide a copy of each leaflet in English so pilots could understand the purpose of their mission. In spite of a marked improvement in pilot attitude, British colonel L. G. Barbrook, who headed PWE–PWB Bari at the end of the war, called the whole system by which bombing aircraft carried leaflets "essentially amateurish and exhausting." He noted that it produced a state of mind in PWE of "I never miss a lb of lift," that is that getting the leaflets aloft is what came to matter rather than a concern for where and when they should be dropped.[18]

In addition to the complexities of framing propaganda for the Balkans and of organizing its dissemination by air, a new challenge for PWE at this time was to emphasize the growing danger to Axis sympathizers from the advancing Russian front. One of Plante's leaflets, preserved among his papers, shows how his work supported this aim. It is a striking black and white drawing of a German soldier standing on a map of Albania being attacked by a pair of two-headed eagles, the Albanian national symbol. In rough translation the caption reads "Merger Brings Power: It is Better with Many Brave Friends: Union for Freedom." On the other side of the leaflet was a map of the whole region showing the western allies advancing up the boot of Italy while Soviet forces pushed west toward Romania and Poland. The sense of the caption was that all those nations that were marching together for security and freedom greeted Albania. This sentiment is also evident in issue No. 46 of the weekly Greek leaflet *H Epithesis* that quoted a statement from one of President Roosevelt's most recent speeches: "In this common war we fight as one man, for one victory." As one leaflet trumpeted, "Now the German satellites who sought land and plunder under the shadow of the swastika will learn that he who sups with the devil must pay the bill."[19]

As Bruce Lockhart pointed out in his memoirs, the information for propaganda messages relied significantly on input from both military and civilian sources. Information came from SOE and OSS agents on the ground as well as from other informants, from prisoner of war interrogations, from newspapers obtained from occupied countries, from digests of enemy broadcasts put out by the monitoring services of British and American intelligence agencies, and from bombing raid photo analysis. The leaflets, single sheets, and miniature booklets, often satirical and usually replete with artwork, frequently quoted defiant speeches from exiled leaders to help boost morale at home. In September, for example, one leaflet aimed at Greece highlighted a speech by Emmanuel Tsouderos, prime minister in the Greek government in exile in Cairo. In many areas Allied propaganda leaflets were the only source of news and were, therefore, in great demand. Even where it was dangerous to do so these leaflets were secretly passed from hand to hand, adding to their impact.[20]

All these materials were delivered by air over wide swathes of the eastern Mediterranean. In the course of September tens of thousands were dropped on Salonika, Imotski, Livno, Arginion, Corfu, Patras, Kalamata, Levkas (Lefkos), Tripolis (Tripoli), Rhodes, and Samos, as well as Sophia, Bucharest, Pristina, and "all German targets including Crete." Many leaflets had to be jettisoned due to bad weather or inability to reach the designated drop zone, while many more had to be cancelled when the information they contained was overtaken by events. Dissemination was also affected by periodic stand-downs of aircraft for various reasons, including lack of serviceable planes. The British had constructed airfields at Tocra, a town on the coast of Cyrenaica in northeastern Libya that became a main dissemination point for PWE leaflets. By October 1943, most Cairo leaflets were sent to Tocra by daily fast airfreight made available by the USAAF while others were sent forward by RAF airfreight. From then on only "standby" stock had to be sent to the airfield by road or rail.[21]

Until the beginning of 1944, RAF aircraft of 234 Wing based at Tocra carried out the dissemination of most leaflets in the

Mediterranean theater. According to PWE records RAF squadrons 148 and 624 undertook the majority of this work. PWE maintained its own air liaison officer and staff at the airfield to brief the crews and supervise the storage and loading of leaflets.[22]

PWE ME's propaganda efforts continued with the full support of London until the end of the war, in spite of periodic changes in organizational structures. During the month of October 1943 alone, PWE in Cairo printed 49,492,600 leaflets of which 34,743,400 were actually disseminated. But to what effect? Paul Vellacott included in his report to Bruce Lockhart in London what he knew would be well-received information about the results of the leafleting campaigns. In November he wrote that the interrogation of a person who had recently escaped from Nazi-occupied mainland Greece, "shows the eagerness with which PWE leaflets are picked up, and the rapidity with which their contents are circulated." When leaflets had been dropped on Salonika on 1 August, for example, "Germans were seen chasing people who were collecting them in the streets with drawn pistols." Although the Germans then proclaimed a curfew from 6 p.m. onward, according to Vellacott's informant "this did not prevent the news from circulating rapidly."[23]

Later in November, Vellacott reported that German prisoners from Rhodes who had been questioned by a member of the PWE Middle East stated that "nearly all the German troops in that area listened to the German broadcasts from Cairo and Jerusalem" and that "two of the prisoners knew the times off by heart." These same prisoners also told their PWE interrogator that German headquarters ordered the immediate collection of all leaflets dropped but that "about 50% found their way into the pockets of the collecting troops and were often taken by them when they left on leave." Apparently the daily newssheet in German made a considerable impression on these men who told PWE that the news they got otherwise was often stale and anyway was given a very obvious propaganda slant![24]

Anecdotal feedback about the effect of these propaganda efforts continued to be reported. That fall, PWE Cairo had a conciliatory letter from General Angelo Carta to General Bruno Bräuer, commander of German forces on Crete, printed in Italian, German, and Greek and dropped in leaflet form over Crete. As a colonel in May 1941, Bräuer—a paratrooper distinguished by his short stature, his cigarette holder, his slight stammer, and his bravery—had jumped into Crete with the initial German assault on the island. Promoted and given command of Crete from fall 1942 until spring 1944, Bräuer had proved himself, according to historian Antony Beevor, "the most humane German general on the island during the war." Carta surely knew this when he wrote to Bräuer, even though the German general had vigorously opposed resistance activities as well as opposing any collaboration with the British.[25]

In November 1943 an Italian officer, "recently escaped from Crete" reported that General Carta's letter to General Bräuer was "a great morale raiser to the Italians and the Greeks, and thoroughly annoyed the Germans." The same officer also reported that listening to Cairo radio transmissions in Greek and German (as well as those in English) was widespread among isolated German garrisons. He further stated that General Bräuer himself paid particular attention to Cairo broadcasts. In fact, the general "designated a special officer" to monitor those broadcasts and to immediately give him copies of them and to send copies to the mainland by air.[26]

In the week of 12 November, PWE printed 3,560,000 daily newssheets in both Greek and German. The longer they were at the job, of course, the more PWE ME was able to refine and improve their output. By December they had figured out how to give the daily Greek and German newssheets a more typical newspaper style on both back and front and had added photographs, which had previously been mechanically impracticable.[27]

By this time in late fall, the pace of the anti-Nazi campaign had quickened, even though poor weather conditions for much of the month of November hampered leaflet dissemination. The Cairo situation report of 20 November noted, "The production of Rumanian and Bulgarian leaflets at short notice was a priority printing requirement in the early part of this week." In a November issue of the Bulgarian leaflet *Truth*, under the heading "Food for Thought," a cartoon showed Hitler reaching into a garbage can and extracting a flat and dirty Mussolini. Hitler dusted him off, pumped him up with a foot pump, and propped up the now fully inflated former Italian dictator on a balcony with his arm raised in the Nazi salute. RAF 148 Squadron dropped 100,000 of these leaflets on Bulgaria during the week of 13–19 November. The message for Bulgarians was clear: As were the Italians, now it is you who are merely Hitler's tools.[28]

This phase of the propaganda campaign also included a focused attack on Nazi-dominated Yugoslavia. Plante's black and white sketches on one of the typical two-sided leaflets show a vast armada of U.S. and British bombers flying overhead. The symbolism was not subtle and the great punishment meted out to Germans from the air was used to bolster the morale of all who resisted the Nazis. Plante's bomber leaflet, S/121, was addressed to the Serbs, the Croats, and the Slovenians of Yugoslavia from the "United Nations" and as usual was printed in all three languages. It informed the Yugoslavs "with heartfelt congratulations," that Allied armies were fighting Germans on the Italian mainland. "Even the Italians have joined the fight against the common enemy of all mankind, against the German enemy," it stated. Each of the remaining three pages also had Plante's pen and ink sketches, one of a German soldier with his hands raised, above the caption "The Allies admire all those who are openly fighting against the Axis invaders." On the last page Plante drew the figure of a German soldier lying on the ground—seemingly dead—under the heading: "All our friends, be constantly on guard against a cunning foe who never gives up trying to trick you."[29]

Because much of the impact of propaganda leaflets continued to depend on the immediacy of their information, the PWE/PWB artists often had to improvise. Sketches were frequently reused, in various different formats, for different countries and to illustrate different points. Plante's drawings of British and American bombers flying overhead that was used in the November leaflets aimed at warning the

Serbs, Slovenes, and Croats of the unbeatable Allied airpower were used again in the Italian pamphlet (also for Albania) AI/19. This time, though, Plante added Allied tanks advancing on the ground below the planes. The caption read: "On the march and there is nothing that can stop them."[30]

Eventually, leaflets were also aimed at paving the way for the planned temporary phase of Allied occupation. PWE propaganda frequently referred to the Atlantic Charter of August 1941 emphasizing that the Allies had no interest in territorial aggrandizement and that the "destiny of every country was based on self-determination." The agreements reached by the foreign ministers of the United States, Great Britain, and the Soviet Union at the Moscow Conference in October–November 1943 were widely publicized in leaflets used to demonstrate the collaboration among the Allies in their plans for the postwar world. So too were the agreements reached between Roosevelt, Churchill, and Stalin at Teheran in December. Of course, with hindsight it is hard not to regard those assurances with cynicism. At the time, however, the goal was to end the war. All evidence of cooperation that furthered that end was touted widely and enthusiastically.[31]

After Teheran, Churchill and Roosevelt met in Cairo again in early December with both Macmillan and Makins in attendance. At the conference Roosevelt informed Churchill that Eisenhower would be the supreme leader for the anticipated invasion of France the following spring. In light of Eisenhower's planned departure for Europe they agreed to amalgamate the Cairo and Algiers command structures under his replacement as supreme Allied commander in the Mediterranean, British general Henry Maitland "Jumbo" Wilson. Wilson was in charge of all the operations in the theater until December 1944. Meanwhile, British general Harold Alexander was given command of the Fifteenth Army Group in Italy composed of the American Fifth Army and the British Eighth Army. Thereafter, Mark Clark, an American, held the command until the end of the war.

While rumors about top-level meetings among Allied leaders were rife in Cairo that fall and winter, apparently very few people knew anything specific and even fewer knew what was on the agenda. Nevertheless, Plante's work was directly affected by the decisions made in Cairo and the determination to remain focused on Italy and the Balkans. Cairo continued to churn out leaflets aimed at Greeks, Albanians, Yugoslavians, Bulgarians, and Germans. One aimed at German troops that must have been particularly unsettling was referred to in the situation report of 4 December as the "Christmas version of *The Lonely Soldier*," produced by the PWE and the OWI together. One million copies of the leaflet were printed by 3 December and widely disseminated to German overseas troops. As the year came to a close, control of PWB shifted gradually from the American military to civilian leaders and on 24 December 1943 the much-criticized colonel Charles Hazeltine was suddenly relieved of his post as head of PWB.[32]

"The building up of this mission has been an interesting task," Paul Vellacott had reported to Bruce Lockhart that November.

> It is not only on personal grounds that I am anxious to see its activities constantly improved and applied in the most effectual manner possible to the prosecution of the war. We have got to a certain point in the journey and it would be a thousand pities if there should be any going back from that point through lack of first class minds which have been exercised and trained in the techniques of political warfare.[33]

Vellacott saw that big changes were in the works as the war progressed in the Allies' favor, particularly around the Mediterranean. Although Vellacott's deputy, Ralph Murray, was still headquartered in Cairo, Murray's responsibilities were described as necessarily "peripatetic between Cairo, Algiers, [and] . . . southern Italy." Since October 1943 Bari had been in Allied hands and PWB had taken over the radio station and had established priority access to local printing facilities. In order to make maximum use of these centrally located resources for psychological and political warfare aimed at Italy and the Balkans it made sense for PWB and PWE to share them. Negotiations between

Cairo and Algiers took place with speed and by November it had been agreed that PWE ME would operate in Bari within the already established PWB organization. By that December a PWE sub-mission had been established in Bari and within three weeks it had produced its first leaflets.[34]

In practice, however, it was found that PWB and PWE could not work effectively as separate entities because of the obvious duplication of two political warfare units using the same transmitters and printing presses with separate control from Cairo and from Algiers. By February 1944 they had amalgamated their operations in all but formal terms. When the fusion of PWE with PWB for the whole Mediterranean was decreed that May, Bari had already accomplished the change.[35]

In March 1944, Macmillan moved much of his operation from North Africa to Caserta, Italy, joining the forward section of AFHQ. In July the whole of AFHQ moved from Algiers to Caserta while PWB set up its operations in nearby Naples because of the superior printing facilities there. Meanwhile, in April, PWE ME had begun a substantial reorganization making it an integral part of an overall PWB for the Mediterranean while also reflecting acceptance by the British of the change in terminology to describe their propaganda from political to the American-preferred psychological warfare.

Although Paul Vellacott had been on sick leave in England since the beginning of January, he had been kept informed of the proposed restructuring. As he wrote Bruce Lockhart, he had studied the proposed changes "very carefully and think that the conclusions reached are sensible and should in the main be adopted." Until that time, the Cairo mission had been a largely British organization. The general doctrine of PWB had not called for equal numbers of British and American personnel, but had operated on the basis of securing the best person available for any given post regardless of nationality. At this point, however, it was clear to PWE Cairo that "we must now work for a greater degree of American participation in Balkan operations." Accordingly, PWE Cairo was to be merged with PWB, and a

PWB Allied Force Headquarters under Vellacott would be situated in Algiers.[36]

The reorganization of PWE ME and the new PWB structure caused considerable friction at the upper reaches of the organization. Vellacott returned to Cairo briefly but left again for Britain in July 1944, giving his continued ill health as the reason. However, Bruce Lockhart noted in minutes addressed to Foreign Secretary Anthony Eden that Vellacott had personally informed him that even were he well he would not stay. There was nothing for him to do in the Mediterranean, as long as the Americans were determined to direct political warfare in the area.[37]

This was hardly fair as General Wilson had initially selected Vellacott to head the PWE/PWB in Algiers and it was only Vellacott's delayed return due to ill health that led to the appointment of an American, Russell Barnes, in his place. As before, the PWB continued to report to the U.S. Army's Information and Censorship Section of AFHQ. So Lockhart went on criticizing American military control of propaganda, calling it "incompetent," adding that both British and American civilian propagandists—OWI officers as well as American members of PWB—had welcomed Vellacott's return hoping he would be able to rectify an intolerable situation. Somewhat more temperate in his postwar memoir, Lockhart noted that after the center of activity had moved north to Europe "much of the glory had departed from Allied Force Headquarters, Algiers. Inevitably," he concluded, "Anglo-American integration did not work as smoothly as under General Eisenhower."[38]

David Garnett noted that there was no disagreement between British PWE authorities in London and American OWI staff there—the "civilian agencies" as they were called—and Lockhart confirms this in his memoir. He quotes an April 1944 letter to him from American playwright Robert Sherwood, speechwriter and confidante of Franklin Roosevelt, and of FDR's adviser Harry Hopkins. Roosevelt and Hopkins had dispatched Sherwood to England in September 1941 on a confidential mission to study British propaganda warfare, and while there he had established a close relationship with the MOI and PWE. The following year Sherwood became the permanent head of the Overseas Branch of the OWI in London. In 1944, Sherwood—who had worked closely and well with Lockhart—wrote thanking him for "all the generous co-operation you have given me and my associates." The letter continues: "It is a source of great satisfaction to me to realize that in political warfare we achieved combined staffs long before the armed forces thought of doing so."[39]

Unfortunately, when Eisenhower had moved to London at the end of 1943, he took with him the cream of the talent of PWB Mediterranean. This included General Robert A. McClure, a psychological warfare expert whom Eisenhower had appointed to head the Information and Censorship Section of AFHQ in Algiers. The section included military and civilian personnel from OWI, OSS, PWE, and the U.S. Army and was responsible for public relations and censorship as well as for psychological warfare. McClure had been invaluable in seeing that the mixed Anglo-American PWB team operated smoothly.[40]

Once in London, the PWB team from Algiers was renamed the Psychological Warfare Division (PWD) attached directly to SHAEF (Supreme Headquarters Allied Expeditionary Force) under Eisenhower. It was essential that the new PWD continue to work closely and cooperatively with Lockhart's PWE headquarters and with the OWI under Sherwood, in the coordination of political warfare planning. This was accomplished by instituting regular meetings of the three entities under Lockhart's chairmanship resulting in what he called a "reasonably satisfactory system." This was greatly assisted by the support of General McClure, who was appointed the military head of PWD and who Lockhart described as a "model of fairness and square dealing." The PWD would continue to conduct its propaganda in conformity with the policy guidance from its parent agencies, the PWE and the OWI, although the PWE was already beginning to fade in importance. The OWI, too, had started to wind down, although it did not finally leave London until September 1945.[41]

In the meantime, Anglo-American cooperation accomplished perhaps the most significant, not to say unprecedented, success of the war—Operation Overlord—the June 1944 landings in Normandy. D-Day and its aftermath were a brilliant affirmation of joint planning and execution made all the sweeter by the American capture of Rome two days earlier.

While none of this would have been possible without wholehearted commitment to Anglo-American integration at the highest levels in London (including, in addition to McClure, General Bedell Smith, Eisenhower's chief of staff), after General McClure's departure from Algiers the situation in the political warfare operation in North Africa quickly changed for the worse. Some local rivalries were bound to persist, weakening the organization still further. Terry G. M. Harman, the British deputy head of PWB, described the political/psychological warfare situation in the Mediterranean in the summer of 1944 as an "overall muddle." Following the Operation Dragoon landings in the south of France in August, the military situation was changing fast and it was not clear how best to structure the new propaganda units for Italy and the Balkans, or whether they should be under British or American control. American colonel (later brigadier general) Arthur J. McChrystal had replaced General McClure as head of the Information and Censorship Section of AFHQ, to which PWB reported under its new head, American Russell Barnes.[42]

Harold Macmillan, in his role as British resident minister in the Mediterranean, took the long view of the situation. Macmillan pointed out to Lockhart that giving up the leadership of the whole of political warfare to an American, in order to keep the peace with the Americans, was actually quite painless since the real power would reside in control of the actual operating theaters, most of which were under complete British control. The Mediterranean theater was, in fact, being organized with respect to political warfare in true Jeffersonian fashion, Macmillan pointed out, with states' rights maximized and federal rights minimized. Aware that many of his colleagues may not have been students of American history, Macmillan understood that many of them would simply see the arrangement as "yet another example of the poor, stupid British representatives having been 'outsmarted' by the slick Americans. It is a pity they do not sometimes hear the American view of these affairs," he wrote.[43]

Richard Crossman, the British director of psychological warfare in Algiers, later recalled Macmillan instructing him along those same lines. "We, my dear Crossman," he had told him,

> are Greeks in this American empire. You will find the Americans much as the Greeks found the Romans—great big, vulgar, bustling people, more vigorous than we are and also more idle, with more unspoiled virtues but also more corrupt. We must run AFHQ as the Greek slaves ran the operations of the Emperor Claudius.

Macmillan's biographer, Alistair Horne, notes that there was nothing cynical in Macmillan's view of Americans. Rather he credits his affinity for the "vitality, spontaneous warmth, breezy informality and generosity endemic" in his allies with bringing out in Macmillan a new relaxed self-confidence that "undoubtedly contributed to the success of his relations with his US colleagues."[44]

Also writing to Bruce Lockhart from the resident minister's office in Caserta three days after Macmillan had written, Roger Makins, Macmillan's invaluable deputy, further clarified the thrust of Macmillan's argument maintaining that he, Makins, really did not understand what all the sound and fury was about. The accusation that they had somehow surrendered British interests in the Mediterranean by allowing political warfare to fall under "senior American control" was nonsense. Political warfare policy was jointly controlled from London and its execution in their theater anyway was mostly under the direction of British officers. As Makins pointed out, the accusations seem to have been based on the fact that locally, an American headed the organization. However, Makins wrote:

> You have met that ingenious and hesitating product of the Middle West, General [Arthur J.] McChrystal. Were you to meet that ornament of the South, Mr. Russell Barnes, you would not, I think, discover in him a paladin of American Imperialist policy. Indeed he is, I fear, not a very efficient officer. But that makes the situation rather easier, for surely what you want and what British interests demand is a policy of measures not men. Provided your measures are carried out you can be indifferent to the fact that the titular heads of the organisation which carries them are American.

In ending his note to Lockhart, Makins noted that it was apparently impossible for the bureaucrats in London to understand the organization and functioning of Allied agencies in the Mediterranean. They could not grasp that control of any particular activity did not depend on whether the head of it was British or American.[45]

Makins was well suited to understand the workings of Anglo-American relationships. He had served in the United States, had an American wife, and had worked closely and well with General Eisenhower. Makins played a central role in building a close relationship between Americans and Britons in North Africa and after the war he was a popular and esteemed British ambassador in Washington, D.C. Indeed, throughout the course of his career Makins worked consistently and successfully to ensure a smooth and mutually beneficial connection between the two countries. His critical comments on McChrystal and Barnes were not partisan and were widely shared by Americans and Britons alike. Robert Sherwood described McChrystal and Barnes to Bruce Lockhart as "useless" and that good teamwork was "almost impossible if both the captain and vice-captain are inefficient and incapable of performing their proper functions."[46]

To be sure, such rivalries were by no means exclusive to North Africa. In Asia, too, a similar rivalry flourished between the highly competitive secret services of Britain and America. As Max Hastings explains, "Much British intelligence material was marked 'Guard'—not to be shown to Americans—and many US documents were stamped 'Control'—to be hidden from British eyes."[47]

At the end of July 1944, Vellacott summed up for Foreign Secretary Eden his own view of what had transpired in North Africa. "In May 1944," he wrote, "following an order by the Supreme Allied Commander, General Maitland Wilson, this PWE Mission was incorporated within PWB Mediterranean." Meanwhile, Vellacott had agreed to head PWB Mediterranean—with the concurrence of interested parties in the Foreign Office, the PWE, the OWI, and AFHQ—but his illness in England had delayed his return to Algiers until late May. "You already know, I think," he wrote Eden, that by the time he, Vellacott, arrived in Algiers General Wilson had taken the view, "in consultation with Mr. Macmillan, that, for the avoidance of further difficulties in Anglo-American relationships at AFHQ, PWB Mediterranean should continue to be controlled by Americans; that consequently I should return to England."[48]

By the summer of 1944, Bruce Lockhart could do nothing further to change the political warfare situation in the Mediterranean. Much of the problem seems to have come from a difference of opinion between the diplomats and the propaganda people on the ground. Naturally, PWE headquarters found the diplomats too complacent about issues of poor military and civilian leadership. "We must get on with our work," Bruce Lockhart wrote Eden on 11 August, "and my main concern now is to raise the morale of the PWE personnel in the Mediterranean which has sunk very low. I admit that propagandists are temperamental," he continued, but "Mr. [Terry] Harman, the senior PWE official in the Mediterranean," whom he regarded highly, "is very properly rallying his British staff to carry on and do their best." Lockhart, moreover, later admitted that he came to think highly of Russell Barnes, Harman's boss, whom he credited with overseeing the harmonious operation of the PWB as an integrated Anglo-American operation until the end of the war.[49]

As far as Plante is concerned there is little hint in his letters of any of this high-level politicking. The move of some propaganda responsibilities to Italy in the fall of 1943 had done little to ease the intensity of the work required of Plante and his fellow Kasr El Aini artists as the weekly situation reports from Cairo in 1944 continued to indicate. The report for the week of 7–14 April 1944, for example, notes that "the Bulgarian and Rumanian leaflet campaign plus the material in preparation for the Yugoslav Partisan Conference and the special Greek leaflets extended the Production Section and the Process Dept. to the limit this week." The number of leaflets actually dropped fluctuated quite dramatically depending, as usual, on the weather and the availability of aircraft so that it was normal for Cairo to have some five hundred thousand leaflets in stock at the Kasr El Aini Press and another seven hundred thousand or so in stock at the airfields, ready to be dropped, as well as some further thousands in preparation. Even with the war progressing well there was to be no let-up in the Anglo-American propaganda offensive.[50]

As long as German soldiers remained in southeastern Europe, psychological warfare had a vital role to play in support of military operations there. The propagandists in Egypt continued the work in spite of bureaucratic uncertainties. An 11 May issue of *Soldaten-Nachrichten* led off with a front-page article on uninterrupted attacks on Romania and another on "Hot Ground in Sunny Dalmatia." In a graphic spread covering parts of the second and third pages of the newsletter an article entitled "How Are Operations Carried Out?" featured one of Plante's characteristically dramatic sketches of a British plane attacking the large German Möhne dams. Later famous as the "Dam Busters," the heroic pilots of this attack were memorialized in print and film.[51]

During the period from 19 to 25 May 1944 Cairo printed 20,300 36-page booklets and 10,000 40-page booklets. The week's report drew "particular attention . . . to the 36-page German magazine and the 40-page Nazidammerung booklets completed this week. Each presents considerable technical difficulties for the limited resources of K. A. Press and the finished booklets can only be described as a credit to all concerned in their production."[52]

The ups and downs of the complex Anglo-American relationship that was so critical to the successful outcome of the war reverberated throughout the propaganda offices in North Africa and Italy. By working well with Americans in Cairo and Bari, Plante played his own small part in cementing the Anglo-American alliance. Vellacott, who had recruited him, was now gone and the focus of the war was shifting north following the advancing Allied forces. With them went the propaganda personnel. Anticipating the possibility of a speedy end to all fighting in PWE's areas of responsibility it was even suggested that as the war inevitably wound down, PWE "should not now hold on too desperately to anyone who is only superficially qualified—either by knowledge of a language [Plante had German] or of a function of our work [in which Plante was highly experienced] but who is, at the same time, fit for active service." Apparently Plante had once again avoided being sent to slog away in the infantry.[53]

CHAPTER NINE

"[PWE produced] countless millions of copies of a vast collection of . . . special newspapers, magazines, leaflets and miniature books."

As the war progressed north the American Fifth Army advanced up the western side of the Italian peninsula while the British Eighth Army was simultaneously pushing up the eastern side. Together they comprised the Fifteenth Army Group under General Harold Alexander, engaged in the slow attritional warfare that characterized the fighting in Italy. With the capture of Rome in June, the Naples–Caserta area had become the center for Anglo-American activities in the country. Eventually, most of the PWB personnel engaged in propaganda were posted to Italy, among them Russell Barnes (as head of PWB AFHQ), Terry Harman (as deputy head), Brigadier W. F. Jeffries (as British military director), and Colonel Donald F. Hall (as American military director). In August they were joined by Ralph Murray as Balkans policy adviser. Within the closely-knit Anglo-American PWB organization this left Bari a mostly British PWE operation, with only a small contingent of Americans. Propaganda support for the Allied landings in the south of France that summer was largely a PWB operation and did not involve PWE propagandists in Cairo or in Bari. At the same time, Bari's functions were extended to include responsibility for Hungarian, Yugoslavian, and Albanian propaganda while Cairo, where Plante was still stationed, remained primarily responsible for Greece, Bulgaria, and Romania.[1]

The relationship of political propaganda to official policy, which Lockhart noted was always difficult, was especially so in the confusing situation now prevailing, although the close relationship with bombing policy remained a constant. The conditions in Italy were among the nastiest faced by the Allies anywhere as they struggled northward through what historian Brian Bond has described as "two appalling bleak winters: that of 1943–44 marked by almost continuous rain and freezing temperatures with the following winter the worst Italy had suffered in twenty years." In the Balkan area, military operations in the first half of 1944 were limited to supporting the activities of resistance movements and national liberation armies. In this situation, intelligence was never timely enough to carry out any tactical propaganda and PWE could only emphasize the long-term themes of encouragement to its allies and opposition to its enemies.[2]

Among Plante's signature contributions to propaganda during 1944 was his work producing covers and illustrations for miniature booklets of 30–35 pages. One of these booklets, aimed at Greece and called *Allied Voice,* had a photograph on the pale blue cover of paratroopers lined up preparing to board the planes of "our friends" the RAF and the American air forces. Included on the front cover and repeated on the back was the usual injunction to pass this booklet on to others after reading it. Placed at the head of one article, "Russia's Back Door," was a sketch by Plante of ships steaming in convoy on the Murmansk Run carrying desperately needed supplies to the USSR. Plante illustrated the article "The Liberation of Corsica" with a drawing of a bearded, pipe-smoking Italian partisan holding a rifle. For an article about America—the "arsenal of democracy"—Plante drew the famous New York skyline, with which he was so familiar, and on the next page he drew a scene with men at work in a factory. Plante headed an article on news of the war at sea with one of his characteristic sketches of a naval vessel under way, smokestack billowing and guns elevated. On the following page he added a sketch of two warships firing their great guns. For an article on German submarine losses, Plante drew a swastika-adorned U-boat exposed on the surface under a full moon near an Allied convoy. A final article in the booklet, on the

British Parliament, was adorned by Plante's sketch of the Houses of Parliament seen from across the River Thames.[3]

In addition to producing these booklets, Cairo also continued to churn out large amounts of printed propaganda in other forms. Operation Shingle, the Allied landings at Anzio, was the most significant news item emphasized by the PWE in January 1944. Although Anzio was a disaster, and the extraordinarily speedy German reaction kept the Allies contained and under constant fire until May, the propagandists gave it a positive spin. Leaflets and newssheets pointed to the importance of sea power to the success of the amphibious landings and leaflets aimed at bolstering Greek resistance noted the participation of Greek naval units in these actions. At the same time, to raise morale in all occupied countries and to confound enemies, "The gravity of Germany's general situation was continually stressed," as was "the unrest and discontent among the satellite countries." Cairo created and widely disseminated leaflets with Russia's warning to Bulgaria that she should break from Germany before it was too late, and newssheets reminded Romanians of their subjection to air raids and of the Russian advance on their territory. Other leaflets clearly pointed out Hungary's vulnerabilities.[4]

Arranging to transfer the printing of some leaflets from Cairo to Bari presented PWE/PWB with new challenges. In Cairo, the Production Section was able to work efficiently with local printers but in Bari, initially, they had had to supply all their own type, paper, metals, chemicals, transport, and even staff, in order to be able to produce the full range of publications now appearing in thirteen different languages—Italian, German, French, Slovak, Polish, Russian, Hungarian, Romanian, Albanian, Greek, Bulgarian, Turkish, Armenian—and in three Yugoslav dialects, Slovenian, Serbian, and Croatian. It took Bari more than seven days to produce its first leaflet and the result was "open to more than a little criticism," as their own year-end report freely admitted. In a business so dependent on the timeliness of the topic this delay was unacceptable and the sub-mission moved fast to accelerate the process.[5]

By December 1944 the situation in Bari had improved to such an extent that, under favorable circumstances, leaflets could be "conceived at five o'clock one afternoon, pass through the drafting, layout, proofreading, printing, packing, transport, briefing, and loading processes"—all except the printing being done directly by PWE/PWB personnel—and disseminated five hundred miles away by nine the next evening. By then, Bari was responsible for printing and disseminating not only its own leaflets for Yugoslavia, Hungary, and Albania, but had long since taken over the printing and dissemination of Cairo's leaflets for Greece, Romania, and Bulgaria, many leaflets produced by PWE/PWB in Naples for Italy, and leaflets produced by all three centers for German troops.[6]

The initial leaflet distribution problem from Italy was soon addressed when aircraft of 234 Wing were transferred from North Africa to airfields at Brindisi, on the heel of Italy. A chapter in PWE history was closed with the departure of the last RAF squadron from Tocra in Cyrenaica in January 1944. After their move to Italy, the aircraft were engaged mainly in supplying resistance movements in Greece, Albania, Yugoslavia, and Poland. On most of their sorties they also carried leaflets for dissemination. In addition, when they were available, aircraft from the wing made special sorties carrying only leaflets to targets chosen by PWE/PWB Bari.[7]

When American and British wings of the strategic Fifteenth Army Air Force also established themselves on the large complex of airfields at Foggia, PWE/PWB was able to negotiate new channels for leaflet dissemination. From March onward, some of the bombers in each formation, spread over a dozen bases in the area, began carrying leaflets, eventually as many as twenty thousand per plane, with the Americans flying by day and the British by night. In addition, when other commitments allowed, the planes of RAF 205 Group carried out lone leaflet missions over France, Germany, Austria, Italy, Czechoslovakia, Hungary, Romania, Albania, Bulgaria, and Greece. PWE/PWB increased the reach of its leaflets even farther when 267 Squadron established itself in Bari and when light bombers and fighter-bombers of the Balkan Air Force (BAF) undertook to carry leaflets to operational targets in the Balkans.[8]

Based in Bari, the Balkan Air Force was created in June 1944 to simplify command arrangements for air activities in the Balkans. It was subordinate to Mediterranean Allied Air Forces, the overall allied air formation in the Mediterranean, and had operational and administrative control of RAF formations operating over the Balkans as well as coordinating operations undertaken by the USAAF and the Italian air force in the same area. In addition to dropping leaflets for PWE/PWB, this multinational force, with men from eight nations, provided air support for SOE operations in the Balkans, including support for Yugoslav partisan groups.[9]

At this point in the war, the earlier hesitation among airmen to support leaflet dissemination had long dissipated, replaced by very effective cooperation. In December 1944, J. D. Stewart, head of the Bari PWE/PWB unit, submitted a year-end report to PWE London. Stewart's report gave two examples of the good relationship with airmen then prevailing. When the date for the invasion of Greece had been moved forward suddenly, the 15th Air Force flew three Liberators to Bari for the sole purpose of picking up leaflets, then flying with them directly to Athens because there was no time to have them delivered from Bari to their base. On another occasion, when all operational aircraft were otherwise engaged, "the Group Captain Commanding at Brindisi flew his own plane with a load of leaflets over heavily defended Sofia so that we should not miss our momentary propaganda targets."[10]

Gaining that kind of cooperation from the air forces was essential to leaflet dissemination, but another concern was the need to improve the accuracy of drops on targets. It had long been realized that "snowstorm" dissemination from heights of up to twenty thousand feet might suit large, sparsely populated areas, but was far less effective when dropped on towns and cities with their concentration of populations. In consequence, fighters and fighter-bombers attacking German targets in low-level raids were induced to also drop some leaflets. PWE/PWB now operated so close to the front lines that they could also arrange for forward artillery units in the Balkans to fire leaflet shells at appropriate German targets.[11]

In addition to dissemination of leaflets over the Balkans by air and by artillery, PWE/PWB organized the infiltration of large numbers of leaflets to various points in Yugoslavia, Albania, and Greece by naval vessels and by British or friendly forward units. For the benefit of resistance movements, the various military missions attached to them were regularly supplied with a large range of British and American publications. As Freya Stark noted with regard to her work in Cairo, "There is only one way of conducting lasting propaganda, and that is to work wholeheartedly for the people whose goodwill you are anxious to obtain."[12]

As successive towns in the Balkans were liberated, they were inundated with British and American display materials, newsreels, and feature films. This campaign was impressive in its numbers and reach. In the six weeks leading up to the end of October 1944, some five hundred thousand news and other leaflets representing over three hundred issues of more than a hundred different publications were infiltrated into Nazi-occupied areas in these ways. A further two hundred thousand publications from Cairo, Washington, and London were also dispatched, while Yugoslav partisans stationed on the Italian mainland also received publications.[13]

Many years later, Plante told his family of accompanying flights from Bari to drop leaflets over occupied territory. On these occasions, he said, he was issued the uniform of an army captain in case the plane went down. He also spoke of chatting with resistance fighters on these flights and of watching them parachute out into the night on their perilous missions. Most likely, these were Balkan Air Force flights.[14]

Although control of PWE activities in the Balkans was to be centered in Bari, propaganda intelligence and leaflet designs continued to be fed to Bari from Cairo, where Plante went on churning out sketches and paintings until his move to Bari in November 1944.

Increasingly, however, PWE Cairo forwarded only the matrices or the blocks for their anti-Nazi leaflets that were then to be printed in Bari. Payment for necessary supplies in Italy—always an issue for Plante in Cairo—was to be made from British or American funds, according to the country of origin of the supplies, making shortages much less of a problem given the abundance of American products. In a sign of the success of Anglo-American cooperation it was clearly understood that "all facilities available for psychological warfare against the Balkans, in whosesoever hands they now happen to be, should be pooled for the common effort."[15]

PWE's Bari headquarters—with postal address for private mail at 9. Polindep Unit (Political Intelligence Department, PWE's cover name, Unit 9) CMF (Central Mediterranean Force)—soon became the major leaflet-printing center for the entire Middle East and Mediterranean region as well as the main leaflet dissemination organization for the area. As the official historian of the PWE noted, "In nine months Bari produced almost *one billion leaflets* [emphasis added]—a production greater than that of PWE London during the same time." The Bari center was described as "something of a mongrel," perhaps because of its mix of nationalities and its civil–military mix. It also provided additional central and ancillary services such as news for the Balkan leaflet services as well as news for southeastern Italy and it was the liaison with Hungarian, Romanian, Bulgarian, and Greek country sections helping with leaflet production until the country sections themselves left Cairo for Italy.[16]

Bulgaria remained a challenge for the propagandists because of its convoluted politics. This, as elsewhere in the area, mostly involved a struggle for power between various right-wing groups sympathetic to the Nazis—including many of the military—and a number of Communist groups, some more influenced by the Soviet Union than others. The devastating Allied air raids on Sofia, beginning in late 1943, and the movement westward of the Red Army against the retreating Germans in 1944, reenergized pro-Nazi elements in Bulgaria, determined to shore up the German presence. It was in this climate that Kasr El Aini leaflets for Bulgaria became increasingly blunt. One single-sheet flyer with a heading designed by Plante showed a black cloud inscribed with one word only: "Recompense." The text read in part, "The bombs falling from the sky over Sophia are only a partial recompense. Each bomb that falls is fair repayment for the misery caused to your neighbors." A similar line had been taken with regard to the heavy bombing inflicted on Italy. Mussolini "insisted in participating in the bombing of England," one leaflet read, "and so doing sowed the wind and condemned [Italians] to harvest the tempest."[17]

A more elaborate leaflet with the question "Back to the Bloody Regime?" showed three knives dripping with blood, inscribed with the names of the leaders of the notorious 1923 military coup that was eventually endorsed by King Boris. "These three evildoers," the leaflet intoned, "whose indelibly bloodstained hands betray their bestial past, mean a revival of the system of man-hunts, of torture chambers, of traceless disappearances and of wholesale slaughter of opponents which became associated with their names in the past." The coup—still vividly remembered—had been a tragedy of the first order. The Bulgarian prime minister, Alexander Stambolisky, was a reformer and a democrat who was seized and brutally tortured to death. Many of his followers were then successfully hunted down and murdered in a similar manner. The large Bulgarian Communist Party did nothing, considering Stambolisky more of a threat than either the king or the army. According to the leaflet, three of the men implicated in the 1923 coup were now calling for a new, strong regime to ward off the Allied advance. If that were to happen, "countless thousands of Bulgarians will fall defending Germany against the final assault which is now commencing." On the reverse of the "Bloody Dagger" leaflet was the outline of a map of Bulgaria with a swastika-emblazoned dagger embedded in its heart. The caption read: "Bulgaria is an outpost of Germany. It could be a spearhead of the justice and freedom of all people. The decision rests with you. History awaits." This and other similar leaflets prepared in Cairo in 1944 were sent to Bari for printing and dissemination.[18]

By May 1944, the situation in Bulgaria had become so precarious that it was decided in Cairo to saturate the principal towns with leaflets as quickly as possible. Mats were sent to Bari where twenty-six thousand leaflets were especially printed and all were dropped in four nights, from Sophia in the west to Varna and Burgas on the Black Sea, and from Ruse on the Danube to Smolyan near the Greek frontier. Among these Bulgarian leaflets was one appearing under a drawing by Plante of a torrent of bombs raining down from the sky.[19]

In the case of Yugoslavia, by the summer of 1944 it was clear to the British government that Tito was the stronger of the two main resistance leaders and the one who might be able to secure Yugoslav unity, although those who favored Mihailović were still accusing Tito supporters of favoring Communism. In August, King Peter of Yugoslavia put an end to the issue when he dissolved General Mihailović's command and urged all Yugoslavs to rally behind Tito. At this point PWE/PWB organized a leaflet, poster, and radio campaign supporting the drive by Tito's Yugoslav Army of National Liberation, by Allied air forces, and by Allied landing forces against German lines of road and rail communications. The propaganda was also designed to drive home to the Germans their increasingly precarious position. The campaign was fully coordinated with the Allies' operational intentions by daily conferences with HQ Balkan Air Force.[20]

Meanwhile, British anxiety about the prospect of a takeover of Greece by the Communist-dominated Greek resistance group ELAS had been growing. Churchill had hoped to intervene in early 1944 on behalf of the Greek government in exile but could not get support from the Americans who were concentrating on the invasion of France. The predominance of British interests in the Eastern Mediterranean area and the divergence of British and American national policies there meant that propaganda activities in the region eventually became a mostly British operation with input from the OWI representing

American views. As Russian forces advanced into Romania and Bulgaria in the second half of the year, and as British landing forces made an appearance on various coastlines, PWE was able to frame part of its output to directly support specific operations. The situation for the Nazis and their allies began to deteriorate more rapidly and propaganda messages raced to keep pace with developments on the ground. British forces finally landed on mainland Greece in October and PWE/PWB supported the landings with leaflets and posters with messages from the Greek government, from the supreme Allied commander in the Mediterranean, General Wilson, and from the commander of Allied forces in Greece. Copies of these publications were printed in Bari and widely disseminated throughout Greece in the space of only a few hours.[21]

At the same time, PWE/PWB leaflet campaigns supported attacks against various German-held Dalmatian Islands as well as supporting British military and partisan operations in southern Albania. The situation on Corfu is perhaps most convincing with regard to the influence of psychological warfare. In mid-October the island was flooded with leaflets dropped at low levels by fighter-bombers demanding the surrender of the German garrison. "The reaction was immediate," according to Stewart's report from PWE/PWB Bari, "and the surrender was complete within eighteen hours of the falling of the leaflets." To be sure, Hitler was already withdrawing his forces from Greece to avoid their being cut off by the Soviet advance into Bulgaria and Hungary, and Athens itself was liberated that same day. Nevertheless, the evidence strongly suggests the positive influence of PWE/PWB's propaganda efforts, although this did not prove sufficient in the long run to forestall a Greek civil war.[22]

Late in the war, in addition to the tangled politics of the region, a number of other factors further complicated Allied propaganda initiatives in the Balkans. In the event of a German collapse, or withdrawal, there would have to be some clarification of the division of responsibilities between the Anglo-American and Russian high commands. It seemed clear that PWE/PWB would be unlikely to be allowed free scope for propaganda in Russian-occupied territory. According to Bruce Lockhart, many East Europeans in exile in London feared—presciently—that the Russian advance would be so rapid that they would settle these problems by occupation before the Allies were even ready to discuss them.[23]

At this point, all the propagandists could do was to look ahead to a postwar world and try to prepare the ground for future propaganda activities. It had always been understood that the liberation of any of the Balkan countries would involve a change in the character of the propaganda issued by PWE/PWB. Plans for new types of printed materials were drafted early in 1944 in Cairo and work had begun on some fifty new publications when the British element of PWE was transferred to Bari that October and November. By then much of the material dispatched from London and Washington was being channeled through the Bari Propaganda Servicing Unit, a change that can be clearly seen in the publications where Plante's later work appeared. Plante was assigned to produce work for countries beyond PWE ME's original area of responsibility. One of these assignments was to design the cover for a miniature booklet in French celebrating the RAF. *La RAF en Guerre*—to be dropped on France as the Allies advanced—was filled with photographs of British aircraft as well as articles on all aspects of the RAF at war. The cover showed a British fighter in the air against a sky blue background with the RAF red, white, and blue bull's-eye logo on the upper right hand side.[24]

At the end of October 1944 Plante had a few days leave and traveled up the Nile to Luxor. In general he had found Cairo "filthy, disease ridden, corrupt and completely unattractive," although he admitted that for people living as well as he did, with minimal contact with the *real* Egypt, it was "quite pleasant." On his arrival in Upper Egypt, however, Plante was forced to revise his opinion. He woke in his comfortable sleeper train to a most beautiful sunrise. "It shone through the palms and the waterlogged Nile Valley looked most thrilling." As Freya Stark observed, "very few tourists have any idea how agreeable the Egyptian country is; neither have the Egyptians, at any rate in the north, and you would think them unaware of anything between Cairo in the winter and Alexandria in the summer."[25]

In Luxor he found "the usual stench, squalor, goats, donkeys, their excretions, and millions of flies." He was even forced to buy a flywhisk. The only motor traffic he saw was a few Egyptian army trucks and vans, which had been given by the British to help fight the raging malaria epidemic. "These are used for joy riding by the Egyptian Army and are driven like mad through the town." But his hotel was near the river and he was delighted to pronounce it "really very good," with a freshly painted room, a luxurious bathroom attached, and a most impressive view of the Temple of Luxor. After dinner on the first evening in Luxor Plante met Sergeant Bruce, his assistant in the Production Unit who was just finishing his leave. Plante broke the news to him "that he was bound for Italy as my vanguard."[26]

Over the next few days Plante thoroughly enjoyed the sights, including the Temple of Karnack with its beautifully engraved pillars. The ruins of Roman columns on the grounds of the Temple of Luxor, by comparison with the Egyptian ones, looked "like toothpicks," and everything Roman was considered modern by the locals. After crossing the Nile on another day and enduring a harrowing donkey ride at a gallop, Plante visited the Valley of the Kings. He crept around the tombs holding candles, admiring the beauty of the pictures and symbols carved and painted on walls and ceilings. On the return he sailed on the Nile for a bit and watched "one of those glorious technicolour sunsets."[27]

On 2 November Plante took a side trip to Aswan staying at the Cataract Hotel. He visited the famous dam, completed in 1902 (predecessor of Nasser's gigantic Aswan High Dam project of the 1960s), as well as the granite quarries where the obelisks for the temples were hewn out of the sold rock. Cleopatra's Needle in London had come from there, as had the obelisks in New York, Paris, and Constantinople. The following day Plante took another donkey ride to the alabaster quarries, the source of all the alabaster used in the royal tombs.[28]

Plante's leave ended on Saturday 4 November and he returned to Cairo by train where he planned to equip himself for an Italian winter, putting his affairs in order before taking off for Bari. "The chances of my being posted to London in this job are non-existent," he explained to Evelyn. "The London equivalent just barely exists now. You see we are not needed much once a country is freed from the enemy. But if I can get a transfer to the US in some capacity it would be a wonderful opportunity—and you know I won't miss any chance." Optimistic as ever, he thought Italy would be a good ground for planning his future. Sergeant Bruce was in Bari already, and he himself was standing by, scheduled to leave by plane or boat, with only an hour or two notice to embark. That turned out to be the first week in November. "When the signal came through for me to leave I couldn't say I was exactly sorry, though I have some very good American friends here."[29]

Surely Plante wrote to Evelyn from Italy, but none of these letters have survived. Apart from the few anecdotes he enjoyed telling years later, the propaganda art he produced provides the best evidence of his activities in Bari. By the time Plante arrived there he joined a very diverse organization. The staff comprised British and American military and civilian personnel, foreign employees who had been hired in Cairo and transferred to Italy, refugees from half a dozen overrun countries, and numerous local employees totaling some seven hundred people. Together they ran five warehouses, handled 250 tons of paper a month, accumulated stockpiles for publications and sent forward masses of propaganda to missions in the Balkan countries.[30]

By then, though bitter and costly fighting went on until the very end of the war in May, sensibilities were shifting. Since the Allies were claiming to be "liberating" Greece, Albania, and Yugoslavia from Nazi tyranny they had to tread carefully. While the Germans had been driven out of mainland Greece in October 1944 they continued to occupy the Dodecanese Islands until the German surrender at which point they became a British Protectorate until 1947 when they were returned to Greece. One of Plante's contributions to this delicate interim situation was a miniature leaflet in English—"The

Dodecanese"—aimed at the British soldiers who were to occupy the Dodecanese Islands on their liberation from the Germans. "This book has nothing to do with planned military operations," read the information inside the front cover. "It deals only with civilian life in the Islands and the way you should behave to the islanders." Plante's pen-and-ink sketches illustrated the text throughout. He drew typical Greek street scenes; British Tommies, guidebook in hand, conversing with the locals; Greek fishing boats; and impressive classical ruins. In addition to conversational phrases and the Greek alphabet, the leaflet contained sections on Greek history and traditions, and one on "Do's and Don'ts." Over Plante's sketch of a bunch of men arguing, arms in the air, hats flying, is the wise admonition, "Don't talk local politics."[31]

Any attempt to control the indigenous publicity media—whether of newly liberated Greece or Albania or Yugoslavia—was bound to be deeply resented, particularly as PWE/PWB had been praising their local resistance movements so highly. The best that could be planned for the end of hostilities was to generate goodwill by supplying the media in those countries with the materials they lacked such as films, ink, and newsprint. In erstwhile enemy countries such as Romania and Bulgaria, the situation would be much simpler, assuming straightforward military control. The only question was—in the event of Russian occupation of Romania—what to do about Bulgaria? The contentious situation in Bulgaria continued until the very end of the war. When the Red Army approached Bulgaria in the summer of 1944, Bulgarian Communist forces incited a pro-Russian armed rebellion against the pro-Nazi government. But with the unanticipated Soviet declaration of war and invasion of Bulgaria in September, the Bulgarian government changed sides—like the Romanians a month earlier—and themselves joined the Soviets in the struggle against Nazi Germany.[32]

Although the war was moving fast it was far from over. The bloody battle of Budapest raged from December 1944 to February 1945, killing tens of thousands of soldiers and civilians. Shortly thereafter, the Soviets began their operation to seize Berlin, a battle that lasted from March to May of 1945. When Plante reached Bari, there were still over forty-five enemy divisions in action against the Allies in southeastern Europe. This was an even more extensive target than there was in Italy and it was Bari's responsibility to aim its propaganda at those forces. Even while the area under German control was shrinking, Bari still had a vital role to play in supporting military operations. In addition, the propagandists were now closer to the front lines than they had ever been, making it possible to conduct tactical propaganda, including the use of loudspeakers designed to capitalize on morale assessments done on the spot. Bari now also turned more of its attention to creating propaganda aimed at the liberated territories. It embarked on an extensive program of publications for infiltration to areas as soon as they were freed of their occupiers while also addressing the growing importance of Germany and Austria as targets, even after their forces evacuated southeastern Europe. A report from Bari issued in December 1944 claimed that practical results in these endeavors had "already been obtained."[33]

One of PWE/PWB's most persuasive arguments supporting the effectiveness of their propaganda efforts thus far, and one that appears frequently in the 1944 year-end report, is the evidence obtained from their liaison officers on the ground and from the interrogation of prisoners. Liaison officers in Yugoslavia, Albania, and Hungary, in addition to Greece, reported that Bari had a considerable audience amongst the locals, both for radio and printed propaganda. Interrogation reports from those areas, as from Corfu, also documented the effect of propaganda on the Germans. The 1944 report noted the "adequate evidence from all the Balkan countries that our leaflets have been seen and read by the population and the occupying Germans." They also noted that radio Bari was received widely in Yugoslavia, Albania, and Greece, broadcast publicly over loudspeakers in some towns. Radio Bari was less widely received in Hungary, though it was at least audible in Romania and Bulgaria. However, the report also acknowledged that evidence of reception was not in itself enough. "It is the action or reaction which follows which indicates the degree of success."[34]

Although not a great deal of information filtered out of the Balkans in the course of 1944, enough arrived to supply concrete examples of the good effect of PWE/PWB's propaganda output. PWE/PWB's year-end report gave specific success stories from Albania, Yugoslavia, Bulgaria, Greece, and Romania. In some of these cases, the titles of news leaflets had become household words with the populations to which they were directed. The reaction of Germans and German sympathizers also indicated that they, too, were very aware of the leaflets and concerned about their influence. This concern prompted them to produce some cleverly forged editions of PWE/PWB publications, which at first sight would pass for the real thing, giving misinformation to the intended recipients.[35]

Into this tangled morass of forces operating on Balkan politics was added the by now customary divisive ingredient: policy differences between the Allies. Many years later, whenever Plante mentioned his time in Bari, he spoke of the confusion over whether the PWE was supporting the Yugoslav resistance forces of Mihailović, favored by Britain, or those of Tito, favored by the Americans. Of course, by the time he arrived in Bari the question had just been settled in Tito's favor. But his vivid recollection—more than fifteen years later—of the ambivalent and sometimes contradictory directives he received on the subject is eloquent testimony to the influence on the propagandists of a political environment in flux.

Since Plante was working for an explicitly Anglo-American organization the uncertainties of national policy directly affected his day-to-day work and greatly complicated the task of propaganda. Nevertheless, as with his tales of belly dancers and giant cockroaches in Cairo, so Plante's reminiscences of his work in Italy were mostly not political, but personal and irreverent. He delighted, for example, in regaling the family with tales of a very attractive young woman who, in spite of her appeal, represented the closest he came to facing actual danger while working for the PWE. In all those years—he wrote in one brief account—he never incurred "any real personal risk, apart from dating a Yugoslavian Partisan girl with four hand grenades slung from her belt."[36]

In the months leading up to the German surrender and after, Plante was kept as busy as in Cairo making propaganda art. For the front page of an edition of *Pojeda,* the Yugoslav newssheet *Victory,* he drew a cartoon sketch of two swastika-adorned U-boats sinking bow first with a caption to the effect that "there go the best hopes for Germany." Plante also designed and painted the colored cover for a miniature booklet version of the Yugoslav magazine *Glas Pobede, The Voice of Victory.* The cover showed five soldiers, one each from Yugoslavia, France, America, Britain, and the USSR advancing together with rifles at the ready, each under his own nation's flag. The articles inside, profusely illustrated with photographs, showed some of the high points of Allied victories that included the successful Normandy landings, De Gaulle striding along in liberated Paris, American troops storming the French coast, American and British planes flying over Europe, Allied tanks driving past the Coliseum and Scottish pipers parading through Rome. On the back cover of the booklet was a photograph of Marshall Tito. All in all, the magazine was a persuasive demonstration of the military power and unstoppable success of the Allies.[37]

Bari's activities for the last weeks of 1944 and the first two weeks of 1945 were largely dominated by the crisis situation in Greece. On the withdrawal of German forces from Greece the Communist and Royalist guerrillas had reluctantly agreed on a coalition government, but the agreement disintegrated quickly. The first phase of a bitter civil war broke out that was suppressed with a good deal of bloodshed, and only temporarily, by British forces. Meanwhile, PWE/PWB Bari produced a number of leaflets devoted to calming the fast changing situation—as well as producing issues of the regular news leaflet *Tachydromos* (Postman)—and focused on ferrying these materials to Athens for onward dissemination by locally based aircraft.[38]

During the early months of 1945, the work of PWE/PWB Bari began to change from purely psychological warfare to efforts that could usefully be carried on after the liberation of occupied countries and even after the peace. As each country was liberated from Axis forces the responsibility for information services devolved from the PWE/PWB to the OWI on the American side and to the MOI on the British. Soon enough, like MacArthur's old soldier, the wartime propaganda apparatus itself would just fade away.[39]

In the interim, among the projects Plante worked on in Bari was a large format version of *Glas Pobede*, the magazine aimed at Yugoslavia. It had a monthly circulation of a hundred thousand and contained articles in Bosnian, Serbian, and Slovenian. *Glas Pobede* was part of the *Londinski Vestnick* (London Gazette) series that ran from 1944 to 1945. There is no indication on the magazine itself of its provenance although the back cover reads: "This magazine is dedicated to the people of Yugoslavia. When you have read it let others read it too." The magazine is filled with long articles with color illustrations and many photographs. By this time, the sophisticated Italian production facilities in Rome had been mobilized in the service of Allied propaganda enabling the superior printing of news pictures by the rotogravure process.[40]

Plante created the cover for issue No. 13 of March 1945. In somber earth tones he showed a crowd of square-jawed German soldiers in their characteristic flared-bucket helmets waving white flags with hands held high in surrender. Inside were articles on FDR's Tennessee Valley Authority bringing electrification to the countryside, the new democracy of the Chinese guerrillas, lots of photographs of happy English children in school and at play, and an article on Ernest Bevin, British trade unionist and minister of labour and national service in Churchill's war cabinet.[41]

Among other issues of *Glas Pobede* that he worked on, Plante created and signed the cover for No. 14 of April 1945, showing an obviously happy farmer shouldering a scythe and walking away from a ruined house with his wife and daughter. The message of the cover was that the family was moving on to a new and better future leaving the devastation of war behind. The articles inside, buttressed by many photographs, supported that theme. One was on the defeat of the Japanese unfolding in the Pacific, another about the miracle of DDT, and a third on planning a new, modern city.[42]

On 4 April 1945 PWE/PWB came out with issue No. 353 of *Nachrichten fur die Truppe* with the headline: "American Tanks Storm the Heart of the Reich—Nuremberg and Leipzig Are Threatened." Plante's contribution was a map on the front page showing that the Allied western and eastern fronts were now only 320 kilometers apart. Germany was being squeezed to death and Berlin was very close to being swallowed up by the advancing Russians. The end was near.[43]

April 1945—the eve of the surrender of German forces in Italy engineered by the head of OSS Europe—was a busy time for Plante. On the 13th of the month he produced a map for the front page of a Dutch newssheet, *De Vliegende Hollander*, showing the American Ninth Army approaching the Elbe River and Patton's forces racing toward Leipzig. He also produced maps for the front page of *Votre France*, a newssheet in French, as well as drawing headings for sections of the newssheet entitled "Presse Libre" (A Free Press) and "On Vous Attend" (We Await You) with advice for prisoners of war on their liberation and repatriation.[44]

Finally, Plante contributed to the 24 April issue No. 14 of *S. H. A. E. F.*, the four-page newssheet calling itself "The Daily Organ of Supreme Headquarters." The front page, with Plante's map showing the Allied forces converging on Berlin was in English, with following pages in French, German, and Polish. The purpose of the paper was clearly laid out by the editor in a special box on page one:

> Designed for the information of displaced persons, *S. H. A. E. F.* carries the official instructions of Supreme Headquarters for Allied nationals in unoccupied Germany and in areas recently occupied. The present issue contains standstill instructions to Russian and Polish nationals in the gap between the Allied and Russian armies, instructions for foreign workers recently

> liberated, and the United Nations warning about mistreatment of prisoners, internees and deportees.[45]

Germany finally surrendered to the Allies unconditionally on 7 May 1945 and PWE/PWB Bari integrated operations ended a week later with anticipated final closure of the agency by 26 May. Most PWB operations in Italy, as an integrated program, ended on 15 July. All leaflets in stock were pulped while all but a final core of staff, both civilian and military, were moved to Naples. Many of the other PWE regional sections for the occupied countries were also closing down. As a temporary department, which would not continue after the war, PWE headquarters in London had already been raided for personnel, particularly by the Foreign Office because of the foreign policy expertise of many of its members. Even before the war in Europe ended the Admiralty had taken back Lockhart's deputy, General Brooks, who some months later became commandant-general of the Royal Marine Corps.[46]

After the German surrender, the exodus from the PWE accelerated. And yet, although political warfare now seemed a misnomer, against all expectations PWE's work in Germany and the Far East had not decreased. Indeed, the process of gradually closing down was complicated, and even retarded, by the unexpected addition of new commitments. Military information services for Germany, though provided by the Psychological Warfare Division that had been created in early 1944, had been financed by the OWI and the PWE. As there were no other organizations to take up the slack of the OWI and the PWE, they were instructed to continue their functions for as long as a military government of Germany lasted. The two organizations handled this by immediately organizing a daily press service for Political Warfare Division.[47]

Plante's departure from PWE was tinged with the same enigmatic aura that infused all his war stories and, like many of them, was somewhat hazily corroborated in interviews he gave years later. In 1975 he was asked to contribute a series of autobiographical essays to

Campaign magazine, discussing his thirty years in advertising. Setting the scene in the first of those essays he noted that at the end of the war in Europe the Foreign Office "must have pressed a few buttons or pulled a few wires" because he "unexpectedly" found himself working "in an American Intelligence Office in Grosvenor Square" in London. This sheds light on the American slant to the propaganda work Plante produced next, much of it clearly derived from information provided by OWI.[48]

After the war, Lockhart praised the wartime cooperation between OWI and PWE largely crediting the Americans, especially Bob Sherwood. The materials Plante kept in his collection make clear that this cooperation between British and American information services continued into peacetime. Not long after the German surrender, OWI produced a large (12 by 9 inches) magazine called *Heute* (Today) the first issue of which offered a German populace starved of news of the outside world a remarkable introduction to what had actually been happening since 1939. The magazine's sixty-three pages were replete with photographs and accompanying text covering most of the high points of what it termed the "Sechs Jahre Weltkrieg," or "Six-Year World War." On the back of the magazine, in German, was the following: "Issued on Behalf of the US Information Service. Enquiries should be addressed to 'Editor, Heute, Information Control Service, APO 757, US Army,' or submitted to the nearest military government office." There is also the PWB/PWE country designation "USMG1," (U.S. Military Government), for propaganda leaflets intended for German consumption.[49]

"The United Nations have fought a two-front war against the Axis Powers," the opening *Heute* article proclaimed in German. "The war in Europe ended victoriously; the war in the Far East continues." There followed a photographic history of the war from the Italian campaign in Abyssinia in 1935 through the Japanese invasion of China in 1937, the London Blitz of 1940, Dunkirk, the Japanese ambassador in Germany, Panzers attacking the Soviet Union in 1941, the attack on Pearl Harbor, Rommel in North Africa, Operation Torch and General

Eisenhower, Guadalcanal, Midway, Stalingrad, Tarawa, the liberation of Paris, the U.S. return to the Philippines, and finally, the German surrender on 7 May. Next came a photo essay on English women doing men's factory jobs and their important contribution to the war. This was followed by five pages of text and harrowing photographs describing the Holocaust. Photos and biographies of several generals—Montgomery, Eisenhower, Zhukov, and De Gaulle—preceded an article on the progress of the war in the Far East. Four pages of photos of the destruction wrought by German forces in the Netherlands led to an article about how the democracies mobilized for war and the part played by trade unions and other labor organizations, and more.

The subheading of one article, "Convoy to Murmansk," read: "The United Nations surmounted the greatest difficulties to keep the Russians supplied with vital war materiel on the North Cape route." Three following pages told the tale of the perilous Murmansk Run brought to life by Plante's three-quarter page illustration of an Allied convoy fighting off German air attacks, and another half-page sketch of the successful unloading of cargo in Russia. Here his art was harnessed to support immediate postwar propaganda explaining the Allied victory over Germany while the "United Nations" were still united and Zhukov could be depicted standing heroically next to Eisenhower, Montgomery, and De Gaulle.[50]

In the meantime, on 12 May, Plante contributed a number of sketches to the newssheet *Die Wochenpost* (the Weekly Mail) one on "Democracy," depicted by an open book, and another "Ratsel" ("Mystery") showing a man with paper, pen, and ink trying to solve a variety of crosswords and other word puzzles.[51]

Allied propagandists understood that immediately after the end of hostilities the situation in many previously German-occupied countries would be tense and uncertain, particularly those where the government had collaborated with the Nazis. This was true of Norway and Plante was put to work on the delicate job of helping facilitate the transition to peace by illustrating a miniature booklet explaining the devastation caused by the Nazis and their complete defeat by the

Allies. The booklet, *Det Frie Norge* (Free Norway), appeared in May 1945 and was filled with photographs of significant recent events. These included an account of the death of President Roosevelt the previous month, maps showing the shrinking size of the Third Reich and the territories under its control in the early months of 1945, the destruction of German cities by Allied bombs, and an address by Foreign Secretary Anthony Eden.[52]

Plante's contribution to the booklet was a full-page pen-and-ink sketch of a German military motorcyclist at a fork in a forested road following a sign pointing the way to a German engineer battalion. The caption above the sketch reads: "German Tactical Signs and Markers" and the message to Norwegians anticipated postwar prosecutions of Germans for war crimes. Norwegians were told that it was important to learn the German signs and markers in order to be able to distinguish between the different departments so that they could accurately answer questions about German war crimes they had witnessed. They were assured that this knowledge would provide valuable help to Norwegian and Allied forces when the time came. Plante filled the next three pages of the booklet with hand-drawn illustrations of German signs with translations in Norwegian.

Transatlantic magazine—with thirty-four issues published by Penguin between September 1943 and June 1946—was another effort put out with the cooperation of the information services. The lofty goal of the series was to "assist the British and American peoples to work together in majesty and peace!" As Plante was already determined to continue a close association with America and Americans, he must have welcomed the opportunity to help strengthen a postwar Anglo-American alliance from his new post in the American Intelligence Office in London. The June 1945 issue of *Transatlantic* described its cover as "an unusual view of the RCA Building in Rockefeller Centre. It was drawn by George Plante from a photograph by Paul J. Wolf." Plante's rendition showed the immensely tall, floodlit RCA building rising high into the night sky, reflecting the bright stars surrounding it, a romanticized version of a scene Plante knew well. Four of the major articles in the magazine were by Americans—writers and journalists—dealing with subjects as varied as "some aspects of the Southern race problem," and a photographic essay about Pittsburgh. The British editor of the magazine addressed the "War efforts, US and UK," in his "Transatlantic Commentary" section. While all the many advertisements were for British products such as Peek Frean's ("Britain's Crispest Biscuits") and Guinness beer, some of the photographs were credited to the OWI. To emphasize even further the ongoing Anglo-American partnership, it was pointed out that the British editor of *Transatlantic* worked on the magazine in collaboration with the American Writers' War Board in New York.[53]

Plante painted at least one other *Transatlantic* cover—that of August 1945. It showed a weathered cowboy in checked shirt and bandana holding his saddle while cattle in the background grazed on the prairie that stretched out to the distant mountains. The content of this issue included a topographical and political map of the northeastern region of the United States and an insert showing the five boroughs of greater New York with adjoining areas of New Jersey and Westchester. A full-page, full color ad by Plante extolling "Guinness for Strength" featured a line of longshoremen struggling to carry one large crate each from a ship down a gangway to shore. The punch is delivered by showing one longshoreman easily carrying a stack of ten crates while proudly balancing a bottle of Guinness on the very top.[54]

By the summer of 1945, Plante had spent two years devoting his creative talents to support his country's psychological warfare goals. At the end of that time it is fair to ask whether his work and that of his colleagues in political warfare had any significant influence. Obviously, the PWE wanted to know the same thing and over the years of its existence it had taken considerable effort to determine the effectiveness of its propaganda. It routinely monitored neutral and enemy media for reaction to its radio broadcasts and leaflets. It also studied the transcripts from interrogation of enemy prisoners of war as well as examining captured documents and other sources. The results of these investigations were circulated to interested parties in "Evidence of Reception" reports.[55]

However, in a postwar conversation Colonel L. G. Barbrook, who took over PWE/PWB Bari after J. D. Stewart left, maintained that "the chief lack which Bari felt was intelligence regarding the effects of their propaganda." Having spent five years in the Albanian Police Force before the war, Barbrook certainly knew the territory and would have been a well-informed observer. He obviously believed the lack of feedback regarding their work was a substantial weakness. A 1949 top secret report on the major developments in political warfare during the war, prepared for the records of the historical section of the cabinet office and based on all the available official documents, suggested that in fact very little was known of the effect of the leaflets or the broadcasts. The evidence that did exist, the report stated—and other sources suggested—consisted mostly of the numbers of those who read the leaflets or heard the radio broadcasts, rather than the effect they generated.[56]

In Britain, an elaborate system of weekly "Home Intelligence Reports" was developed. These reports were sent to the MOI from thirteen regional offices to help assess, as accurately as possible, British public opinion, and to guide the ministry in its creation of propaganda. Obviously, such an institutional approach was not available when dealing with enemy and enemy-occupied territories. Moreover, David Welch, noted historian of propaganda, points out that how we measure success when it comes to propaganda remains "a recurring issue."[57]

In his memoir of his years at the helm of the PWE, Lockhart noted the "countless millions of copies of a vast collection of printed material in the form of special newspapers, magazines, leaflets and miniature books" that PWE had sent out. He admitted that it was difficult to estimate the result of this enormous effort and that opinion at the highest levels was divided. Perhaps surprisingly, he also believed that political warfare and propaganda had a "most noxious influence," but that in war they were a "necessary evil." Lockhart maintained that in total warfare results are not to be gauged only by their effects on frontline troops. There were other ways to contribute to the collapse of the enemy will to resist and British leaflets had played their part in the demoralization of the German people. By holding close to the truth, he wrote, PWE's propaganda was also the single most important factor in sustaining British influence in the occupied countries. It provided the only news from the outside world, kept alive the hope of victory, and nurtured resistance movements.[58]

Military historian Brian Sullivan, an authority on Italy in the World War II era, noted that several Italian friends of his were children or adolescents living in northern Italy from 1943 to 1945. They told him of their great appreciation of British broadcasting and leafleting in that period. Their families were old anti-Fascists, some of whom had died in prison while others were still imprisoned. Some of those men had joined the partisans. "To listen to the BBC at night, read leaflets and pamphlets urging resistance and promising liberation were," according to what they told Sullivan, "a source of hope and encouragement at a time of hunger, bombing, deportations to labor in Germany and Nazi-Fascist terror. It's impossible to quantify or get human statistics on such communication and the comfort it brought," Sullivan concludes, "but there is no doubt about how precious it was."[59]

Harold Macmillan, the wartime resident minister in North Africa and Italy, agreed, as did General Eisenhower. After the capture of Naples, Eisenhower had praised the important work of the PWE/PWB in encouraging the friendly and cooperative attitude of the Italians and he later testified that political warfare had "unquestionably made its contribution as an integral part of the fighting forces." But others disagreed and such evidence as exists is largely anecdotal. Arguing statistically, Richard Overy, in his comprehensive study of the air war over Europe, maintains that "on the actual effect of leaflet drops the evidence remains speculative." Max Hastings' assessment was blunt: "The military achievements of resistance were very modest," he wrote, "the moral ones immense." Bruce Lockhart, who was heavily invested in ensuring maximum PWE successes, was nevertheless under no illusions as to the effectiveness of propaganda that in his opinion could never "replace military success."[60]

If it is impossible to gauge with any confidence the effect of propaganda on the course of World War II, the significance of George Plante's contribution to the war is less difficult to assess, in part because characteristic examples of the two distinct forms of his work survive. At the very least it can be said that his contribution was an unusual one. There were not many war artists altogether, and there were even fewer whose wartime artistic output was produced in two such totally different spheres.

His life in uniform and out, the rhythms of his occupations at sea and ashore, the expectations of productivity, the weather, the climate, the topography, and the geography in which he labored—each was dramatically distinct, one from the other. As a painter documenting the war at sea he was his own boss, directed only by his own artistic inclinations, following his own timetable and working alone. To be sure, he had other duties to perform as radio officer and as a member of a militarized crew, but after the first year at sea these were limited. His working conditions, though, were hardly conducive to the production of art of any sort. The constant motion of a ship at sea, the incessant noise of the engines, the eternal comings and goings of a busy crew, and the ever-present exposure to the elements certainly challenged any activity involving the careful application of images to paper. Perhaps the most inhibiting factor of all was that from the moment his ship sailed until the moment it arrived back in port, George Plante was in danger. His creative output in light of these impediments was a tribute to his powers of concentration, to his dedication to his art, and to his confidence in the importance of what he was doing. In so far as he was engaged in propaganda it was indirect, as part of a cultural offensive.

Working for the PWE was altogether different. In Cairo, Plante was one cog in a complex machine. He worked as part of a largely civilian team to meet demanding deadlines imposed from the outside and was required to produce art to meet the very specific needs of a direct political propaganda offensive. On the other hand, he worked in a clean, bright studio with minimal distractions, with no other responsibilities, and with generally adequate if at times skimpy materials. And although he had to work in the heat he was otherwise sheltered from the elements, his drawing board did not heave and buck, and he was never in danger.

Plante had been a novice when introduced to each of these two very different worlds, yet he adapted to each. In each he produced enduring art and left a rich legacy that broadens our understanding of the extraordinary tapestry of war. Beyond that, in the course of his work he learned much from his experiences. He found a way to develop his own skills and artistic sensibilities in each situation and he nurtured an Anglo-American spirit that stood him in good stead for the rest of his life.

CHAPTER TEN

"All these things evolve through a process of constructive thinking. It's not just mad, wild inspiration."

In July 1945, only two months after the Allied victory in Europe and while the war still raged in Asia and the Pacific, Britain held a general election. To the profound shock of many Americans, Winston Churchill was swept out of office by a weary nation that looked to Clement Attlee and the Labour Party to repair the war-ravaged economy. With the defeat of Japan, when the Americans left Britain for home, the new prime minister wished them good luck. In the last London edition of the U.S. Army paper, *Stars and Stripes*, Attlee said "Now, with the immense tasks of war brought to a glorious conclusion, we look forward to continuing an ever-growing friendship with the United States in the achievements of peace."[1]

But the friendship had changed in the course of the war. While the United States was virtually unscathed, Britain had lost one quarter of its wealth and two thirds of its export trade. Food rationing continued more stringently than ever. It even came to include such staples as bread and potatoes once the United States stopped Lend-Lease food shipments—which by one account had been "a savior for democracy." Clothing was also in short supply, and the bombings had left millions of Britons without permanent housing, many living in makeshift homes of wood and corrugated iron. Bomb damage was still in evidence for much of the next decade and some rationing continued well into the 1950s. The country was virtually bankrupt and it would take years to restore the economy and begin serious rebuilding. As the correspondent Edward R. Murrow had broadcast from England to his fellow Americans, "We are the only nation engaged in this war which has raised its standard of living since the war began. We are not tired, as all Europe is tired."[2]

For six years Britain's production had been devoted entirely to the war, while the United States had been able to continue to produce some consumer goods. It is true that, among other measures, American civilian automobile construction had been suspended, food rationing had been imposed, and civilian housing construction stagnated, but when Plante visited New York he always found the standard of living and the availability of goods astounding. Once peace was restored, the United States was soon in a position to supply not only its own domestic needs but also to flood world markets, including many previously dominated by Britain. By then, too, many Americans were tired of supporting Britain, while most members of Congress had only reluctantly approved the Lend-Lease program in the first place, and only as a wartime measure. They ended it immediately. As soon as Japan announced its surrender, American ships bound for all allied countries were ordered home. Since British agricultural production had been disrupted by war this sent the nation's already meager food supplies plummeting causing severe shortages and driving the Attlee government into economic cooperation with the Soviets, a consequence surely not foreseen by the U.S. Congress.

Ultimately, after considerable wrangling, the United States agreed to help Britain out of its financial crisis with a $3.5 billion loan. But the price exacted in return was steep, and to many Britons—and even to some Americans—unfair. Britain had had little choice but to agree to the plan hammered out at Bretton Woods, New Hampshire, in 1944 creating a new international economic order by, among other things, making the dollar the world's leading currency and greatly benefiting U.S. trade in general. Harry Hopkins, one of Roosevelt's closest advisers, believed these terms were unacceptably harsh given that Britain had twice "saved" the United States—once with France in 1917–18 and again, alone, in 1940. But Truman and his advisers did not share Roosevelt and Hopkins' understanding of the importance of the Anglo-American alliance. They were focused on the future and the looming Cold War, not on the past. It was only with the advent of the Marshall Plan in 1948 that Britain could begin to emerge from the economic prostration caused by the war.[3]

In addition, Britain still had many worldwide responsibilities that helped to slow its recovery. Paramount among these was the need to keep large numbers of troops under arms until well into 1948 to police the empire. British troops were engaged in keeping peace in Palestine, preventing the worsening Moslem-Hindu slaughter in India, and disarming the large number of Japanese troops in Indochina and the Dutch East Indies. Britain also had a large occupation zone in Germany, which, particularly after the Cold War turned serious in 1948, required a considerable army stationed there. Moreover, unwilling totally to cede British global power, Attlee felt he had to undertake the enormous expense of developing nuclear weapons since Congress passed the McMahon Act in 1946 forbidding the United States from sharing nuclear weapons technology with Britain.

In spite of this continuing global presence, it was clear to many that Britain had dropped to a position of strategic dependence on the United States that now assumed a dominant role in the partnership and on the world stage. Nevertheless, even in the face of serious challenges, the transatlantic special relationship survived the peace—much to the advantage of both nations. This was particularly important as they joined forces to confront the threat of a hostile Soviet Union. Many Britons who had worked closely and well with Americans during the war continued to do so after its end, Plante among them. He himself benefited directly from his wartime experience and from the contacts he had made, although in an economic environment where even necessities were scarce, advertising must have seemed like a quixotic career choice.

In May 1941, Plante had heard from a former colleague in London that in an effort to keep advertising agencies going until after the war, Everetts Advertising had joined a kind of studio pool where four studios cooperated to work together from one office. He hoped it would work. "I can tell you one thing I'm sure of," he wrote his wife at the time, "and that is that if any agency survives, Everetts will be the one." But Plante had returned from war a changed man, not just because of the suffering and carnage he had witnessed but more because he had been introduced to another side of life—one that was affluent, urbane, and cosmopolitan. In Manhattan he had come face-to-face with the real life he had seen previously only in glossy images in American magazines and he was attracted by what he saw. Moreover, his time spent visiting American advertising agencies and his growing familiarity with their work greatly increased his appreciation for how the modern advertising methods they were developing led to increased competition to improve products and to broaden their dissemination.[4]

Young & Rubicam, the advertising agency that had shown an interest in Plante's work when he was in New York with the Merchant Navy, was often regarded as the first "creative" agency in America. Since the 1920s it had been a mecca for talented creative types, as it had been for Plante. With offices at 285 Madison Avenue, Y&R was the reason that the term "Madison Avenue" had become shorthand for the advertising industry as a whole. After the war, the national and international situation spurred a rapid flowering of American advertising. At home, wartime profits enabled businesses to expand, sparking a rush to retool from military production back to domestic goods as businesses hastened to meet the long pent-up consumer demand. The G.I. Bill put money in the pockets of sixteen million veterans and a soaring birth rate further increased the pressure for more and better goods. Defense spending and foreign aid—particularly through the Marshall Plan—enabled war-stricken countries to purchase American products, further stimulating the economy as well as the advertising industry that both drove demand and grew with it.

As a result of Plante's keen interest in these developments his ambitions had changed and he did not return to Everetts, having set his heart on continuing to work with Americans. No doubt this decision was made all the easier by the difficult economic situation in

England. Working for a prosperous American company had obvious advantages in postwar London, but the risk of going into advertising was still great. Scarcities of all sorts meant that British newspapers could only muster four pages and magazines, as Plante recalled, "were slender, and reproduction dreadful." "Colour wasn't available," he continued, "and photographic materials [were] in short supply."[5]

Even during the war years, however, Young & Rubicam had flourished and in 1943, not long before buzz bombs would begin falling on London, it opened an office there, its first outside North America. It was only natural that when he was released from his wartime service obligations, Plante should be one of the first British employees hired by Y&R's American managing director in London. Looking back years later, Plante wrote that "the scale and professionalism of American advertising appealed to me, but the life-style of London suited me better."[6]

In Cairo, Plante had learned how his art could influence behavior and his work in the ad business now reflected what he had learned, especially as he was not alone in his appreciation for American advertising. The large numbers of Americans living in Britain during the war, civilians as well as military, brought with them many new ideas, looks, and products that inevitably influenced British attitudes and interests. Just the exposure to the apparent affluence of even ordinary G.I.s changed the way Britons viewed their world making them ever more aware of the material comforts previously unknown to them.

Thus the end of the war ushered in a change in advertising in Britain as the industry gradually moved closer to the rapidly evolving American ideas and practices. In October 1945 a group of British advertisers set up an organization called the Advertising Creative Circle. Its major objectives were to raise the general status of advertising in Britain "by encouraging high standards of creative skill, and of providing opportunities for the interchange of ideas amongst advertising creative people." Membership was by invitation only and at first was limited to fifty individuals of whom Plante was one.[7]

For the next thirty years, Plante's career in advertising was marked by the same embrace of change that had enabled him to weather the extraordinary shifts in his wartime environment and occupation. Y&R prospered in Britain, as did he. He quickly rose to be creative director, staying at the leading edge of developments that took him from print, to black-and-white television, to color television, and to film. He was always creative, innovative, and eager to try something new.

While much of Plante's work for Y&R involved the promotion of specific products such as Lifesavers, Mars chocolate bars, Fairy Liquid detergent and Fairy Snow soap flakes, he also kept his hand in with some sketches that had much in common with his wartime propaganda caricatures. The December 1951 issue of *Advertiser's Weekly*, for example, featured a two-page spread of Plante cartoons headed "THE AGENCY AS SEEN BY THE CLIENT (as feared by George Plante)." The sketches included caricatures titled the "Managing Director," the "Art Director," the "Home Economist," the "Copywriter" (female), the "Research Man," and others. Plante drew the Managing Director with a bag of golf clubs over his shoulder; the Copywriter was a chain-smoking, hard-bitten journalist with hat and large glasses, wreathed in cigarette smoke, pounding away at an ancient typewriter. Plante's Home Economist was shown standing bemused, with a wooden spoon in hand, beside a stove holding a bubbling pot and young children clinging to her apron. Plante lampooned himself as the Art Director, bearded and barefoot, standing before his easel in a smock. In front of him was a voluptuous nude model holding a box of soap powder but the image the artist was painting, with a gleeful smile, showed only the box of detergent.[8]

Plante's complaints to Evelyn about the hygiene and sartorial habits of his fellow countrymen in Cairo found a strong echo in an article he illustrated for the *Sunday Graphic* in 1954. The first sentence of the article, "Could it be You?" by Phyllis Digby Morton, the glamorous British fashion journalist, made clear its point: "A man who will work hard for hours polishing his new car wouldn't dream of giving his teeth the same attention." "Brush up—or be brushed off," she admonished.

"Bathe daily or you'll be in hot water. Eat badly and you'll eat alone." The strong American influence in this campaign against British slovenliness was openly avowed. The article advised men to take care of their teeth, to bathe and use deodorant, and to avoid cleaning teeth at the table "with tongue or fingernail," if they wanted to look like "those lovely full-page color advertisements in American magazines . . . of college boys or diplomats brandishing mouthwashes, deodorants, talcum powers etc."—or if they wanted to have Gregory Peck's dazzling smile.

As Plante had learned in his work for the PWE, good information about the prospective audience for propaganda was critical. One of the uphill battles he waged at Y&R for many years was to sell British men on the use of those health and hygiene products that market research confirmed were widely considered slightly effeminate. He later wrote that the campaign for Gleem toothpaste, for example, "which had been so successful in the States, didn't have the same impact in Britain, where people didn't give a damn about cleaning their teeth." Plante's contribution to Phyllis Digby Morton's *Sunday Graphic* article was just one effort in this long battle. It was a drawing of an unkempt, paunchy man smoking a pipe and holding a mug of beer. Tags surrounding him pointed to "six-monthly haircut," "wipe out those stains [on his jacket front]," "pockets stuffed with junk," "forsaken fingernails," "waistline gone to seed," "trousers crying for a press," and finally, "shine those shoes." Here Plante put to good use the classic psychological warfare technique of lampooning bad behavior in order to elicit change.[9]

During his years at Y&R Plante also spearheaded numbers of products that were standard by then in America, but were still novel and often viewed with suspicion in Britain. At that time, most British housewives shopped for food daily. Many still did not have refrigerators at home or if they did they were small, with minimal freezer space if indeed they had any. Selling women on the benefits of frozen vegetables was another long, slow slog and one that depended on the improving economy, the increased availability and affordability of consumer products such as refrigerators, and the change in daily habits of British housewives. The Birds Eye brand, promoted by Y&R, eventually took off, helped by Plante's frozen peas campaign and by the increasing number of women entering the workforce. The same was true of one of Plante's other notable ad campaigns for Gibbs SR toothpaste; it ran the first commercial shown on British television on the opening night of ITV, the independent channel that broke the BBC's television monopoly and its freedom from ads.[10]

In 1951, when his American boss returned to New York, Plante was offered the managing directorship of Y&R in England. He rejected it "because I couldn't see myself having any satisfaction with my struggles to read and understand balance sheets, the leasing arrangements for office buildings, and so on, while trying to explain the English way of doing things to someone constantly breathing down my neck from New York." Also, by then he was separated from Evelyn and anticipating a painful divorce and he did not think he could undertake the social side of the job, with all its required entertaining. Moreover, he had fallen in love with an attractive and vivacious young American woman who was also in the process of disentangling herself from an unhappy marriage. So instead of accepting a promotion he continued at Y&R London as deputy managing director and creative director.[11]

In 1956 George Plante and Jane Shenfield married in the London suburb of Hampstead, where they lived until they moved to the United States in 1980. Their Anglo-American ménage mirrored the close ties still maintained by the two nations. That same year Cairo was in the news again and this time the "special relationship" with Britain almost foundered less than fifteen years after it had passed its first test on those same North African shores.

The Suez Crisis was a total disaster for the British government. When the United States abruptly stopped funding the construction of the Aswan Dam on the Nile River that summer, Britain also withdrew its support. In response to the denial of funding, Gamal Abdel Nasser, Egypt's president since the overthrow of King Farouk, nationalized the Suez Canal and took over its operation and collection of transit fees that had been handled by Britain and France since the canal's construction in the nineteenth century.[12]

Given Britain's desperate struggle to defend the critical waterway during the war, the canal's continuing importance for access to Middle Eastern oil, and its historic significance as a vital link through the Mediterranean to overseas dominions, the British determined to stop Nasser, even in the face of U.S. opposition. Although lacking American support, Britain did not have to go it alone. British and French troops landed at Port Said on 5 November and headed down the canal toward Cairo, with Israeli forces already in the vanguard. On 6 November Eisenhower, who won reelection overwhelmingly that same day, demanded an immediate ceasefire in Egypt. Clearly grasping the bind they were now in, and perhaps influenced by public opposition in Britain to the invasion, the British (to the fury of the French and the Israelis) agreed to withdraw their forces. The Suez fiasco demonstrated definitively the change in the Anglo-American alliance. Not only was Britain obviously the junior member of the special relationship, but it had declined to such an extent that it had sunk from "great power" status to that of a middle-ranking power.[13]

Thinking back to the patronizing attitude of so many British involved in decision-making toward Americans during the war, the Suez Crisis must have been a seriously damaging blow. No wonder Plante followed the events closely. Like those who had early thrown their weight behind cooperation with America, he had chosen a winning strategy. And yet, it cannot have been easy to watch Britannia lose her far-reaching power, status, and worldwide empire. What bothered Plante most about the debacle was not just that he recognized how it brought into glaring focus Britain's change in status nor even that it challenged the Anglo-American relationship he valued. His most vivid reaction was worry about the plight of his Anglophile Egyptian friends. The speedy resolution of the crisis was a huge relief. Eventually, his old friend Milo left Nasser's Egypt and moved to New York; Plante remained in touch with him for many years. Apparently Seddy and Max left Cairo too—for the UK. In 1963 a notice in the *London*

Gazette showed that Seddy Beauty Products (London) Limited had been dissolved although no record has been found of how long it had been in existence nor whether Plante had maintained any contact with the owners.[14]

Another friend who influenced Plante's wartime career continued to play an even more important part in his postwar life than did his Egyptian friends. This was Robert Harling, Ian Fleming's former colleague in naval intelligence. When the masterful PWE black propagandist Sefton Delmer first met Harling in Fleming's NID office, he described him as "a young man with the laughing, big-eared, long-nosed face of a medieval court jester and the shrewd appraising eyes of a physician." Fleming thought so much of his friend Harling that he named the Nassau commissioner of police for him in his novel, *Thunderball*. After the war, Harling became the editor of *House & Garden* magazine. The cover of the January 1960 issue featured George and Jane Plante's new house in the London suburb of Hampstead. Harling's article about the house, "An unusual experiment in a modern house," revealed both his jester's nature and his shrewdness. "*House & Garden*, having introduced client and architect," he noted, "here reports with some relief, on a felicitous conclusion to this dangerous practice." Those who did not know of the wartime exploits of Harling and Plante could hardly appreciate the appropriateness of the comment. Both men had embraced humor, experiment, and dangerous practices, and both continued to do so in their later careers.[15]

Plante was described in the article as "a director of Young & Rubicam, one of the top advertising agencies in the world. He is also an established artist whose paintings have been shown in London and New York. His work gives him an absorbing interest in the whole field of design. His American wife and wide experience of life in America have added to his enthusiasm for the freedom and comfort that a really well-designed modern home can give."[16]

Trevor Dannatt, the architect recommended by Harling, went on to a highly successful career and a fellowship in the Royal Society of Arts. But in 1960 he was just getting started and audaciously created a one-story semi-courtyard plan with ceiling-to-floor windows; the house was tucked into what before had been an orchard. Although screened from the street by walls and trees, the house caused considerable consternation among the neighbors, ensconced in their large, formal, red-brick Edwardian homes. Indeed, many condescendingly called the house a bungalow, equating it with the cheap, single-story homes put up in Britain in the interwar depression. Others felt antipathy toward what was seen as an American-style house, reflecting the resentment felt by many and the injured pride of those who had suddenly become junior partners. Evidently, the readers of *House & Garden* were more discerning; they were certainly more receptive to modern trends in architecture and design.

Fifteen years later, the Plantes' house was again featured in *House & Garden*, this time with four pages of photographs demonstrating "the unusual flexibility of the original plan," as the owners adapted to their new status as empty nesters. "These adaptations come naturally to George and Jane Plante," the article maintained, "for they must be amongst the most resilient couples in Britain." Later still, their home was also featured as a cover story in a coffee table book published by *House & Garden*.[17]

During these years, and certainly helped by his knowledge of American trends, Plante carved out a respected name for himself in the advertising industry. He kept a substantial collection of clippings from industry publications such as *Advertiser's Weekly*, in which he was frequently interviewed, quoted, and photographed, often at social events with his glamorous American wife. Years later, in an autobiographical article for the advertising magazine *Campaign*, Plante explained that once Y&R had business from virtually all the important packaged goods companies, they decided to diversify. "It wasn't long," Plante wrote, "before we were working for Bristol Siddley aero-engines and also handling a brassiere account. What a wonderful business to be in," he noted. "It was all summed up for me one afternoon," Plante continued, "when I flew up from Bristol on a proving flight for the Bristol Britannia 'whispering jet' to Heathrow to jump straight into a taxi so I could attend a show of the latest bras and corsets. The outsizes swaying down the catwalk made a big impression on me!"[18]

In an article of October 1962 Plante neatly summarized his thinking about his profession. "Nineteen sixty-two," he was quoted as saying, was proving to be a vintage year. The article continued:

> "Like grapes," he explained, "we have people treading all over us." Advertising, he said, had become big news and anyone could get into the headlines, or in front of huge television audiences—especially on BBC—simply by uttering a lot of half truths about the work of the advertising profession. He continued that it was "surprising how often the critics of advertising use the very techniques—distortion of facts, half truths, and so on—that they accuse us of exploiting, to promote their own points of view." But it was noticeable, he said, that there was a great reluctance on the part of the critics to develop their argument and discuss the consequences to this nation if they succeeded in eliminating advertising. It was a fact, he said, that the countries with the highest standard of living also had the highest expenditure on advertising. Advertising was part of, and essential to, the development of a higher standard of living. "Nevertheless, we appear to be held responsible for all the evils of our age and there seems to be very little understanding of the contribution we make."[19]

That same year, after seventeen years in advertising, Plante felt his career at Y&R had run its course. He was ready for a change and to his surprise he received telegrams, letters, and phone calls with more than thirty offers from agencies in London and Paris. Eventually, he decided to accept the newly created position of world wide creative director for Unilever International. There he directed the work of artists, writers, filmmakers, and television producers at their thirty-six Lintas advertising offices across the globe. Ever sensitive to a changing environment, Plante's move to Unilever was brilliant. He saw that major companies were moving toward globalism and that to move with them advertising had to take on an international perspective. "I found that there were only a relatively few people in advertising who work and think globally," he later recalled. "Most people think that they want to know about the world but they are really very parochial." In his new job Plante traveled all over the world lecturing, consulting, advising, and participating in international advertising film festivals.[20]

Interviewed in Australia in 1974, Plante denied—with his characteristic deprecatory humor—that his job was as a "creative astronaut descending from the skies to produce brilliant, instant creative solutions." At the PWE, he had absorbed the lesson that informed local intelligence was vital for effective propaganda, so he would not try to tell the locals what to do, but only how to harness their own creativity to best effect. His role, he noted, was "selecting and nurturing creative people who don't act like a bunch of prima donnas, each believing he has a private line to his God." And that is what he continued to do for Lintas International in Indonesia, India, Brazil, South Africa, Australia, New Zealand, and so forth, until, as he put it, "I decided I better get out of this and [get] back to painting." Again, he was lucky and got commissions from Caltex that took him to Java and Sumatra while the ruler of Bahrain commissioned some paintings specifically for his own private collection.[21]

Among the many honors he accumulated during these years, Plante became a fellow of the Royal Society of Arts in London, and served on the council and as president of International Practitioners in Advertising. He continued as an active member of the Advertising Creative Circle serving as its president from 1955 to 1956. He was always sought after as a speaker guaranteed to amuse with his humor as well as inform with his good sense.[22]

Eventually, Plante realized it was time to settle down and although he and his wife loved London they were drawn to a place without the hassles and pressures of the large cities they could still visit whenever they wished. In 1980 the Plantes moved to Hilton Head Island in South Carolina, where they built another new house. Robert Harling was still the editor of *House & Garden* and arranged to feature his friend's new home in the October 1983 edition of the magazine. This time, there was no controversy. The ultra-private site of the house at the tip of a small peninsula had a 360-degree view of creek, marshland, and lagoon. As described in the *House & Garden* article it was "not only very beautiful, but possessed of the qualities that any artist needs: the tidal waters with their dramatic colour changes; marvelous sunsets; and plentiful natural wildlife." The Plantes' preference for the house itself, according to its architect, Jake Lee, was that the design be "understated, site-sensitive, and compatible with its environment and its neighbors." Consequently, it was timber built and left in natural colors. With the exception of Plante's "vast studio under the sloping cedar roof," all the rooms, as in the London home, were at ground level. There were no complaints from their neighbors.[23]

On Hilton Head Plante was able to once again throw himself vigorously into his passion for painting. It is an irony of his life that until he retired from business he had had more freedom to paint during the war than he had in his peacetime career. Perhaps that made it even more gratifying to receive much favorable attention from local media outlets. As he himself loved to say, he had gone from being a small fish in a very big pond to being a big fish in a small pond. A typical example of the notice he received was an article from March 1982: "Plante Paintings Bring World to Hilton Head." The article announced, "With the paintings of George Plante in his new show which opened at the Red Piano Gallery Sunday, we enter the world's remote and poetic areas, such as Bahrain, India, Indonesia and Greece."[24]

Another article from October 1985 described the thirty paintings in Plante's most recent show, "Places and Boats around the World." They ranged, according to the journalist Kathryn Hodgeman, "from large to very small, in oils and watercolors. Most are painted in glowing colors and are 'personal interpretations,' not representations, of the colors of scenes." Plante's paintings in the show documented his wide travels from the UK to Portugal, Italy, Java, Greece, Mexico, the Bahamas, and even the Lowcountry in South Carolina. "George Plante asserts," Hodgeman noted, "[that] he is a colorist first and foremost. He draws the scene carefully in pencil, on location. Then he recreates it as it has been translated by his own memories and sensations."[25]

In November 1988, Plante again appeared in the British edition of *House & Garden*. An article called "Southern Comfort" featured two pages of his paintings of his house on Hilton Head and "describes how he came to his island life." Robert Harling was still the editor of the magazine, cementing a friendship and mutual admiration that stretched back more than fifty years. Describing the attractions of the location on a sea island off the coast of South Carolina, Plante noted the "tremendous magnolia trees and huge live oaks festooned with *Gone with the Wind* Spanish moss sheltering wild deer, great blue herons and alligators." Harking back to his student days in Germany, Plante said the house was "every bit as functional as anything ever conceived by the Bauhaus, but it is designed to blend with nature, not compete with it."[26]

Plante continued to receive glowing reviews of his work. The summer 1995 edition of the *Beaufort and South Carolina Low Country* magazine devoted the front cover to a full-page photograph of Plante in his studio. Inside was a four-page spread of "the Portrait of an artist: George Plante. . . . A transplanted Scotsman." The article celebrated Plantes' landscapes and seascapes from his world travels, with color photographs of several of them, and noted that they were based on the small pencil and pen-and-ink sketches in his ever-present sketchbook. "His color harmonies are unexpected delights," the article enthused, melding "poetry into paint and subject matter." In the judgment of the article's author, who noted that he had "seen a lot of art in his lifetime, the work of George Plante ranks among the best contemporary art anywhere."[27]

Perhaps the best way to understand Plante, the artist, is to listen to how he explained himself in interviews. He usually differentiated between two different aspects of his art. When painting for himself, he said, "I don't like to paint what I see in front of me. I look upon nature as an abstraction. Nature does a pretty good job, and I don't want to try to compete with nature. So I make my paintings an abstraction from nature, I use colors that will evoke an emotion, an emotional response in the person looking at the picture, and that is sometimes better by not doing what is done in nature." On the other hand, painting to fulfill a particular assignment—for example, creating a poster for the Red Piano Gallery on Hilton Head Island—involved a specific problem to be solved. Plante would start by defining the problem. For the gallery poster, he concluded that it should say Hilton Head and nowhere else, which meant, like it or not, the iconic lighthouse. "So if we do something with a picture of a lush marsh, a lighthouse, the sky, and we put a red piano in the middle of the marsh—something totally unexpected—this would get attention for a poster. All these things evolve through a process of constructive thinking. It's not just mad, wild inspiration." It seems clear, then, that much of Plante's later work was built on the solid foundation of what he had learned in World War II. His propaganda art had been created by careful observation and hard, persistent work, and that same approach later made him a top-notch advertiser.[28]

In December 1994, George Plante became a U.S. citizen—the culmination of a life-long love affair. He continued to paint until his death from leukemia in 1995 and his ashes remain in the adopted country he loved. The warrior-artist left a brilliant legacy to museums and galleries that deepens our understanding of the many faces of war, while the artist's peacetime work adorns and enriches private homes and public spaces across the globe. The Red Piano Gallery held a memorial retrospective exhibition of his work in 1997 including seventy-two works, among them watercolors and drawings, paintings from before the war and from the war years, oils and acrylics, and figure studies. "George's style," according to the exhibition brochure, "is highly recognizable and all his own."[29]

Competent and workmanlike in his habits, his perceptive eye and innovative spirit enabled him to thrive wherever he landed. During the war he was dedicated and productive at sea and ashore and after the war those qualities kept him at the forefront of a fast-changing profession. The two impulses that drove him—his innate creativity and his instinctive attraction to America and Americans—propelled him through a long, prolific, and successful life. Once billed as "the man who made Jack Benny look like a hypertension case," George Plante's relaxed and ever-present humor was the outward face of a thoughtful and sensitive artist.[30]

NOTES

Prologue.

1. Churchill quote is in Hastings, *Secret War,* 96.
2. For a discussion of war artists and their art see Rabb, *The Artist and the Warrior.*
3. Bond, *Britain's Two World Wars,* 163.

Chapter One. *"I had chosen my own battleground. Well . . . up to a point."*

1. George Plant birth certificate (sometime in the 1930s George would add an artistic "e" to his last name), George Plante Papers (hereafter GPP); George Plante, letter to his son Derek, 6 Feb. 1995 (hereafter GP to DCP), GPP.
2. George Plante, "A Very Personal View of World War Two," typescript in GPP (hereafter Plante Memoir), 7.
3. Unless otherwise noted, this account of George's youth is based on his letter to his son Derek, 6 Feb. 1995, GPP.
4. GP to DCP, 6 Feb. 1995, GPP.
5. GP to DCP, 6 Feb. 1995, GPP; emails from Derek Plante to author, 7 Feb. 2016 and 5 June 2016; Papers filed by W. Addiscott of Lincoln's Inn, "In the High Court of Justice, Divorce and Admiralty Division (Divorce), Plant against Plant and Handwerck, Petition Filed 27 Apr. 1922, Cause Set Down 26 Sep. 1922, Decree Nisi 13 Feb. 1923, Final Decree 19 Nov. 1923, Und 240, case 08859," United Kingdom National Archives (hereafter UKNA), Kew, UK. At the time of the divorce, which was uncontested, Harry was living in Staffordshire, England, where he continued to live for the rest of his life.
6. According to information from Plante cousins Eric and Marjorie Clinch, and from Northilt Handwerck, Rudolph Handwerck eventually moved to Florida where Northilt, one of his daughters, still lives. Information on the Handwerck's is from http://www.sussexpostcards.info/publishers.php?PubID=130.

7. Emails from Derek Plante to author, 7 Feb. 2016 and 5 June 2016; quotes are from GP to DCP, 6 Feb. 1995, GPP.
8. Plante Memoir, 1, GPP.
9. George Plante to Evelyn Smith, who George marries in 1939 (hereafter GP to EP), 39 Arden St., Edinburgh, 3 April 1933, GPP.
10. Plante Memoir, 1, GPP.
11. Plante Memoir, 1; The "gay, mad Berlin" quote is from a one-page, undated, typewritten autobiography, GPP.
12. Plante Memoir, 2, GPP; West, *Black Lamb and Grey Falcon*, 32.
13. Plante Memoir, 2, GPP.
14. Plante Memoir, 3, GPP.
15. Plante Memoir, 4, GPP; Graves and Hodge, *Long Week-End*, 305, 309–11.
16. Plante Memoir, 5, GPP. For a description of his first studio see "Southern Comfort," *House & Garden*, Nov. 1988, 154, GPP.
17. Email from Derek Plante, 5 Jan. 2016, GPP. According to Graves and Hodge, *Long Week-End*, 45–46, there were some two hundred thousand self-styled artists in Britain in 1939, fewer than two hundred of whom were able to support themselves solely on their art.
18. For opposition to Chamberlain see, for example, Sampson, *Macmillan*, 57; the "minor country" quote is from Olson, *Troublesome Young Men*, 145.
19. GP to EP, Handwerck, Berlin–Tegel, Schloss Strasse 20, Monday, GPP.
20. GP to EP, Handwerck, Berlin–Tegel, Schloss Strasse 20, Monday. GPP.
21. GP to EP, Handwerck, Berlin–Tegel, Schloss Strasse 20, Monday's letter, continued "later," GPP.
22. GP to EP, Berlin–Tegel, Schloss Str. 20, Tuesday, GPP.
23. GP to EP, Berlin–Tegel, Schloss Str. 20, Tuesday, GPP. Information on Uncle Rudolph from Derek Plante and Northilt Handwerck.
24. Plante Memoir, 9, GPP.
25. Plante Memoir, 9, GPP.
26. Quote is from Olson, *Troublesome Young Men*, 230.
27. Plante Memoir, 10, GPP; Foss, *War Paint*, 11.
28. Olson, *Troublesome Young Men*, 186–87.
29. Plante Memoir, 10, GPP.
30. Plante Memoir, 10–11, GPP; Slader, *The Fourth Service*, 14; Middlebrook, *Convoy*, 24.
31. For an overview of the Battle of the Atlantic see Williams, *Secret Weapon*, Chapter One. A fascinating report was put out in 1944 by the Ministry of Information for the UK Ministry of War Transport called

Merchantmen at War: The Official Story of the Merchant Navy: 1939–1944. It is full of firsthand information, quotes, and personal stories about the experiences of merchant seamen and the impact of their work during the first five years of the war.

32. Slader, *The Fourth Service*, 21, 40, 42; Plante Memoir, 17, GPP.
33. Plante Memoir, 12, GPP.
34. United Kingdom of Great Britain and Northern Ireland, Special Certificate of Proficiency in Radiotelegraphy issued to George Plante, 31 Dec. 1941, GPP.
35. Ministry of Information, *Merchantmen at War*, 13–14; Slader, in his 1995 book *The Fourth Service*, 14–15, puts the number of merchant sailors at 185,000, while Alston Kennerley, in his article "Vocational Further Education and Training for British Merchant Navy Ratings: The National Sea Training Schools, 1942–1972," published in 2000, wrote that "the effective Merchant Navy manpower was estimated at not more than 145,000," 302. Middlebrook, *Convoy*, 21, puts the number at 190,000.
36. Middlebrook, *Convoy*, 19.
37. GP to EP, Friday a.m. [28 Feb. 1941, Edinburgh], GPP; Plante Memoir, 12, GPP.
38. GP to EP, Friday a.m. [28 Feb. 1941, Edinburgh], GPP.
39. Plante Memoir, 12, GPP.
40. Plante Memoir, 12, GPP.
41. Plante Memoir, 14–16, GPP.
42. GP to EP, Thursday, n.d. but other evidence dates this as 6 Mar. 1941, Arden St., Edinburgh, GPP.
43. GP to EP, Thursday [6 March 1941], Arden St., Edinburgh, GPP.
44. GP to EP, Thursday [6 March 1941], Arden St., Edinburgh, GPP.
45. GP to EP, Thursday [6 March 1941], Arden St., Edinburgh, GPP.
46. GP to EP, Thursday [6 March 1941], Arden St., Edinburgh, GPP.

Chapter Two. *"My main duty was to be tethered by the ears to the radio."*

1. GP to EP, 39 Arden St., Edinburgh, 27 April [1941], GPP; GP to EP, 39 Arden St., Edinburgh, Wednesday [7 May 1941], GPP. For Edinburgh at war see Lockhart, *Comes the Reckoning*, 280.
2. GP to EP, 39 Arden St., Edinburgh, [11 May 1941], GPP.
3. GP to EP, 39 Arden St., Edinburgh, 27 April [1941], GPP. For the Merchant Navy Shipping Pool see Ministry of Information, *Merchantmen at War*, 14–15, and Middlebrook, *Convoy*, 24.

4. GP to EP, 39 Arden St., Edinburgh, 27 April [1941], GPP. For Topolski see Foss, *War Paint*, 35, 71, 87, 118, 162, 165, and for Ardizzone 3, 24, 25, 67, 117, 181, and for Nash, 3, 11, 137, 200, and for Ravilious, 3, 11, 25, 125, 139; GP to EP, 39 Arden St., Edinburgh, Sunday [11 May 1941], GPP; Foss, *War Paint*, 24.
5. GP to EP, 39 Arden St., Edinburgh, Sunday [11 May 1941], GPP.
6. GP to EP, 39 Arden St., Edinburgh, 27 April [1941], GPP; GP to EP, 39 Arden St., Edinburgh, Wednesday [7 May 1941], GPP.
7. GP to EP, 39 Arden St., Edinburgh, Wednesday [7 May 1941], GPP; Blair, *Hitler's U-Boat War: The Hunters*, 226–28; Gardner, *Decoding History*, 20; Churchill's quote is from Cull, *Selling War*, 143.
8. GP to EP, Mersey, Dingle Jetty, Tuesday [13 May 1941], GPP.
9. GP to EP, Mersey, Dingle Jetty, Tuesday [13 May 1941], GPP.
10. Slader, *The Fourth Service*, 36–40.
11. Monsarrat, *The Cruel Sea*, 163.
12. Plante Memoir, 22, GPP. For the state of public transportation in Liverpool see Slader, *The Fourth Service*, 40.
13. GP to EP, Mersey, Dingle Jetty, Tuesday [13 May 1941], GPP; Plante Memoir, 23, GPP; for *Sourabaya* see http://uboat.net/allies/merchants/ships/2302.html, and http://iancoombe.tripod.com/id24.html.
14. Plante Memoir, 23, GPP; Cargo and Passenger Report (hereafter C&P Report) (Vessels Departing from United States Ports), left New York 25 April, arrived Liverpool 8 May 1942, Indian Division Special File #25 (hereafter file #25), boxes 11–12, Record Group 48 (hereafter RG48), National Archives and Records Administration, College Park, MD (hereafter NARA). For British Ministry of War Transport and SS *Sourabaya* see documents in box 5934, SS Sourabaya, Maritime Individual Ship Files (hereafter Ship Files), RG178, NARA; Slader, *The Fourth Service*, 45.
15. GP to EP, Mersey, Dingle Jetty, Tuesday [13 May 1941], GPP; Slader, *The Fourth Service*, 39.
16. GP to EP, Mersey, Wednesday [14 May 1941], GPP.
17. GP to EP, Mersey, Dingle Jetty, Tuesday [13 May 1941], GPP; Plante Memoir, 24, GPP.
18. GP to EP, Mersey, Dingle Jetty, Tuesday [13 May 1941], GPP; Plante Memoir, 24, GPP; Middlebrook, *Convoy*, 110; for rum in the hot tea see Monsarrat, *The Cruel Sea*, 84. For many years, all museums in New York City, including even the Metropolitan Museum of Art and the Frick Collection, had free admission. Only the Museum of Modern Art charged.

19. GP to EP, SS *Sourabaya*, Thursday, [15 May 1941], GPP.
20. GP to EP, SS *Sourabaya*, Thursday [15 May 1941], GPP; GP to EP, Monday [2 June 1941], GPP.
21. GP to EP, Birkenhead, Friday [16 May 1941], GPP.
22. GP to EP, somewhere in the Irish Sea, Monday [19 May 1941], GPP; Milner, *North Atlantic Run*, 53. Ships that could sail faster than 14.8 knots were routed independently and those capable of speeds between 7.5 and 8.9 knots were grouped in slow convoys and sailed between Britain and Sydney, Cape Breton Island. Ships in convoy setting out from Liverpool, wrote Nicholas Monsarrat, "were of all shapes and sizes: tankers, big freighters, small ships which would surely have been better off in the coasting trade than trying the hazards of an Atlantic passage. Some were deep laden, some were in ballast and uncomfortably high out of the water; they steamed in single file from the narrow Mersey channel: their pendants" flying bravely, Monsarrat, *The Cruel Sea*, 76–77.
23. GP to EP, Somewhere in Irish Sea, Monday [19 May 1941], GPP. See Middlebrook, *Convoy*, 24, for wartime watch keeping by radio operators.
24. GP to EP, somewhere in the Irish Sea, Monday [19 May 1941], GPP; GP to EP, Birkenhead, Friday [16 May 1941], GPP.
25. GP to EP, Tuesday 0100 [20 May 1941], GPP.
26. Plante Memoir, 26, GPP.
27. GP to EP, Tuesday 0100 [20 May 1941], GPP; Plante Memoir, 32, GPP; Middlebrook, *Convoy*, noted that "most men slept fully clothed with a lifejacket close by," 110. As Monsarrat observed of the shortage of escorts in the early years, "It was clear that many chances would have to be taken with the safety of merchant ships for a long time to come." Later, he noted that escorts could provide only a "thin token screen" between the merchant ships and the "growing force of U-boats." Monsarrat, *The Cruel Sea*, 87, 115.
28. Plante Memoir, 27–28, GPP.
29. Plante Memoir, 28, GPP; the quote is from Middlebrook, *Convoy*, 23.
30. GP to EP, Wednesday [21 May 1941], GPP.
31. GP to EP, Wednesday [21 May 1941], GPP. An example of these concrete slabs can be seen in a photograph of the wheelhouse of a merchant ship in the collection of the Library and Archives Canada. The caption on the photograph reads: "On wheelhouse deck, the skipper, right, keeps incessant watch on his convoy through his glasses, peering through mere slits of concrete which protected all merchantmen wheelhouses and chart rooms during World War II." PA-213733, N. Morant, National Film Board of Canada, Library and Archives Canada (hereafter LAC).

32. GP to EP, Wednesday [21 May 1941], GPP.
33. GP to EP, Thursday [22 May 1941], GPP; Plante Memoir, 30, GPP.
34. Middlebrook, *Convoy*, 109; Plante Memoir, 31, GPP.
35. GP to EP, Friday [23 May 1941], GPP; GP to EP, Saturday [24 May 1941], GPP.
36. GP to EP, Saturday [24 May 1941], GPP.
37. GP to EP, Saturday [24 May 1941], GPP.
38. GP to EP, Wednesday [21 May 1941], GPP; for re-radiation, see Middlebrook, *Convoy*, 110.
39. GP to EP, Sunday [25 May 1941], GPP.
40. GP to EP, Sunday [25 May 1941], GPP. Quote is from Plante Memoir, 30, GPP.
41. GP to EP, Monday [26 May 1941], GPP.
42. GP to EP, Monday [26 May 1941], GPP.
43. GP to EP, Tuesday [27 May 1941], GPP; Slader, *The Fourth Service*, 125.
44. GP to EP, Tuesday [27 May 1941], GPP; GP to EP, Wednesday [28 May 1941], GPP; GP to EP, Wednesday 4th June [1941], GPP.
45. GP to EP, Wednesday [28 May 1941], GPP; GP to EP, Tuesday [27 May 1941], GPP.
46. GP to EP, Wednesday [28 May 1941], GPP. For blackouts see Gannon, *Operation Drumbeat*, 185–87.
47. GP to EP, Thursday [29 May 1941], GPP; GP to EP, Saturday [31 May 1941], GPP.
48. GP to EP, Sunday [1 June1941], GPP.
49. GP to EP, Monday [2 June1941], GPP; Plante Memoir, 35–36, GPP. For the role of Halifax in the Allied war effort see White, "Conscripted City."
50. GP to EP, Monday [2 June1941], GPP.
51. GP to EP, Once more in the Atlantic, off the coast of Canada, Tuesday 3rd June [1941], GPP. In addition to the civilian clubs in Halifax, "bootleggers bought up ration books or peddled their own vile concoctions." Moreover, "Large shipments of liquor inbound or outbound rarely crossed the wharves without black marketeers taking their share." White, "Conscripted City," 30.
52. GP to EP, Once more in the Atlantic, off the coast of Canada, Tuesday 3rd June [1941], GPP.
53. GP to EP, Wednesday 4th June [1943], GPP.
54. GP to EP, Thursday 5th [June 1941], GPP.
55. GP to EP, Friday [6 June 1941], GPP.

56. GP to EP, Friday [6 June 1941], GPP.
57. GP to EP, Sunday [8 June 1941], GPP. *Sourabaya* arrived at the port of New York on 7 June 1941, C&P Report (Vessels Entering United States Ports), file #25, boxes 11–12, RG48, NARA.

Chapter Three. "*New York . . . is simply magnificent.*"

1. Plante Memoir, 39, GPP.
2. GP to EP, Sunday [8 June 1941], GPP.
3. GP to EP, Sunday [8 June 1941], GPP.
4. GP to EP, Sunday [8 June 1941], GPP.
5. GP to EP, Sunday [8 June 1941], GPP.
6. GP to EP, Tuesday [10 June 1941], GPP.
7. GP to EP, Tuesday [10 June 1941], GPP.
8. GP to EP, Tuesday [10 June 1941], GPP.
9. GP to EP, Tuesday [10 June 1941], GPP.
10. Director, Maintenance and Repairs to British Ministry of War Transport, Subject: SS *Sourabaya*, Jun 11, 1941, box 5934, Ship Files, SS *Sourabaya*, RG178, NARA.
11. GP to EP, Thursday [12 June 1941], GPP.
12. GP to EP, Thursday [12 June 1941], GPP.
13. GP to EP, New York, Tuesday 17 June [1941], GPP; GP to EP, New York, Thursday [19 June 1941], GPP.
14. GP to EP, New York, Saturday [14 June 1941], GPP.
15. GP to EP, New York, Saturday [14 June 1941], GPP.
16. GP to EP, New York, Tuesday 17 June [1941], GPP. Quentin Reynolds, a journalist and a war correspondent, was an associate editor of *Collier's* magazine.
17. GP to EP, New York, Wednesday 18 June [1941], GPP.
18. GP to EP, Wednesday [18 June 1941], GPP.
19. GP to EP, Friday [20 June 1941], GPP.
20. GP to EP, Friday [20 June 1941]—letter continued on Saturday [21 June], GPP.
21. GP to EP, Friday [20 June 1941], GPP. A 1940 Gallup poll showed that although only about 7 percent of Americans wanted to declare war on Germany nearly three-quarters thought that the United States was not giving enough help to Britain and France. Conant, *The Irregulars*, 200.
22. GP to EP, Wednesday 24th [actually 25 June 1941], GPP; "Visiting British Radio Officer Saw Reuben James Attacked: Sinking of U.S. Destroyer but One of Many Thrills for Former Artist," *Canton Repository*, Canton, Ohio, n.d. but 1942, newspaper clipping in GPP.

23. GP to EP, Wednesday 24th [actually 25 June 1941], GPP. Lauriston Castle, dating from the sixteenth century, is in Edinburgh, overlooking the Firth of Forth.
24. GP to EP, Wednesday 24th [actually 25 June 1941], GPP. In 1940, eighty-four children of employees of the Hoover Co. in Britain were evacuated to North Canton to avoid the bombings. See Helen Manfull, "Hoover Evacuees, Part 1: A Haven for Children during WWII," CantonRep.com, updated 29 August 2011, www.cantonrep.com/article/20110829/news/308299891.
25. GP to EP, Wednesday 24th [actually 25 June 1941], GPP.
26. GP to EP, Bayonne, Monday 31st June [1941]. GPP; Plante Memoir, 40–41, GPP.
27. GP to EP, Bayonne, Monday 31st June [1941], GPP; C&P Report (Vessels Clearing United States Ports), 7/1/41, file #25, boxes 11–12, RG48, NARA.
28. GP to EP, Thursday July 3rd [1941], GPP; C&P Report (Vessels Clearing United States Ports), 7/1/41, file #25, boxes 11–12, RG48, NARA.
29. Gardner, *Decoding History,* 19–20.
30. C&P Report (Vessels Entering United States Ports), 8/19/41, file #25, boxes 11–12, RG48, NARA; C&P Report (Vessels Clearing United States Ports), 8/25/41, file #25, boxes 11–12, RG48, NARA; Plante Memoir, 47–48.
31. For *Sourabaya*'s requisition orders see, for example, Director, Maintenance and Repairs, to British Ministry of War Transport, Subject: Whaler Sourabaya, General deck and engine repairs, Aug. 20, 1941, box 5934, Ship Files, SS Sourabaya, RG178, NARA; for warehouse bombing see "Visiting British Radio Officer Saw Reuben James Attacked: Sinking of U.S. Destroyer but One of Many Thrills for Former Artist," *Canton Repository,* Canton, Ohio, n.d. but 1942, newspaper clipping in GPP; personal recollection of author.
32. C&P Report (Vessels Entering United States Ports), 10/9/41, file #25, boxes 11–12, RG48, NARA; British Ministry of War Transport to Director of Maintenance and Repair, Subject: Whaler Sourabaya Voyage #3, Oct. 9, 1941, box 5934, Ship Files, SS Sourabaya, RG178, NARA; Plante Memoir, 42, GPP.
33. Plante Memoir, 44, GPP. See GP to EP, New York, Saturday [14 June 1941], GPP, for a slightly different version of the same story.

34. Plante Memoir, 44–45, GPP; "Visiting British Radio Officer Saw Reuben James Attacked," *Canton Repository*, newspaper clipping, n.d., in GPP.
35. Jan Juta to E. M. Dickey, 15 April 1942, File # GP/55/327, Second World War Artists Archive, Imperial War Museum (hereafter IWM); Conant, *The Irregulars*, 17, 36–37.
36. Cull, *Selling War*, 3, 9–10, and 154 for Lindbergh quote.
37. Jan Juta to E. M. Dickey, 15 April 1942, File # GP/55/327, Second World War Artists Archive, IWM; Conant, *The Irregulars*, 17, 36–37.
38. Plante Memoir, 45, GPP.
39. In addition to having been the European lightweight amateur boxing champion, Stephenson was an acknowledged hero. A World War I fighter pilot he had been awarded the Military Cross for gallantry as well as the Distinguished Flying Cross. He was also rich, having made his first million before the age of thirty. Pearson, *The Life of Ian Fleming*, 107–108; Cabell, *Ian Fleming's Secret War*, 56–58; Conant, *The Irregulars*, xiii-xiv; Hastings, *Secret War*, 99; Winks, *Cloak and Gown*, 166–74.
40. Pearson, *The Life of Ian Fleming*, 107–108; Cabell, *Ian Fleming's Secret War*, 56–58; Conant, *The Irregulars*, xiii-xiv.
41. Conant, *The Irregulars*, xiv-xv, 92–83, 90–92, 196; Cull, *Selling War*, 131. For Fleming and the Naval Intelligence Division see NID Staff and Distribution of Work, Feb. 1940–Oct. 1945, ADM 223/257, UKNA.
42. Conant, *The Irregulars*, xv, and 75–78 for quote.
43. Cull, *Selling War*, 3, 9–10, 65–57, 66, 149, and 38 for "propaganda phobia" quote; Foss, *War Paint*, 158 for Reith quote; Plante Memoir, 45, GPP.
44. Plante Memoir, 45, GPP; Cull quote is from Cull, *Selling War*, 201.
45. C&P Report (Vessels Clearing United States Ports), 10/17/41, file #25, boxes 11–12, RG48, NARA; Plante Memoir, 51, GPP; Cull, *Selling War*, 28.
46. Plante Memoir, 49–52, GPP. For attack on *Kearny* see Padfield, *War beneath the Sea*, 164, and "A Brief History of U.S. Navy Destroyers," http://www.navy.mil/navydata/nav_legacy.asp?id=142.
47. Plante Memoir, 52–53, GPP.
48. "Visiting British Radio Officer Saw Reuben James Attacked: Sinking of U.S. Destroyer but One of Many Thrills for Former Artist," *Canton Repository*, Canton, Ohio, n.d. but 1942, newspaper clipping in GPP. For *Reuben James* see Blair, *Hitler's U-Boat War: The Hunters*, 375.

Chapter Four. *"I am not seeking financial gain or desirous of leaving the sea."*

1. C&P Report (Vessels Entering United States Ports), 12/3/41, file #25, boxes 11–12, RG48, NARA; British Ministry of War Transport to Director of Maintenance and Repair, S. S. Sourabaya, Voyage #4, at New York, December 5, 1941, box 5934, Ship Files, SS Sourabaya, RG178, NARA; Plante Memoir, 53, GPP; Rohwer and Hummelchen, *Chronology of the War at Sea*, 100–101.
2. C&P Report (Vessels Clearing United States Ports), 12/10/41, file #25, boxes 11–12, RG48, NARA; Slader, *The Fourth Service*, 93; Rohwer and Hummelchen, *Chronology of the War at Sea*, 111, 113, 115. For Operation Drumbeat see, for example, Gannon, *Operation Drumbeat*. For the Canadian answer to this threat, particularly to their oil supply, see Robert C. Fisher, "We'll Get Our Own: Canada and the Oil Shipping Crisis of 1942," *Northern Mariner/Le marin du nord* III, No. 2 (April 1993): 33–39.
3. Slader, *The Fourth Service*, 97. For King as Anglophobe see, for example, Milner, *The U-Boat Hunters*, 29.
4. Blair, *Hitler's U-Boat War: The Hunters*, 455; Williams, *Secret Weapon*, 14, 145; MacIntyre, *Battle of the Atlantic*, 137, 140–43.
5. C&P Report (Vessels Entering United States Ports), 1/30/42, file #25, boxes 11–12, RG48, NARA; C&P Report (Vessels Clearing United States Ports), 2/21/42, file #25, boxes 11–12, RG48, NARA; C&P Report (Vessels Entering United States Ports), 4/4/42, file #25, boxes 11–12, RG48, NARA; C&P Report (Vessels Clearing United States Ports), 4/25/42, file #25, boxes 11–12, RG48, NARA.
6. British Ministry of War Transport to Director of Maintenance and Repair, S. S. Sourabaya, Voyage #5, Pier 54, New York, January 29, 1942, box 5934, Ship Files, SS Sourabaya, RG178, NARA; British Ministry of War Transport to Director of Maintenance and Repair, S. S. Sourabaya, Voyage #6, Pier 24, Brooklyn, April 4, 1942, box 5934, Ship Files, SS Sourabaya, RG178, NARA.
7. Plante Memoir, 58–59, GPP.
8. Plante Memoir, 59, GPP. For the twenty-five pounds of rationed food see Middlebrook, *Convoy*, 25.
9. Plante Memoir, 59–60, GPP.
10. Plante Memoir, 48, GPP. For *Normandie* and the Mafia see, for example, Rankin, *Ian Fleming's Commandos*, 182.
11. Foss, *War Paint*, 1.

12. Roger Tolson, "A Common Cause: Britain's War Artists Scheme," Canadian War Museum, https://www.warmuseum.ca/cwm/exhibitions/artwar/essays/britain_war_artists_scheme_e.shtml; Foss, *War Paint*, 19, 23.
13. Quotes are from Tolson, "A Common Cause"; Foss, *War Paint*, 1, 28; File # GP/55/327, Second World War Artists Archive, IWM.
14. Foss, *War Paint*, 210 n. 59.
15. George Plante to E. M. O'R. Dickey, Esq., 11 March 1942, File # GP/55/327, Second World War Artists Archive, IWM; Foss, *War Paint*, 24–25.
16. Foss, *War Paint*, 3.
17. George Plante to E. M. O'R. Dickey, Esq., 11 March 1942, File # GP/55/327, Second World War Artists Archive, IWM; E. M. O'R. Dickey to Mr. Plante, 17 March 1942, File # GP/55/327, Second World War Artists Archive, IWM.
18. Juta to E. M. Dickey, 15 Apr. 1942, File # GP/55/327, Second World War Artists Archive, IWM.
19. Dickey to Juta, 29 April 1942, File # GP/55/327, Second World War Artists Archive, IWM; Memo signed by E. M. O'R, 19 May 1942, File # GP/55/327, Second World War Artists Archive, IWM; Plante to Dickey, n.d., File # GP/55/327, Second World War Artists Archive, IWM.
20. Plante Memoir, 45–46, GPP. Advisory Committee see "War Artists Advisory Committee."
21. Howard Devree, "A Reviewer's Notebook," *New York Times*, Sunday 17 June 1942, GPP; Plante Memoir, 46, GPP; for Henry Moore see Alan Bowness, *Enyclopaedia Britannica*, s.v. "Henry Moore," www.britannica.com/EBchecked/topic/391533/Henry-Moore. For John Nash see "John Nash, 1893–1977," http://www.tate.org.uk/art/artists/john-nash-1689; 124th Meeting, 30 June 1943 to Mr. Caddy "Payment of 21 pounds to Mr. George Plante authorized" (signature illegible), File # GP/55/327, Second World War Artists Archive, IWM; To Dear Miss Melville, from Plante, 4 July 1943 and stamped MoI 5 July 1943, with handwritten note added by Miss Melville saying "Can this be paid please. We have the picture," File # GP/55/327, Second World War Artists Archive, IWM.
22. Monsarrat, *The Cruel Sea*, 244; the quote is from Monsarrat, 80–81. Slader, *The Fourth Service*, 180.
23. C&P Report (Vessels Arriving at United States Ports), 6/8/42, file #25, boxes 11–12, RG48, NARA; GP to EP and Oscar or Judy, off the Virginian Coast [Tuesday 16 June 1942], GPP; Devree, "Reviewer's Notebook," *New York Times*, Sunday 17 June 1942, GPP.

24. Plante Memoir, 54, GPP; Blair, *Hitler's U-Boat War: The Hunted*, 593–97.
25. Slader, *The Fourth Service*, 93–97.
26. Plante Memoir, 54, GPP; GP to EP and Oscar or Judy, off the Virginian Coast, Saturday [13 June 1941], GPP; GP to EP and Oscar or Judy, off the Virginian Coast [Tuesday 16 June 1942], GPP; Monsarrat, *The Cruel Sea*, 93. For descriptions of similar journeys see Gannon, *Operation Drumbeat*.
27. GP to EP and Oscar or Judy, off the Virginian Coast, Saturday [13 June 1942], GPP.
28. GP to EP, and Oscar or Judy, off the Virginian Coast [Tuesday 16 June 1942], GPP.
29. GP to EP and Oscar or Judy, off the Virginian Coast [Tuesday 16 June 1942], GPP; Plante Memoir, 54–55, GPP.
30. GP to EP and Oscar or Judy, off the Virginian Coast [Tuesday 16 June 1942], GPP; Blair, *Hitler's U-Boat War: The Hunted*, 594 for Adm. King's quote about getting every ship under protection, and 605–606.
31. GP to EP and Oscar or Judy, 2 July [1942], GPP; GP to EP, New Orleans, July 10th [1942], GPP.
32. Blair, *Hitler's U-Boat War: The Hunted*, 613.
33. GP to EP and Oscar or Judy, 2 July [1942], GPP; Plante Memoir, 56, GPP.
34. For Higgins boats see "Research Starters: Higgins Boats," The National WWII Museum, www.nationalww2museum.org/search.jsp?query=higgins+boats; Plante memoir, 57, GPP.
35. GP to EP, New Orleans, July 10th [1942], GPP.
36. GP to EP, New Orleans, July 10th [1942], GPP; Plante Memoir, 57–58, GPP.
37. GP to EP, New Orleans, July 10th [1942], GPP.
38. Foss, *War Paint*, 169.
39. C&P Report (Vessels Departing from United States Ports), 7/11/42, file #25, boxes 11–12, RG48, NARA; boy's dream quote is from GP to EP, Off Florida, 20 July 1942, GPP; Plante Memoir, 56–57, GPP.
40. Plante memoir, 56–57, GPP.
41. GP to EP, 20th July [1942], GPP; Blair, *Hitler's U-Boat War: The Hunted*, Appendix 17, 764–67; Williams, *Secret Weapon*, 43.
42. GP to EP, 29th July [1942], GPP.
43. Blair, *Hitler's U-Boat War: The Hunted*, 628.
44. GP to EP, New York, Tuesday [4 Aug. 1942], GPP.

45. GP to EP, New York, Tuesday [4 Aug. 1942], GPP.
46. C&P Report (Vessels Departing from United States Ports), 7/11/42, file #25, boxes 11–12, RG48, NARA; C&P Report (Vessels Departing from United States Ports), 8/7/42, file #25, boxes 11–12, RG48, NARA; GP to EP, New York, Tuesday [4 Aug. 1942], GPP.

Chapter Five. *"I didn't feel panicked so much as angry that this should happen to me when I had so much I wanted to do."*

1. C&P Report (Vessels Departing from United States Ports), 10/16/42, file #25, boxes 11–12, RG48, NARA; Rohwer and Hummelchen, *Chronology of the War at Sea*, 169–70; Blair, *Hitler's U-Boat War: The Hunted*, 43–44; http://uboat.net/allies/merchants/ships/2302.html; quote is from "War Diary, U-436 from 6th Oct. 42 to 12th Nov. 42," Directorate of History and Heritage, National Defence, Ottawa, Canada (hereafter DHH) 83/665 box 3 file 23.
2. Rohwer and Hummelchen, *Chronology of the War at Sea*, 169–70; Blair, *Hitler's U-Boat War: The Hunted*, 43–44; http://uboat.net/allies/merchants/ships/2302.html; Slader, *The Fourth Service*, 94 and Appendix XVII, 317.
3. Slader, *The Fourth Service*, 94; http://uboat.net/allies/merchants/ships/2302.html.
4. See letter dated 22 December 1942 from Assistant Counsel Arthur Y. Tarastine, regarding three vessels, including *Southern Princess*, box 5935, Ship Files, SS Southern Princess, RG178, NARA. For repairs, etc., see, for example, Director of Maintenance and Repairs to British Ministry of War Transport, Subject: S. S. Southern Princess, June 11, 1941, box 5935, Ship Files, SS Southern Princess, RG178, NARA; Director of Maintenance and Repairs to British Ministry of War Transport, Subject: S. S. Southern Princess, Voyage #2, SEP 30, 1941, box 5935, Ship Files, SS Southern Princess, RG178, NARA; British Ministry of War Transport to Director of Maintenance and Repair, S.S. Southern Princess, Voyage #3, "Dear sir: the above vessel has arrived in New York and requires rudder, and general deck and engine repairs which we would request be handled under the Lease Lend Act. Cunard White Star Limited will act as our agents. The formal requisition is being put through in the usual manner." November 14, 1941, box 5935, Ship Files, SS Southern Princess, RG178, NARA; British Ministry of War Transport to Director of Maintenance and Repair, S.S. Southern Princess, Voyage #3 [actually #4—the error was spotted in a subsequent letter], January 3, 1942,

box 5935, Ship Files, SS Southern Princess, RG178, NARA; British Ministry of War Transport to Director of Maintenance and Repair, S.S. Southern Princess, Voyage #5, April 2, 1942, box 5935, Ship Files, SS Southern Princess, RG178, NARA. For these voyages in British records see Southern Princess, BT/389/27, UKNA.

5. British Ministry of War Transport to Director of Maintenance and Repair, S.S. Southern Princess Repair #5, May 8, 1942, box 5935, Ship Files, SS Southern Princess, RG178, NARA.
6. Monsarrat, *The Cruel Sea*, 259.
7. George Maranz, "The Man Who Painted the Atlantic Battle," *Palestine Illustrated News* (Jerusalem), n.d., in GPP.
8. Quotes about how he managed to paint are from Maranz, "The Man Who Painted the Atlantic Battle," GPP; "Blossom of flame" quote is from "Visiting British Radio Officer Saw Reuben James Attacked," *Canton Repository*, n.d., GPP.
9. C&P Report (Vessels Arriving at United States Ports), 2/24/43, box 490, Southern Princess, RG178, NARA; C&P Report (Vessels Departing from United States Ports), 3/6/43, box 490, Southern Princess, RG178, NARA; Plante Memoir.
10. Syrett, *The Defeat of the German U-Boats*, 25. For the twenty-nine Distressed British Seamen (DBS) hitching a ride home on *Southern Princess* in March 1943 see Middlebrook, *Convoy*, 190; Gardner, *Decoding History*, 20–21.
11. Plante Memoir, 60–61, GPP; Middlebrook, *Convoy*, 101, puts the total number of ships at 141; Slader, *The Fourth Service*, 152, puts the number of ships in HX 229A at 39. For this battle see Padfield, *War beneath the Sea*, 322–24; Terraine, *The U-Boat Wars*, 553–54, 556–57; Syrett, *The Defeat of the German U-Boats*, 23–24.
12. For signals intelligence see Gardner, *Decoding History*, 124–25; Hastings, *Secret War*, 218.
13. Middlebrook, *Convoy*, 101, 107–108, Slader, *The Fourth Service*, 151–53.
14. Middlebrook, *Convoy*, 188.
15. Middlebrook, *Convoy*, 189.
16. Middlebrook, *Convoy*, 188–92, 302–03; Padfield, *War beneath the Sea*, 325–26.
17. Plante Memoir, 61, GPP; nobody undressed quote is from Maranz, "The Man Who Painted the Atlantic Battle," GPP.
18. Plante Memoir, 62, GPP.

19. Maranz, "The Man Who Painted the Atlantic Battle," GPP. For commodore's report see HX-229 "Extracts from Report by Commodore (Londonderry) re. HX-229," March 1943, DHH 81–520–8280, box 254 file 25; for blistered paint see Middlebrook, *Convoy*, 190.
20. Plante Memoir, 62, GPP; "Torpedo Hit Ship 'Exactly on the Hour,'" *New York Times*, 17 June 1943, clipping in GPP.
21. For reports of screams coming from the *Southern Princess* see Middlebrook, *Convoy*, 190; In addition to Middlebrook, *Convoy*, see, for example, Gardner, *Decoding History*; Ireland, *Battle of the Atlantic*; Milner, *North Atlantic Run*; Offley, *Turning the Tide*; Padfield, *War beneath the Sea*; Rohwer, *Critical Convoy Battles of March 1943*; Syrett, *The Defeat of the German U-Boats*; Terraine, *The U-Boat Wars*; MacIntyre, *The Battle of the Atlantic*.
22. Plante Memoir, 62–63, GPP.
23. Plante Memoir, 63–64, GPP. For an account of the sinking of the *Irénée du Pont* see Middlebrook, *Convoy*, 187–89.
24. Plante Memoir, 65, GPP.
25. Maranz, "The Man Who Painted the Atlantic Battle," GPP.
26. Middlebrook, *Convoy*, 112; Plante Memoir, 66, GPP.
27. Plante Memoir, 66, GPP; Middlebrook, *Convoy*, 190 and Appendix 5, 353.
28. Slader, *The Fourth Service*, 63–64.
29. For the giant fireworks quote see Middlebrook, *Convoy*, 191. Plante's painting of the burning ship is now in the Imperial War Museum in London. The sketches are part of the large collection of Plante's art found in his papers after his death.
30. Southern Princess, BT/389/27, UKNA; HX-229 "Extracts from Report by Commodore (Londonderry) re. HX-229," March 1943, DHH 81–520–8280, box 254 file 25.
31. Middlebrook, *Convoy*, 169–94, 308–15, 322–23; Gardner, *Decoding History*, 184, 190; Padfield, *War beneath the Sea*, 327. Different historians have given different figures for the number of U-boats actually engaged against HX229/SC122. Gardner puts the number at 41, Rohwer, *Critical Convoy Battles of March 1943*, at 38. There is also some disagreement as to the total number of merchant vessels involved.
32. Plante Memoir, 67, GPP; Middlebrook, *Convoy*, 112, 190, 295. For Albert Hocken see T 335/82, UKNA.
33. Plante Memoir, 68, GPP.
34. Plante Memoir, 68, GPP; Maranz, "The Man Who Painted the Atlantic Battle," GPP.

35. Plante Memoir, 67–68, GPP; Middlebrook, *Convoy*, 290. Quote is from Maranz, "The Man Who Painted the Atlantic Battle," GPP.
36. Dönitz quoted in Slader, *The Fourth Service*, 154.
37. Gardner, *Decoding History*, 21; Slader, *The Fourth Service*, 152.
38. Williams, *Secret Weapon*, 232; Slader, *The Fourth Service*, Appendix XII, 312, and Appendix XIII, 313, Appendix XX, 320, puts total UK merchantmen casualties at 31,908. The missing at sea notification is from *New York Times* interview with Plante, "Torpedo Hit Ship 'Exactly on the Hour,'" 17 June 1943, clipping in GPP.

Chapter Six. "*[I was] helping to undermine the enemy in the Middle East and the Balkans.*"

1. For leaflets instead of bombs see, for instance, Lockhart, *Comes the Reckoning*, 55.
2. Plante Memoir, 70, GPP. In April 1943, at about the time Plante was contacted, the Political Intelligence Department of the Foreign Office was merged with the Royal Institute of International Affairs' Foreign Research and Press Service in Oxford, creating the new Foreign Office Research Department. However, the Political Intelligence Department continued to exist as a name until 1946 as a cover for the PWE, Lockhart, *Comes the Reckoning*, 31, 54, 75; for Jeffries and Vellacott see "Middle East—Cairo, PWE Mission, Organisation and Administration, 1942–1945, Staff List No. 2—April 1944," 1, Foreign Office records, FO 898/119, UKNA; for Vellacott see Lockhart, *Comes the Reckoning*, 310.
3. The sobriquet "the Cairo Gang" apparently was not applied to this group until the 1950s; see http://www.cairogang.com/; in any event, the rumors of Jeffries' association with this unit may well be apocryphal.
4. NID Staff and Distribution of Work, Feb. 1940–Oct. 1945, 21, 34, 45, 48, ADM223/257, UKNA; Sefton Delmer, "Ian Fleming, 007—James Bond," http://www.psywar.org/delmer/2030/1001.
5. Pearson, *The Life of Ian Fleming*, 103–14; Cabell, *Ian Fleming's Secret War*, 70–71; Plante Memoir, 70, GPP.
6. Plante Memoir, 70, GPP.
7. Plante Memoir, 70–71, GPP; for "At Own Request," see Plante's Merchant Navy Reserve Pool, Certificate of Discharge from Merchant Navy Service, dated 22 July 1943, GPP.
8. Founded in 1900, Austin Reed was a British fashion retailer known for menswear. For Ministry of War Transport see Slader, *The Fourth Service*, 183; Lockhart, *Comes the Reckoning*, 143; "Psychological

Warfare in the Mediterranean Theater," Part I, Col. Donald F. Hall, Military Director, PWB, 31 Aug. 1945, RG331, NARA.

9. Plante letter to E. M. O'R. Dickey, 11 March 1942, File # GP/55/327, Second World War Artists Archive, IWM; Morgan, Naval Intelligence, 1939–1942, 124, ADM 223/464, TNA; NID Staff and Distribution of Work, Feb. 1940-Oct. 1945, 8, 12, 15, 40, 48, ADM 223/257, TNA. For more on Harling see "Robert Harling: Typographer, Designer, 'House and Garden' Editor and Author of Riveting Novels of 'Old Fleet Street,'" *The Independent*, 7 July 2008. For the work of 30 Assault Unit see Rankin, *Ian Fleming's Commandos*.
10. Vellacott himself, headmaster of the renowned boys' school Harrow (before moving on to Cambridge), when he met a former pupil at a party in Cairo had promptly recruited him away from the Royal Army Service Corps to the PWE ME. For Vellacott's recruiting see Beevor, *Crete 1941*, 328.
11. Undated, typed manuscript in GPP; Avery Chenoweth, "Portrait of an Artist . . . George Plante, a Transplanted Scotsman," *Beaufort Lowcountry*, Summer 1995, 53, GPP; "Non-Golfing Scotsman Creates Poster," *The Island Packet*, newspaper clipping, n.d., GPP; Memorial and Retrospective Exhibition, George Plante, 1914–1995, The Red Piano Gallery, Hilton Head, SC, GPP; Nancy Wellard, "London Exhibit to Feature Plante's Wartime Art," *The Island Packet*, 24 July 1998, GPP.
12. Garnett, *Secret History of PWE*, xii-xiii, 321, 325; Lockhart, *Comes the Reckoning*, 125–26. Murray later served as ambassador to Greece.
13. Andrew Roberts, "Introduction," to Garnett, *Secret History of PWE*, ix–xvi. According to Cull, *Selling War*, 195, this was not the only sensitive postwar history to be buried. The same fate overcame a history of the British Information Service which the Foreign Office considered "too sensitive to publish and buried it in their archives under a high security classification."
14. Lockhart, *Comes the Reckoning*, 126.
15. Cull, *Selling War*, 14, 16.
16. Lockhart, *Comes the Reckoning*, 68, 153; Cull, *Selling War*, 31. Lockhart's book about his work for the Secret Intelligence Service in Russia, *Memoirs of a British Agent*, was a worldwide success, Garnett, *Secret History of PWE*, 18 and *n*; "gangrene of the soul" quote is from Lockhart, *Comes the Reckoning*, 72. For more on Lockhart's view of Chamberlain see Olson, *Troublesome Young Men*, 288. See also Lockhart, *Comes the Reckoning*, 127, for Churchill's lack of interest in propaganda.

17. Lockhart, *Comes the Reckoning*, 3, 31–32, 53–54, 75, and for "wordy warfare" see 123.
18. Simpson, *The Science of Coercion*; Frank Prosser and Sgt. Maj. Herbert A. Friedman (Ret.), "Organization of the United States Propaganda Effort during World War II" at http://www.psywar.org/usa.php; Streatfield, "Major Developments in Political Warfare," 1, CAB 101/131, UKNA.
19. Lockhart, *Comes the Reckoning*, 143, 155.
20. Lockhart, *Comes the Reckoning*, 97, 127, 166.
21. Lockhart, *Comes the Reckoning*, 154–55.
22. Streatfield, "Major Developments in Political Warfare," Introduction, CAB 101/131, UKNA. For detailed descriptions of these conflicts with regard to propaganda in America see Cull, *Selling War.* Quotes are from Lockhart, *Comes the Reckoning*, 159.
23. Vellacott to Anthony Eden, 31 July 1944, FO 898/118, UKNA.
24. The records of FO 898/118, UKNA are headed: "Middle East—Cairo, PWE Missions, Correspondence with Mr. Paul Vellacott (Director), 1942–1944," FO 898/118, UKNA.
25. Horne, *Harold Macmillan: Vol. I*, 151, 217; "instinctive hostility" quote is from Vellacott to Bruce Lockhart, 3 May 1943, FO 898/117, UKNA. See also Vellacott to Bruce Lockhart, PWE MEF, 17 Nov. 1943, FO 898/118, TNA; Vellacott to Bruce Lockhart, Cairo, 26 Nov. 1942, FO 898/118, UKNA. For Glenconner as "God" see Beevor, *Crete 1941*, 272.
26. See, for example, Vellacott to Bruce Lockhart, PWE, MEF, 27 Nov. 1943, FO 898/118, UKNA; Vellacott to Bruce Lockhart, The Master's Lodge, Peterhouse, Cambridge, 21 April, 1944, FO 898/118, UKNA; Draft Telegram from the Director-General to Harman, Repeated to Jeffries, 22 April 1944, FO 898/118, UKNA. Vellacott to Bruce Lockhart, Cairo, 26 Nov. 1942, FO 898/118, TNA; Bickham Sweet-Escott quoted in Beevor, *Crete 1941*, 272.
27. In addition to the PWE records at the British National Archives at Kew, there is a collection of approximately 575 PWE pamphlets and leaflets in the Library of Congress accessible at Call Number D810.P7 G735 WWII Prop Coll. According to David Sharp and Jason Cowley, "Wartime Lies," *New Statesman* 131, no. 4597 (22 July 2002): 53, some records have been destroyed.
28. An excellent account of these campaigns is Atkinson, *An Army at Dawn*.
29. Quotes are from Olson, *Citizens of London*, 198–99; for a slightly different version of green ally, " How green were my Allies," see Lockhart, *Comes the Reckoning*, 217.

30. Beevor, *Crete 1941*, 236.
31. Sampson, *Macmillan*, 60–61.
32. For mutual Anglo-American animosity see, for example, Atkinson, *An Army at Dawn*, 439, 466; Collier, *The War in the Desert*, particularly 130–39 for Montgomery; Warner, "Auchinleck" in Keegan, *Churchill's Generals*, 145. Interestingly, Montgomery's brother was at one time War Office liaison officer with PWE. For Montgomery's brother and PWE see Lockhart, *Comes the Reckoning*, 283. Alexander is quoted in Brian Holden Reid, "Alexander," in Keegan, *Churchill's Generals*, 112–14; French is quoted in Bond, *Britain's Two World Wars*, 37.
33. Johnsen, *The Origins of the Grand Alliance.*
34. Garnett, *Secret History of PWE*, 258–59, 260–62, 322; Streatfield, "Major Developments in Political Warfare," 3, CAB 101/131, UKNA; Hall, "Psychological Warfare in the Mediterranean Theater, 31 Aug. 1945," RG331, NARA.
35. Murray to PWE, undated but May 1944, FO 898/119, UKNA; Garnett, *Secret History of PWE*, 251, 258–9; Minister of Information to Lord Selborne [Minister of Economic Warfare], 12 Nov. 1943, FO 898/141, UKNA. For Hazeltine as an "ignoramous" and as an impediment see Garnett, *Secret History of PWE*, 276.
36. Olson, *Troublesome Young Men*, 352–52; Lockhart, *Comes the Reckoning*, 219. Much to Anthony Eden's chagrin Macmillan had been instructed to report directly back to the prime minister, short-circuiting the Foreign Office and complicating Vellacott's position. Vellacott had been instructed to look to Macmillan for "day-to-day political guidance" although he was not in the PWE chain of command that ran from Vellacott through Lockhart to Eden. Sampson, *Macmillan*, 60; Wevill, *Diplomacy, Roger Makins and the Anglo-American Relationship*, 40; "day-to-day political guidance" quote is from Garnett, *Secret History of PWE*, 154.
37. Wevill, *Diplomacy, Roger Makins and the Anglo-American Relationship*, 40.
38. Wevill, *Diplomacy, Roger Makins and the Anglo-American Relationship*, 41.
39. Lockhart, *Comes the Reckoning*, 171.
40. Overy, *The Bombers and the Bombed*, 332–33.
41. Lockhart, *Comes the Reckoning*, 198, for "hot air arm"; Garnett, *Secret History of PWE*, xiii. The historian, Andrew Roberts, is quoted in his introduction to Garnett, *Secret History of PWE*. The other eight secret organizations were MI5, MI6, SOE, Government Code and Cipher

School, Radio Security, M19, London Controlling Section, and the Auxiliary Units; David Welch, "Radio Goes to War/The Secret History of PWE," *History Today* 52, no. 9 (September 2002); 57; Garnett, *Secret History of PWE*, xii.

Chapter Seven. *"No one dare interrupt during this job. Time is so valuable for this short period each day the pressure is tremendous."*

1. PWE—Leaflets Italian—General Correspondence 1939–1944, FO 898/436, UKNA; Streatfield, "Major Developments in Political Warfare," 35–36, 39, CAB 101/131, UKNA. See also relevant portions of the official British history of World War II, especially Howard, *Grand Strategy*, chapters xix–xxix, and Brooke, *War Diaries*, 397–555.
2. Lockhart, *Comes the Reckoning*, 253–54; Sampson, *Macmillan*, 66.
3. Olson, *Troublesome Young Men*, 354; Horne, *Harold Macmillan: Vol. I*, 191, 201, 211; GP to EP, 19 Sept. 1943, PWE, GHQ, MEF, GPP.
4. Overy, *The Bombers and the Bombed*, 318–19; Rankin, *Ian Fleming's Commandos*, 205–206.
5. Lockhart, *Comes the Reckoning*, 251.
6. Lockhart, *Comes the Reckoning*, 228–29, 252–53, 315, and 158 for "promises" quote; Streatfield, "Major Developments in Political Warfare," 35–36, 39, CAB 101/131, UKNA; Wedemeyer's quote is from Atkinson, *An Army at Dawn*, 294.
7. For F. R. H. (Ralph) Murray see "Middle East—Cairo, PWE Mission, Organization and Administration, 1942–1945, Staff List No. 2—April 1944, 1," FO 898/119, UKNA.
8. "Middle East—Cairo, PWE Mission, Organization and Administration, 1942–1945, Staff List No. 2—April 1944," 6, 16, FO 898/119, UKNA; For "secret building" see Beevor, *Crete 1941*, 254.
9. Streatfield, "Major Developments in Political Warfare," 42, CAB 101/131, UKNA; Lockhart, *Comes the Reckoning*, 158–59, 252–53; "Come Garibaldi! The Germans Have Returned," booklet I/24, GPP.
10. Lockhart, *Comes the Reckoning*, 157; booklets in GPP.
11. "Ordine," flyer I/117, GPP. For General Wilson see, for example, Michael Dewar, "Wilson," in Keegan, *Churchill's Generals*, 166–82.
12. Beevor, *Crete 1941*, 292; poster in GPP.
13. Beevor, *Crete 1941*, 229, 243, 292–94, 297–99, and "ghastly experience" quote is by John Keegan, on the front cover of the paperback edition.
14. Carta's testimony to the PWE is in PWE Middle East Situation Report No. 34, October 2nd 1943, FO 898/121, UKNA.

15. PWE Middle East Situation Report No. 35, October 9th 1943, FO 898/121, UKNA. For "remoralisation" see also Annexe to PWE Middle East Situation Report No. 36, 16 October 1943, FO 898/121, UKNA; Rankin, *Ian Fleming's Commandos*, 207–14.
16. Leaflet I/71, GPP; PWE Middle East Situation Report No. 34, 2 Oct. 1943, FO 898/121, UKNA; Rankin, *Ian Fleming's Commandos*, 206–14.
17. Quote is from PWE ME Situation Report No. 35, 9 Oct. 1943; Annexe to PWE Middle East Situation Report No. 36, 9 October 1943, FO 898/121, UKNA.
18. Vellacott to Bruce Lockhart, PWE, MEF, 14 Oct. 1943, FO 898/141, UKNA.
19. Lockhart, *Comes the Reckoning*, 156–57.
20. GP to EP, 19 Sept. 1943, PWE, GHQ, MEF [Middle East Force], Cairo, GPP; To Glenconner from F, 19 Oct. 1942, FO 898/118, UKNA; Vellacott to Bruce Lockhart, PWE, MEF, 27 Aug. 1943, FO 898/141, UKNA.
21. GP to EP, 19 Sept. 1943 PWE, GHQ, MEF, Cairo, GPP; GP to EP, 23 Sept. 1943, PWE, GHQ, MEF, Cairo, GPP.
22. GP to EP, 19 Sept. 1943, PWE, GHQ, MEF, Cairo; GP to EP, 22 Sept. 1943, PWE, GHQ, MEF, Cairo, GPP; Cooper, *Cairo*, 4–5; Stark, *East Is West*, 60.
23. GP to EP, 22 Sept. 1943, PWE, GHQ, MEF, Cairo, GPP.
24. GP to EP, 22 Sept. 1943, PWE, GHQ, MEF, Cairo, GPP.
25. GP to EP, 19 Sept. 1943, PWE, GHQ, MEF, Cairo, GPP. For Pike see http://www.johnpikeartprod.com/JPikebio.htm and http://americanart.si.edu/collections/search/artist/?id=5755. Born in 1911, John Pike was three years older than Plante. In 1960 he established the John Pike Watercolor School in Woodstock, New York, which attracted many ad agency artists for advanced study. Pike died in 1979. His later career and that of Plante have many common themes but this author has found no evidence that they continued their wartime friendship after their service together in Egypt and Italy; GP to EP, 19 Sept. 1943, GPP.
26. GP to EP, 19 Sept. 1943, PWE, GHQ, MEF, Cairo, GPP.
27. GP to EP, 19 Sept. 1943, PWE, GHQ, MEF, Cairo, GPP.
28. "Middle East—Cairo, PWE Mission, Organization and Administration, 1942–1945, Staff List No. 2—April 1944," FO 898/119, UKNA. For country codes see, for example, "Leaflets in Stock at Airfields," PWE ME Situation Report No. 41, 20 Nov. 1943, FO 898/122, UKNA.

29. "Daily News," Greek flyer GrB/10/29, GPP.
30. Annexe to PWE Middle East Situation Report No. 36, 9 October 1943, FO 898/121, UKNA; GP to EP, 19 Sept. 1943, PWE, GHQ, MEF, Cairo, GPP; Lockhart, *Comes the Reckoning*, 253.
31. GP to EP, 27 Sept. 1943, PWE, GHQ, MEF, Cairo, GPP; Maranz, "The Man Who Painted the Atlantic Battle" [clipping], GPP
32. From Minister of State Resident in Cairo to Foreign Office, 19 Oct. 1943, FO 898/141, UKNA.
33. For *H Epithesis* see, for example, Annexe to PWE Middle East Situation Report No. 34—2/10/43 (2 Oct. 1943), FO 898/121, UKNA.
34. *Notizie del Soldato*, 2 Oct. 1943, IB/10/2, GPP.
35. GP to EP, PWE, GHQ, MEF, Cairo, 27 Sept. 1943, GPP.
36. GP to EP, PWE, GHQ, MEF, Cairo, Monday [August] 30th [1943], GPP; Durrell is quoted in Cooper, *Cairo*, 82.
37. Cooper, *Cairo*, 25, 54, 59–61, 138–39; Manning, *Fortunes of War*, 131–32.
38. The house at 4, Darb al-Labbanah, became known as the "Maison des Artistes." *Al-Ahram Weekly On-line*, 19–25 June 2008, No. 902, http://weekly.ahram.org.eg/2008/902/cu2.htm; GP to EP, PWE, GHQ, MEF, Cairo, Monday [August] 30th [1943], GPP.
39. GP to EP, PWE, GHQ, MEF, Cairo, Monday [August] 30th [1943], GPP.
40. GP to EP, PWE, GHQ, MEF, Cairo, Monday [August] 30th [1943], GPP.
41. GP to EP, PWE, GHQ, MEF, Cairo, Monday [August] 30th [1943], GPP.
42. GP to EP, 23 Sept. 1943, PWE, GHQ, MEF, Cairo, GPP.
43. For the well-connected Britons see Conant, *The Irregulars*, xv; for Noel Coward and the PWE see Roberts, "Introduction" to Garnett, *Secret History of PWE*, xvi.
44. *H Epithesis* No. 24, n.d., GPP.
45. Macmillan is quoted in Horne, *Harold Macmillan: Vol. I*, 245.
46. Annexe to PWE ME Situation Report No. 39, 6 Oct. 1943, FO 898/123; Gregor Kranje, "Fight or Flight: Desertion, Defection, and Draft Dodge in Occupied Slovenia 1941–45," *Journal of Military History* 81, no. 1 (Jan. 2017): 147 and n. 53.
47. Greek photographs in GPP.
48. GP to EP, 27 Sept. 1943, PWE, GHQ, MEF, Cairo, GPP.
49. GP to EP, 27 Sept. 1943, PWE, GHQ, MEF, Cairo, GPP.
50. GP to EP, 27 Sept. 1943, PWE, GHQ, MEF, Cairo, GPP.

51. GP to EP, 27 Sept. 1943, PWE, GHQ, MEF, Cairo, GPP.
52. GP to EP, 27 Sept. 1943, PWE, GHQ, MEF, Cairo, GPP; for "gaberdine swine" see Beevor, *Crete 1941*, 231; Stark, *East Is West*, 69.
53. GP to EP, 30 Sept. 1943, PWE, GHQ, MEF, Cairo, GPP.
54. GP to EP, 30 Sept. 1943, PWE, GHQ, MEF, Cairo, GPP.
55. GP to EP, 30 Sept. 1943, PWE, GHQ, MEF, Cairo, GPP.
56. GP to EP, 30 Sept. 1943, PWE, GHQ, MEF, Cairo, GPP.

Chapter Eight. *"In political warfare we achieved combined staffs long before the armed forces thought of doing so."*

1. PWE ME Situation Report No. 34, 2 Oct. 1943, FO 898/121, UKNA; Annexe to PWE ME Situation Report No. 36, 16 Oct. 1943, FO 898/121, UKNA; Hall, "Psychological Warfare in the Mediterranean Theater," Part III, RG331, NARA.
2. For an excellent, fictionalized account of these events in Romania and Bulgaria see Manning, *The Balkan Trilogy*.
3. West, *Black Lamb and Grey Falcon*. For a detailed study of the complicated situation in Slovenia, for example, see Gregor Kranje, "Fight or Flight: Desertion, Defection, and Draft Dodging in Occupied Slovenia, 1941–45," *Journal of Military History* 81, no. 1 (Jan. 2017): 133–62.
4. Paper written by Lt. Col. Kenneth Johnstone [identified only as Top Secret] dated 4 January 1944 and sent to Vellacott by Mr. Harman, FO 898/118, UKNA; Lockhart, *Comes the Reckoning*, 290; Rankin, *Ian Fleming's Commandos*, 216–17.
5. Croatian flyer "Harmony, Discipline, Endurance, Caution," GPP.
6. Leaflet AB/23, PWE ME Situation Report No. 37, 23 Oct. 1943, FO 898/121, UKNA; Annexe to PWE ME Situation Report No. 37, 23 Oct. 1943, FO 898/121, UKNA. Manning's *Balkan Trilogy*, gives a clearly negative picture of German activities in Romania, especially before the invasion.
7. Lockhart, *Comes the Reckoning*, 213–14.
8. Lockhart, *Comes the Reckoning*, 76.
9. Annexe to PWE ME Situation Report No. 36, 9 Oct. 1943, FO 898/121, UKNA; Annexe to PWE Middle East Situation Report No. 36, 16 October 1943, FO 898/121, UKNA.
10. *Soldaten-Nachrichten*, 16 Oct. 1943, GB/10/15, GPP.
11. *Soldaten-Nachrichten*, 16 Oct. 1943, GB/10/15, GPP.
12. PWE ME Situation Report No. 37, 23 Oct. 1943, FO 898/121, UKNA for Schweinfurt; PWE ME Situation Report No. 39, 6 Nov. 1943, FO

898/121, UKNA for Hamburg; Annexe to PWE ME Situation Report No. 45, 18 Dec. 1943, FO 898/122, UKNA for Berlin.

13. PWE ME Situation Report No. 37, 23 Oct. 1943, FO 898/121, UKNA.
14. PWE ME Situation Report No. 36, 16 Oct. 1943, FO 898/121, UKNA; annex to PWE ME Situation Report No. 37, 23 Oct. 1943, FO 898/121, UKNA.
15. Hall, "Psychological Warfare," Part III, RG331, NARA, for "pilots preferred steel" quote; Garnett, *Secret History of PWE*, 323; Report on the Activities of the Office of War Information, 20, http://www.psywar.org/psywar/reproductions/OWIintheETO.pdf; for work of PWE units on the ground see Annexe to PWE Middle East Situation Report No. 36, 16 October 1943, FO 898/121, UKNA; PWE/PWB Bari, Survey of Year's Activities, 9 Dec. 1944, Leaflet Dissemination, 3, FO 898/142, UKNA.
16. General Anderson was eventually deputy commander of operations to General Carl Spaatz, Lockhart, *Comes the Reckoning*, 348–49; Overy, *The Bombers and the Bombed*, 341.
17. Garnett, *Secret History of PWE*, 189, 323; PWE/PWB Bari, Survey of Year's Activities, 9 Dec. 1944, Leaflet Dissemination, 1–2, FO 898/142, UKNA.
18. "Note of conversation with Colonel Barbrook who was in charge of PWE/PWB Mission at Bari after Mr. J. Stewart left," FO 898/142, UKNA; Garnett, *Secret History of PWE*, 323.
19. Albanian Leaflet and *H Epithesis*, GPP; PWE ME Situation Report No. 36, 16 Oct. 1943, FO 898/121, UKNA.
20. Lockhart, *Comes the Reckoning*, 56, 154–56, 251–53, 290; PWE ME Situation Report No. 34, 2 Oct. 1943, FO 898/121, UKNA. See Gen. Carta's testimony to the PWE, PWE ME Situation Report No. 34, 2 Oct. 1943, FO 898/121, UKNA; Hall, "Psychological Warfare" report, Part I, 31 Aug. 1945, RG331, NARA.
21. See, for example, Annexe to PWE ME Situation Report No. 34, 2 Oct. 1943, FO 898/121, UKNA; Annexe to PWE ME Situation Report No. 36, 9 Oct. 1943, FO 898/121, UKNA; Annexe to PWE ME Situation Report No. 36, 16 Oct. 1943, FO 898/121, UKNA; Annexe to PWE ME Situation Report No. 40, 12 Nov. 1943, FO 898/121.
22. Middle East—Cairo, PWE Mission, Organization an Administration 1942–1945, 6, FO 898/119, UKNA.
23. For October numbers see Annexe to PWE ME Situation Report No. 39, 6 Nov. 1943, FO 898/122, UKNA; PWE ME Situation Report No. 39, 6 Nov. 1943, FO 898/121, UKNA.

24. PWE ME Situation Report No. 41, 20 Nov. 1943, FO 898/122, UKNA.
25. PWE ME Situation Report No. 34, 2 Oct. 1943, FO 898/121, UKNA; Beevor, *Crete 1941*, 75, 132, 274–75. Quote is from 274.
26. PWE Middle East Situation Report No. 40, 13 Nov. 1943, FO 898/121, UKNA.
27. Annexe to PWE ME Situation Report No. 40, 12 Nov. 1943, FO 898/121, UKNA; Annexe to PWE ME Situation Report No. 45, 18 Dec. 1943, FO 898/122, UKNA.
28. For poor weather see, for example, Annexe to PWE ME Situation Report No. 40, 12 Nov. 1943, FO 898/122, UKNA; Annexe to PWE ME Situation Report No. 41, 20 Nov. 1943, FO 898/122, UKNA; Leaflet B/159, Annexe to PWE ME Situation Report No. 41, 20 Nov. 1943, FO 898/122, UKNA.
29. "POSLANICA ZDRUZENIH NARODOV JUGOSLAVIJI." On the last page there is the customary PWE/PWB country identification, in this case an "S" for Slovenia, followed by the number 121. An original leaflet is among the GPP, as is the same leaflet in Serbian, designated Y-121. See Annexe to PWE ME Situation Report No. 41, 20 Nov. 1943, FO 898/122 for numbers of the leaflets dropped on Serbia and Slovenia as well as the same four-page leaflet, designated C/121, dropped on Croatia.
30. See Albanian/Italian leaflet AI/19 in Annexe to PWE ME Situation Report No. 41, 20 Nov. 1943, FO 898/122, UKNA.
31. Annexure "B"—Role of Political Warfare Executive and Units in the Balkans, n.d., FO 898/141, UKNA; PWE ME Situation Report No. 40, 13 Nov. 1943, FO 898/122, UKNA; see, for example, PWE ME Situation Report No. 39, 6 Nov. 1943, FO 898/121, UKNA; Annexe to PWE ME Situation Report No. 43, 4 Dec. 1943, FO 898/122, UKNA; Annexe to PWE ME Situation Report No. 45, 18 Dec. 1943, FO 898/122, UKNA.
32. PWE ME Situation Report No. 43, 4 Dec. 1943, FO 898/122, UKNA; Wevill, *Diplomacy, Roger Makins and the Anglo-American Relationship*, 45; Cooper, *Cairo*, 289; Dewar, "Wilson," in Keegan, *Churchill's Generals*, 177; Hall, "Psychological Warfare" report, Part I, 31 Aug. 1945, RG331, NARA.
33. Vellacott to Bruce Lockhart, PWE, MEF, 27 Nov. 1943, FO 898/118, UKNA.
34. Vellacott to Bruce Lockhart, PWE, MEF, 27 Nov. 1943, FO 898/118, UKNA; PWE/PWB Bari, Survey of a Year's Activities, Dec. 1944, 1, FO 898/142, UKNA.

35. PWE/PWB Bari, Survey of a Year's Activities, Dec. 1944, 1–2, FO 898/142, UKNA.
36. Vellacott to Bruce Lockhart, The Master's Lodge, Peterhouse, Cambridge, 23 April 1944, FO 898/118, UKNA; "Extract of Notes on the Future Structure of PWE ME Sent by Mr. Harman," 10, Apr. 1944, 5, [annotated by Vellacott] included by Vellacott in his letter to Bruce Lockhart from The Master's Lodge, Peterhouse, Cambridge, 23 April 1944, FO 898/118, UKNA.
37. "Minutes" for Secretary of State, signed by Robert Bruce Lockhart, 12 July 1944, FO 898/118, UKNA.
38. "Minutes" for Secretary of State, signed by Robert Bruce Lockhart, 12 July 1944, FO 898/118, UKNA; Lockhart, *Comes the Reckoning*, 310; Hall, "Psychological Warfare" report, Part I, 31 Aug. 1945, RG331, NARA.
39. Lockhart, *Comes the Reckoning*, 132, 236–37; Garnett, *Secret History of PWE*, 351.
40. Lockhart, *Comes the Reckoning*, 309–11; Hall, "Psychological Warfare" report, Part I, 31 Aug. 1945, RG331, NARA.
41. Lockhart, *Comes the Reckoning*, 293–95; Garnett, *Secret History of PWE*, 328, 351–53; Streatfield, "Major Developments in Political Warfare," 60, CAB 101/131, UKNA.
42. "My dear Mr. Vellacott," n.d. Algiers, from Terry Harman, FO 898/118, UKNA; Hall, "Psychological Warfare" report, Part I, 31 Aug. 1945, RG331, NARA.
43. Macmillan to Bruce Lockhart, 25 July 1944, Office of the Resident Minister in the Mediterranean, FO 898/118, UKNA.
44. Horne, *Harold Macmillan: Vol. I*, 160.
45. Makins to Bruce Lockhart, AFHQ, Caserta, 28 July 1944, FO 898/118, UKNA. Writing to Anthony Eden in February 1943 Macmillan referred to Makins as "a most excellent assistant," Horne, *Harold Macmillan: Vol. I*, 175.
46. For opinions on McChrystal and Barnes see, for example, "Minutes" for Secretary of State, signed by Robert Bruce Lockhart, 12 July 1944, where Barnes is described as "persona ingrata to both the British and the American members of PWB." FO 898/118, UKNA. For Roger Makins see Richard Wevill, *Diplomacy, Roger Makins and the Anglo-American Relationship*, particularly p. 23 for his American wife, and p. 29 for his work with Eisenhower and the extent of his influence generally; Bruce Lockhart to Eden, 11 Aug. 1944, FO 898/118, UKNA.

47. Hastings, *Secret War*, 513,
48. Vellacott to Anthony Eden, 31 July 1944, FO 898/118, UKNA. Vellacott returned to his post at Peterhouse College, Cambridge, where he was in the running for the position of vice-chancellor of the university, and he received recognition for his wartime services, including submission of his name for a royal honor.
49. Bruce Lockhart to Eden, 11 Aug. 1944, marked "top secret," FO 898/118, UKNA; Lockhart, *Comes the Reckoning*, 311.
50. Annexe to PWE ME Situation Report No. 62, 14 Apr. 1944, FO 898/123.
51. 11 May 1944, *Soldaten-Nachrichten*, GPP.
52. Annexe to PWE Middle East Situation Report No. 68, 26 May 1944, FO 898/123, UNKA.
53. "Extract of Notes on the Future Structure of PWE ME Sent by Mr. Harman," 10 Apr. 1944, 5, FO 898/118, UKNA.

Chapter Nine. *"[PWE produced] countless millions of copies of a vast collection of . . . special newspapers, magazines, leaflets and miniature books."*

1. Garnett, *History of PWE*, 321–22; Streatfield, "Major Developments in Political Warfare," 47, CAB 101/131, UKNA; PWE/PWB Bari, Survey of a Year's Activities, Dec. 1944, Policy and Propaganda, 1, FO 898/142, UKNA.
2. PWE/PWB Bari, Survey of a Year's Activities, Dec. 1944, Operations and Campaigns, 1–2, FO 898/142, UKNA; Overy, *The Bombers and the Bombed*, 371; Bond, *Britain's Two World Wars*, 371.
3. Miniature Greek booklet *Allied Voice*, GPP.
4. Quote is from Appendix to PWE ME Situation Report No. 51, 29 Jan. 1944, FO 898/122, UKNA; Leaflets in Stock at KA Press, Annexe to PWE Middle East Situation Report No. 68, 26 May 1944, FO 898/123, UKNA.
5. PWE/PWB Bari, Survey of a Year's Activities, Dec. 1944, Printed Propaganda, 1, FO 898/142, UKNA.
6. Annexe to PWE ME Situation Report No. 51, 29 Jan. 1944, FO 898/122, UKNA; Garnett, *Secret History of PWE*, 322.
7. PWE/PWB Bari, Survey of a Year's Activities, Dec. 1944, Leaflet Dissemination, 1, FO 898/142, UKNA; Overy, *The Bombers and the Bombed*, 340–41.
8. PWE/PWB Bari, Survey of a Year's Activities, Dec. 1944, Leaflet Dissemination, 1, FO 898/142, UKNA.

9. Overy, *The Bombers and the Bombed*, 341–43; Wg. Cdr. Jeff Jefford, "The Balkan Air Force," *Royal Air Force Historical Society Journal* 46 (2009) 63–80.
10. PWE/PWB Bari, Survey of a Year's Activities, Dec. 1944, Leaflet Dissemination, 3, FO 898/142, UKNA.
11. PWE/PWB Bari, Survey of a Year's Activities, Dec. 1944, Leaflet Dissemination, 3, FO 898/142, UKNA.
12. Stark, *East Is West*, 70.
13. PWE/PWB Bari, Survey of a Year's Activities, Dec. 1944, Infiltration and Propaganda Servicing, 1, FO 898/142, UKNA.
14. For Plante's memories of those flights see email from Derek Plante to writer, 27 July 2015, GPP, and this writer's personal recollections.
15. "Extract of Notes on the Future Structure of PWE ME Sent by Mr. Harman," 10 Apr. 1944, 9, FO 898/118, UKNA. Quote is from the same source, 6.
16. Garnett, *Secret History of PWE*, 322–23; "Extract of Notes on the Future Structure of PWE ME Sent by Mr. Harman," 10 Apr. 1944, 10–11, FO 898/118, UKNA; PWE/PWB Bari, Survey of a Year's Activities, Dec. 1944, 2–3, FO 898/142, UKNA.
17. PWE/PWB Bari, Survey of a Year's Activities, Dec. 1944, Operations and Campaigns, 1, FO 898/142, UKNA; Lockhart, *Comes the Reckoning*, 227; "Recompense" flyer, B/189, GPP; Overy, *The Bombers and the Bombed*, 360.
18. The "Back to the Bloody Regime?" leaflet is in Annexe to PWE ME Situation Report No. 51, 29 Jan. 1944, FO 898/122, UKNA. The three leaders named in the leaflet are former premier Aleksandar Tsankov, Gen. Ivan Vulkoff who led the 1923 coup, and "Koguharoff."
19. PWE/PWB Bari, Survey of a Year's Activities, Dec. 1944, Operations and Campaigns, 1, FO 898/142, UKNA; Torrent of bombs leaflet C/Bu 103, GPP.
20. Lockhart, *Comes the Reckoning*, 290–292; PWE/PWB Bari, Survey of a Year's Activities, Dec. 1944, Operations and Campaigns, 1, FO 898/142, UKNA; Gregpr Kranje, "Fight or Flight: Desertion, Defection, and Draft Dodge in Occupied Slovenia 1941–45," *Journal of Military History* 81, no. 1 (Jan. 2017): 158–59.
21. PWE/PWB Bari, Survey of a Year's Activities, Dec. 1944, Operations and Campaigns, 1–2, FO 898/142, UKNA; Lockhart, *Comes the Reckoning*, 332–35.
22. PWE/PWB Bari, Survey of a Year's Activities, Dec. 1944, Leaflet dissemination, 3, Operations and Campaigns, 2, FO 898/142, UKNA; Sampson, *Macmillan*, 70–72.

23. Lockhart, *Comes the Reckoning*, 269–70.
24. PWE/PWB Bari, Survey of a Year's Activities, Dec. 1944, Infiltration and Propaganda Servicing, 1, FO 898/142, UKNA; *La RAF en Guerre*, French booklet, GPP.
25. GP to EP, Luxor Hotel, Luxor, Upper Egypt, Tuesday 31 Oct. 1944, GPP; Stark, *East Is West*, 75.
26. GP to EP, Luxor Hotel, Luxor, Upper Egypt, Next Day [Wed. 1 Nov. 1944], GPP. For Sergeant Bruce see "Middle East—Cairo, PWE Mission, Organization and Administration, 1942–1945, Staff List No. 2—April 1944," 6, FO 898/119, UKNA. Malaria epidemics were common in Upper Egypt in those years, Stark, *East Is West*, 75.
27. GP to EP, Luxor Hotel, Luxor, Upper Egypt, Next Day [Wed. 1 Nov. 1944]. GP to EP, Luxor letter continued on Thurs. 2 Nov.
28. GP to EP, Luxor letter continued from Aswan, Fri. 3 Nov. 1944. The earlier Aswan Dam is not to be confused with the High Dam built in the 1960s.
29. GP to EP, Luxor letter continued from Cairo, n.d. but most likely Sunday 5 Nov. or Monday 6 Nov. 1944, GPP.
30. PWE/PWB Bari, Survey of a Year's Activities, Dec. 1944, Administration, 1, FO 898/142, UKNA.
31. "The Dodecanese," 37 page miniature booklet, GPP.
32. For media supplies see paper written by Lt. Col. Kenneth Johnstone dated 4 January 1944 and sent to Vellacott by Terry Harman, FO 898/118, UKNA.
33. PWE/PWB Bari, Survey of a Year's Activities, Dec. 1944, 4, FO 898/142, UKNA.
34. PWE/PWB Bari, Survey of a Year's Activities, Dec. 1944, Effectiveness, 1, FO 898/142, UKNA.
35. PWE/PWB Bari, Survey of a Year's Activities, Dec. 1944, Leaflets, 3–4, FO 898/142, UKNA.
36. Undated, typewritten biography, GPP.
37. *Glas Pobede*, 32-page miniature booklet, GPP.
38. PWB Fortnightly Activities Report No. 1, For the Period Ending 15 January 1945, FO 898/142, UKNA. After a general election in March 1946, a Royalist government took over in Greece and King George, confirmed by a plebiscite, finally returned that September. Nevertheless, civil war broke out again between the Royalist government and the Communists and continued until 1949 when the Communists were finally defeated with the backing of Britain and the United States; Richard Cavendish, "The Greek Civil War Ends," *History Today*, Nov. 1999.

39. PWE/PWB Bari, Survey of a Year's Activities, Dec. 1944, Infiltration and Propaganda Services, 1–2, FO 898/142, UKNA; PWB Fortnightly Activities Report No. 1, For the Period Ending 15 January 1945, FO 898/142, UKNA; PWB Fortnightly Activities Report No. 9, For the Period Ending 15 May 1945, FO 898/142, UKNA; Hall, "Psychological Warfare" report, Part I, 31 Aug. 1945, RG331, NARA.
40. The *Glas Pobede* booklets can be found in FO 898/504, UKNA; For circulation numbers see Report on the Activities of the Office of War Information, 17; Hall, "Psychological Warfare in the Mediterranean Theater," Part III, 31 Aug. 1945, Naples, Italy, RG331, NARA.
41. The magazine *Glas Pobede, Broj 13*, GPP.
42. The magazine *Glas Pobede, Broj 14*, GPP.
43. *Nachrichten fur die Truppe*, No. 353, 4, April 1945, GPP.
44. *De Vliegende Hollander* and *Votre France* newssheets, GPP.
45. 24 April 1945, No. 14, *S. H. A. E. F.*, GPP.
46. PWB Fortnightly Activities Report No. 9, For the Period Ending 15 May 1945, FO 898/142, UKNA; Lockhart, *Comes the Reckoning*, 338–39, 351–52; Hall, "Psychological Warfare," report, Part I, 31 Aug. 1945, RG331, NARA.
47. PWB Fortnightly Activities Report No. 9, For the Period Ending 15 May 1945, FO 898/142, UKNA; Lockhart, *Comes the Reckoning*, 338–39, 351–52.
48. Plante "Autobiography Part 1," *Campaign*, 25 July 1975, 21, GPP.
49. Lockhart, *Comes the Reckoning*, 370; *Heute* Nr. 1, n.d., GPP.
50. *Heute*, Nr. 1, n.d., 42, GPP. For more information on the content and influence of Allied propaganda magazines from 1944 on see: A Report on the Activities of the Office of War Information in the European Theatre of Operations January 1944–January 1945, 16–18, http://www.psywar.org/psywar/reproductions/OWIintheETO.pdf.
51. 12 May issue of *Die Wochenpost*, GPP.
52. *Det Frie Norge*, No. 5 (39) 5 ARG, May 1945, N25, GPP.
53. *Transatlantic*, June 1945, GPP.
54. *Transatlantic*, August 1945, GPP.
55. HS 6/696, UKNA; See also http://www.psywar.org/delmer/8800/1001.
56. Quote from Colonel Barbrook is from "Note of conversation with Colonel Barbrook who was in charge of PWE/PWB Mission at Bari after Mr. J. Stewart left," FO 898/142, UKNA; Streatfield, "Major Developments in Political Warfare," 4–5, CAB 101/131, UKNA.
57. Welch, *Persuading the People*, 15.
58. Lockhart, *Comes the Reckoning*, 372–73.

59. Email from Brian Sullivan to author, Feb. 2017.
60. Eisenhower quote is from Streatfield, "Major Developments in Political Warfare," 4–5, CAB 101/131, UKNA; Garnett, *Secret History of PWE*, 305; Overy, *The Bombers and the Bombed*, 368; Hastings quoted in *Secret War*, 261; Lockhart quote is from Hastings, *Secret War*, 263.

Chapter Ten. *"All these things evolve through a process of constructive thinking. It's not just mad, wild inspiration."*

1. Welch, *Persuading the People*, 212–15; Attlee's quote is in Olson, *Citizens of London*, 365.
2. Olson, *Citizens of London*, 366–68; Slader, *The Fourth Service*, 90 for "savior for democracy" quote; Murrow quote is in Olson, *Citizens of London*, 372.
3. Olson, *Citizens of London*, 368–70.
4. For Everetts quote see GP to EP, 39 Arden St., Edinburgh, Sunday [11 May 1941], GPP.
5. Plante "Autobiography, Part 1," *Campaign*, 25 July 1975, 21, GPP.
6. Plante "Autobiography, Part 1," *Campaign*, 25 July 1975, 21, GPP.
7. "Advertising Creative Circle," Records, History of Advertising Trust Archive (HAT), NRA 30198, UKNA.
8. George Plante, "The Agency as Seen by the Client (as feared by George Plante) . . . ," Dec. 1951, 12–13, GPP.
9. For the Gleam comment see Plante "Autobiography, Part 3," *Campaign*, 8 Aug. 1975, 21, GPP; Phyllis Digby Morton, "Could It Be You?" *Sunday Graphic*, 15 Aug. 1954, 3, GPP.
10. Plante "Autobiography, Part 3," *Campaign*, 8 Aug. 1975, 20–21, GPP.
11. Plante "Autobiography, Part 3," *Campaign*, 8 Aug. 1975, 20, GPP.
12. Wevill, *Diplomacy, Roger Makins and the Anglo-American Relationship*, 105–106, 120, 126–27.
13. Horne, *Harold Macmillan: Vol. I*, 154, 394–96, 410–411, 419–22, 423–25, 430–31, 439, 440; Wevill, *Diplomacy, Roger Makins and the Anglo-American Relationship*, 1, 143–144; Olson, *Troublesome Young Men*, 357–60.
14. *London Gazette*, 25 Oct. 1963.
15. Rankin, *Ian Fleming's Commandos*, 222–23.
16. "Unusual Experiment in a Modern House," *House & Garden*, No. 1, Whole Number 143, Vol. 16, cover and 28–31, GPP.
17. Nancy Stevens Piera, "Islander Visits George and Jane Plante in Baynard Peninsula," *Hilton Head Islander*, Oct. 1982, 49–56, GPP; "A Modern House That Has Coped Smoothly with the Passage of Years," *House & Garden*, June 1978, 76–79, GPP.

18. See, for example, "Much Flair and Sparkle Gone out of Advertising," with photograph of Plante and wife at the Poster Advertising Conference, *Advertiser's Weekly,* 8 June 1962, 10, GPP; "18th Century Splendor," with photograph of Plante and wife at the ad film festival in Venice, *AdWeek,* 24 June 1966, 10, GPP; Plante "Autobiography, Part 3," 8 Aug. 1975, 20, GPP.
19. "Advertising's Vintage Year," by George Plante, *Advertiser's Weekly,* Oct. 12, 1962, 14, GPP.
20. Avery Chenoweth, "George Plante, a Transplanted Scotsman," *Greater Beaufort and the South Carolina Low Country,* Summer 1995, 54, GPP; Nancy Wellard, "London Exhibition to Feature Plante's Wartime Art," *The Island Packet*, 24 July 1998, GPP; quote is from Plante "Autobiography, Part 4," *Campaign*, 15 Aug. 1975, 19, GPP.
21. Quote is from Valerie Lawson, "Lintas Troubleshooter Outlines New Industry Issues," *The Australian*, 16 July 1974, GPP; Plante quotes from Margaret Greer, "Cover Story," *Hilton Head Islander,* Oct. 1982, 74 , GPP. For Plante's works in Bahrain see Nancy Wellard, "London Exhibition to Feature Plante's Wartime Art," *The Island Packet*, 24 July 1998, GPP, and Margaret Greer, "Art and Flower Festival to Honor George Plante, *The Island Packet*, 22 Apr. 1994, GPP.
22. "History of Advertising Trust Archive," National Register of Archives, NRA 30198, UKNA.
23. Jake Lee, "Cover Story," *Hilton Head Islander,* Oct. 1982, 56, GPP; *House & Garden Incorporating Wine and Food Magazine*, Oct. 1983, 134–37, GPP.
24. Kathryn Hodgeman, "Plante Paintings Bring World to Hilton Head," *The Island Packet*, 11 March 1982, 52, GPP.
25. Kathryn Hodgeman, "George Plante Show Is a Round-the-World Tour," *The Island Packet*, 8 Oct. 1985, GPP.
26. "Southern Comfort," *House & Garden Magazine*, British Edition, Nov. 1988, 154–55, GPP.
27. Avery Chenoweth, "George Plante, a Transplanted Scotsman," *Greater Beaufort and the South Carolina Low Country,* Summer 1995, 53–56, GPP.
28. Margaret Greer, "Cover Story," *Hilton Head Islander,* Oct. 1982, 74, GPP.
29. Memorial Retrospective and Exhibition, "George Plante, 1914–1995," GPP.
30. Valerie Lawson, "Lintas Troubleshooter Outlines New Industry Issues," *The Australian*, 16 July 1974, GPP.

BIBLIOGRAPHY

Author's Interviews and Correspondence

Clinch, Eric and Marjorie (Plante cousins)
Gardner, W. J. R.
Handwerck, Northilt (Plante cousin)
Plante, Derek C.
Sullivan, Dr. Brian

Unpublished Sources:

DHH Directorate of History and Heritage, National Defence, Ottawa, Canada

- DHH 81–520–8280, box 254 ("Extracts from Report by Commodore (Londonderry) re. HX-229," March 1943).
- DHH 83/665, box 3 file 23 ("War Diary, U-436 from 6th Oct. 42 to 12th Nov. 42").

George Plante Papers

- Held by Kathleen Broome Williams.

Imperial War Museum, London

- Second World War Artists Archive (File # GP/55/327).

Library and Archives Canada, (LAC)

- PA-213733 (N. Morant, wheelhouse photograph and caption, National Film Board of Canada).

National Archives and Records Administration, College Park, MD

- RG 48, Records of the Secretary of the Interior.
- RG 178, Records of the US Maritime Commission (Files of the Director of Maintenance and Repairs to British Ministry of War Transport).
- RG 331, Military Agency Records (Records of the Psychological Warfare Branch).

United Kingdom National Archives, Kew

- ADM 223—Royal Navy operations in the Second World War (NID History).
- BT 389—Merchant Shipping Movements, 1939–1945.

CAB 101—Official Historical Studies of the Second World War (Streatfield, "Major Developments in Political Warfare").
FO 898—Political Warfare Executive.
HS 6—Intelligence Services (Special Operations Executive).
High Court of Justice and Admiralty Division (Divorce)—Und 240, case 08859.
NRA 30198—Records, History of Advertising Trust Archive (HAT).
T 335—Officers in the Merchant Navy.

Published Sources

Books

Atkinson, Rick. *An Army at Dawn: The War in North Africa, 1942–1943*. New York: Henry Holt and Company, 2002.
Beevor, Antony. *Crete 1941: The Battle and the Resistance*. New York: Penguin Books, 2014.
Blair, Clay. *Hitler's U-Boat War: The Hunters, 1939–1942*. New York: Random House, 1996.
———. *Hitler's U-Boat War: The Hunted, 1942–1945*. New York: Random House, 1998.
Bond, Brian. *Britain's Two World Wars against Germany: Myth, Memory and the Distortions of Hindsight*. Edited by Alex Danchev and Daniel Todman. Cambridge, UK: Cambridge University Press, 2014.
Brooke, Alan Viscount Alanbrooke. *War Diaries 1939–1945*. London: Phoenix Press, 2002.
Cabell, Craig. *Ian Fleming's Secret War*. Barnsley: Pen & Sword Military, 2008.
Churchill, Winston S. *The History of the Second World War*. Vol. 3, *The Grand Alliance*. Cambridge: Houghton Mifflin Company, 1950.
———. *The History of the Second World War*. Vol. 5, *Closing the Ring*. Cambridge: Houghton Mifflin Company, 1951.
Coale, Lt. Cmdr. Griffith Baily. *North Atlantic Patrol: The Log of a Seagoing Artist*. New York: Farrar & Rinehart, Inc., 1942.
Collier, Richard. *The War in the Desert*. Alexandria, VA: Time-Life Books Inc., 1977.
Conant, Jennet. *The Irregulars: Roald Dahl and the British Spy Ring in Wartime Washington*. New York: Simon & Schuster, 2008.
Cooper, Artemis. *Cairo in the War 1939–1945*. London: John Murray, 2013.
Cull, Nicholas John. *Selling War: The British Propaganda Campaign against American "Neutrality" in World War II*. New York, Oxford: Oxford University Press, 1995.

Foss, Brian. *War Paint: Art, War, State and Identity in Britain 1939–1945*. New Haven, CT: Yale University Press, 2007.

Gannon, Michael. *Operation Drumbeat: The Dramatic True Story of Germany's First U-Boat Attacks along the American Coast in World War II*. New York: Harper & Row, Publishers, 1990.

Gardner, W. J. R. *Decoding History: The Battle of the Atlantic and Ultra*. London: Macmillan Press Ltd., 1999.

Garnett, David. *The Secret History of PWE: The Political Warfare Executive 1939–1945*. London: St. Ermin's Press, 2002.

Graves, Robert, and Alan Hodge. *The Long Week-End: A Social History of Great Britain 1918–1939*. New York: W. W. Norton & Company, 1963.

Gretton, (Sir) Peter William. *Convoy Escort Commander*. London: Cassell and Company, Ltd., 1964.

Hall, Roger. *You're Stepping on My Cloak and Dagger*. Annapolis, MD: Naval Institute Press, 2004.

Hastings, Max. *The Secret War: Spies, Codes and Guerrillas 1939–1945*. London: Williams Collins, 2016.

Horne, Alistair. *Harold Macmillan: Volume I: 1894–1956*. New York: Viking Penguin, Inc., 1989.

Howard, Michael. *History of the Second World War*. Vol. IV, *Grand Strategy*. London: The Stationery Office Books, 1972.

Ireland, Bernard. *Battle of the Atlantic*. Annapolis, MD: Naval Institute Press, 2003.

Johnsen, William T. *The Origins of the Grand Alliance: Anglo-American Military Collaboration from the Panay Incident to Pearl Harbor*. Lexington: University Press of Kentucky, 2016.

Keegan, John, ed. *Churchill's Generals: The First Authoritative Look at the Men Who Helped Churchill Win the War*. New York: Quill, William Morrow, 1991.

Lockhart, R. H. Bruce. *Comes the Reckoning*. London: Putnam, 1947.

MacIntyre, Donald. *The Battle of the Atlantic*. London: B. T. Batsford, 1961.

Manning, Olivia. *The Balkan Trilogy*. Middlesex, England: Penguin Books Ltd., 1981.

————. *Fortunes of War: The Levant Trilogy*. New York: New York Review of Books, 2014.

Middlebrook, Martin. *Convoy: The Battle for Convoys SC.122 and HX.229*. New York: William Morrow, 1977.

Milner, Marc. *North Atlantic Run: The Royal Canadian Navy and the Battle for the Convoys*. Toronto: University of Toronto Press, 1985.

———. *The U-Boat Hunters: The Royal Canadian Navy and the Offensive against Germany's Submarines.* Annapolis, MD: Naval Institute Press, 1994.

Ministry of Information. *Merchantmen at War: The Official Story of the Merchant Navy, 1939–1944.* Honolulu, HI: University Press of the Pacific, 2005. First published 1944 by His Majesty's Stationery Office (HMSO), London.

Monsarrat, Nicholas. *The Cruel Sea.* London: Penguin Books, 2009.

Offley, Ed. *Turning the Tide: How a Small Band of Allied Sailors Defeated the U-Boats and Won the Battle of the Atlantic.* New York: Basic Books, 2011.

Olson, Lynne. *Citizens of London: The Americans Who Stood with Britain in its Darkest, Finest Hour.* New York: Random House, 2010.

———. *Troublesome Young Men: The Rebels Who Brought Churchill to Power and Helped Save England.* New York: Farrar, Straus and Giroux, 2007.

Overy, Richard. *The Bombers and the Bombed: Allied Air War over Europe, 1940–1945.* New York: Viking Penguin, 2015.

Padfield, Peter. *War beneath the Sea: Submarine Conflict during World War II.* New York: John Wiley & Sons, Inc., 1998.

Pearson, John. *The Life of Ian Fleming.* New York: McGraw Hill Book Company, 1966.

Persico, Joseph E. *Roosevelt's Secret War: FDR and World War II Espionage.* New York: Random House, Inc., 2001.

Rabb, Theodore K. *The Artist and the Warrior: Military History through the Eyes of the Masters.* New Haven, CT: Yale University Press, 2011.

Rankin, Nicholas. *Ian Fleming's Commandos: The Story of the Legendary 30 Assault Unit.* New York: Oxford University Press, 2011.

Ricks, Thomas E. *Churchill & Orwell: The Fight for Freedom.* New York: Penguin Press, 2017.

Rohwer, Jurgen. *The Critical Convoy Battles of March 1943: The Battle for HX229/SC122.* London: Ian Allan, 1977.

Rohwer, J. and G. Hummelchen, *Chronology of the War at Sea, 1939–1945,* rev. ed. Annapolis, MD: Naval Institute Press, 1992.

Sampson, Anthony. *Macmillan: A Study in Ambiguity.* New York: Simon and Schuster, 1967.

Simpson, Christopher. *The Science of Coercion: Communication Research & Psychological Warfare, 1945–1960.* Oxford University Press, 1994.

Slader, John. *The Fourth Service: Merchantmen at War, 1939–1945.* 2nd ed. New York: ipicturebooks, 2010.

Stark, Freya. *East Is West*. London: Century, 1986.

Syrett, David. *The Defeat of the German U-Boats: The Battle of the Atlantic*. Columbia, SC: University of South Carolina Press, 1994.

Terraine, John. *The U-Boat Wars, 1916–1945*. New York: G. P. Putnam's Sons, 1989.

van der Vat, Dan. *The Atlantic Campaign: World War II's Great Struggle at Sea*. New York: Harper and Row, 1988.

Waters, John M. *Bloody Winter*. Annapolis, MD: Naval Institute Press, 1984.

Welch, David. *Persuading the People: British Propaganda in World War II*. London, UK: British Library, 2016.

West, Rebecca. *Black Lamb and Grey Falcon: A Journey through Yugoslavia*. New York: Penguin Group, 2007.

Wevill, Richard. *Diplomacy, Roger Makins and the Anglo-American Relationship*. Burlington, VT: Ashgate Publishing Company, 2014.

Williams, Kathleen Broome. *Secret Weapon: US High-Frequency Direction Finding in the Battle of the Atlantic*. Annapolis, MD: Naval Institute Press, 1996.

Winks, Robin W. *Cloak and Gown: Scholars in the Secret War, 1939–1961*, 2nd ed. New Haven, CT: Yale University Press, 1996.

Periodicals

Cavendish, Richard. "The Greek Civil War Ends." *History Today*, Nov. 1999.

Fisher, Robert C. "We'll Get Our Own: Canada and the Oil Shipping Crisis of 1942." *Northern Mariner/Le marin du nord*, April 1993.

Jefford, Wg. Cdr. Jeff. "The Balkan Air Force." *Royal Air Force Historical Society Journal* 46 (2009): 63–80.

Kranje, Gregor. "Fight or Flight: Desertion, Defection, and Draft-Dodging in Occupied Slovenia, 1941–45." *Journal of Military History* 81, no. 1 (Jan. 2017): 133–62.

Kennerley, Alston. "Vocational Further Education and Training for British Merchant Navy Ratings: The National Sea Training Schools, 1942–1972." *History of Education*, XXTX, No 4 (2000) 301-327.

"Robert Harling: Typographer, designer, 'House and Garden' editor and author of riveting novels of 'old Fleet Street.'" *The Independent*, 7 July 2008.

Sharp, David, and Jason Cowley. "Wartime Lies." *New Statesman* 131, no. 4597 (22 July 2002): 53.

Sullivan, Brian R. "'A Highly Commendable Action': William J. Donovan's Intelligence Mission for Mussolini and Roosevelt, December 1935–February 1936." *Intelligence and National Security* 6, no. 2 (1991): 334–66.

Welch, David. "Radio Goes to War/The Secret History of PWE." *History Today* 52, no. 9 (September 2002): 57.

Electronic sources

Al-Ahram Weekly On-line, No. 902, 19–25 June 2008. http://weekly.ahram.org.eg/2008/902/cu2.htm.

Bismarck. http://www.history.navy.mil/faqs/faq118–1.htm.

Bowness, Alan. *Enyclopaedia Britannica*, s.v. "Henry Moore." www.britannica.com/EBchecked/topic/391533/Henry-Moore.

"A Brief History of Christian Salvesen Shipping." Christian Salvesen. http://iancoombe.tripod.com/id24.html.

"A Brief History of U.S. Navy Destroyers Part II—World War II (1941–1943)" (*Kearny* attack). America's Navy. http://www.navy.mil/navydata/nav_legacy.asp?id=142.

Delmer, Sefton. "Ian Fleming, 007—James Bond." Psywar.org. http://www.psywar.org/delmer/2030/1001.

Handwerck postcards. Sussex Postcards. http://www.sussexpostcards.info/publishers.php?PubID=130.

Manfull, Helen. "Hoover Evacuees – Part 1: A Haven for Children during WWII." CantonRep.com. http://www.cantonrep.com/newsnow/x1688624942/Hoover-Evacuees-Part-1-A-haven-for-children-during-WWII#axzz2XT0i8zTM.

"John Nash, 1893–1977." Tate. http://www.tate.org.uk/art/artists/john-nash-1689.

"John Pike." Smithsonian American Art Museum. http://americanart.si.edu/collections/search/artist/?id=5755.

"Long and Short Positions." John Pike Art Products. http://www.johnpikeartprod.com/JPikebio.htm.

"OWI in the ETO." Psywar.org. http://www.psywar.org/psywar/reproductions/OWIintheETO.pdf.

"Research Starters: Higgins Boats." The National WWII Museum. www.nationalww2museum.org /search.jsp?query=higgins+boats.

"Sourabaya." Uboat.net. http://uboat.net/allies/merchants/ships/2302.html.

"SS Southern Princess (+1943)." Wreck Site. http://www.wrecksite.eu/wreck.aspx?153529.

"The Cairo Gang." http://www.cairogang.com/.

Tolson, Roger. "A Common Cause: Britain's War Artists Scheme." Canadian War Museum. https://www.warmuseum.ca/cwm/exhibitions/artwar/essays/britain_war_artists_scheme_e.shtml.

"War Artists Advisory Committee." Imperial War Museum. http://www.iwm.org.uk/history/the war-artists-advisory-committee#.

Dissertations

White, Jay. "Conscripted City: Halifax and the Second World War." PhD diss., McMaster University, 1994. Open Access Dissertations and Theses (paper 2549).

INDEX

ABOUT THE AUTHOR

Kathleen Broome Williams was raised in Italy and England and has taught in Puerto Rico, Japan, and Panama, as well as in the United States. She has published extensively in naval history and is spending the 2018–19 academic year at the U.S. Naval Academy as the Class of 1957 Distinguished Chair in Naval Heritage.

The Naval Institute Press is the book-publishing arm of the U.S. Naval Institute, a private, nonprofit, membership society for sea service professionals and others who share an interest in naval and maritime affairs. Established in 1873 at the U.S. Naval Academy in Annapolis, Maryland, where its offices remain today, the Naval Institute has members worldwide.

Members of the Naval Institute support the education programs of the society and receive the influential monthly magazine *Proceedings* or the colorful bimonthly magazine *Naval History* and discounts on fine nautical prints and on ship and aircraft photos. They also have access to the transcripts of the Institute's Oral History Program and get discounted admission to any of the Institute-sponsored seminars offered around the country.

The Naval Institute's book-publishing program, begun in 1898 with basic guides to naval practices, has broadened its scope to include books of more general interest. Now the Naval Institute Press publishes about seventy titles each year, ranging from how-to books on boating and navigation to battle histories, biographies, ship and aircraft guides, and novels. Institute members receive significant discounts on the Press' more than eight hundred books in print.

Full-time students are eligible for special half-price membership rates. Life memberships are also available.

For a free catalog describing Naval Institute Press books currently available, and for further information about joining the U.S. Naval Institute, please write to:

Member Services
U.S. Naval Institute
291 Wood Road
Annapolis, MD 21402-5034
Telephone: (800) 233-8764
Fax: (410) 571-1703
Web address: www.usni.org